"One of the most gut-wrenching stories in recent years was the deliberate, systematic, court-ordered starvation of Terri Schiavo. David Gibbs III, the Christian attorney who fought so valiantly to save her life, has now written a gripping account of the fight to save Terri. This book . . . is a wake-up call to a society that shrugs its collective shoulders as to how we treat the most vulnerable among us."

—D. James Kennedy, PhD, Senior Minister, Coral Ridge
　　Presbyterian Church

"Attorney Gibbs makes the case for people like me to be allowed to live. I am so thankful that my husband didn't let me die because of my 'quality of life.' This could be the most important book you ever read."

—Kate Adamson, Author of *Triumph Over Adversity*

"The tragedy of Terri Schiavo will long be remembered, mourned, and debated. David Gibbs's vital book explains why Terri Schiavo died and why all Americans should care."

—U.S. Representative Tom DeLay (R-TX), retired

"Americans are indebted to David Gibbs for bringing to light a wealth of insider information never reported on the Terri Schiavo case. His expert legal and eyewitness account is unmatched. A must read."

—Joseph Farah, WorldNetDaily.com

"My heart was deeply moved by this touching and thought-provoking account! My husband and I prayed diligently for Terri and for the Schindlers, as he, as well as I, greatly value every precious life.

"I thank God for the compassionate and valiant stand of David Gibbs. May this book be used greatly to promote the value of every single life."

—Joyce Rogers, wife of the late Dr. Adrian Rogers

THE UNTOLD STORY OF **TERRI SCHIAVO**
AND WHAT IT MEANS FOR ALL OF US

FIGHTING
FOR
DEAR LIFE

BY THE ATTORNEY WHO FOUGHT FOR TERRI

DAVID GIBBS
WITH **BOB DeMOSS**

BETHANY HOUSE
MINNEAPOLIS, MINNESOTA

Published by Bethany House Publishers
11400 Hampshire Avenue South
Bloomington, Minnesota 55438

Bethany House Publishers is a division of
Baker Publishing Group, Grand Rapids, Michigan.

Printed in the United States of America

Hardcover: ISBN 978-0-7642-0243-8
Trade Paper: ISBN 978-0-7642-0534-7

Library of Congress has cataloged the hardcover edition as follows:

Gibbs, David (David C.)
    Fighting for dear life : the untold story of Terri Schiavo and what it means for all
of us / David Gibbs with Bob DeMoss.
        p.   cm.
    Summary: "Gibbs, lead attorney for Bob and Mary Schindler, Terri Schiavo's
parents, recounts the legal case to keep her alive and her last days. Discusses
background information on the U.S. judiciary process and value of life issues"—
Provided by publisher.
    Includes bibliographical references.
    ISBN 0-7642-0243-X (hardcover : alk. paper)
    1. Schiavo, Terri, 1963–2005. 2. Right to die—Moral and ethical aspects—United
States—Case studies. 3. Terminal care—Moral and ethical aspects—United States—
Case studies. 4. Coma—Patients—United States—Biography. 5. Medical ethics—
United States—Case studies. I. DeMoss, Robert G. II. Title.

    R726.G52   2006
    179.7—dc22

                                                              2006013760

In keeping with biblical principles of
creation stewardship, Baker Publishing Group advocates the responsible
use of our natural resources. As a
member of the Green Press Initiative,
our company uses recycled paper
when possible. The text paper of
this book is comprised of 30% post-
consumer waste.

green
press
INITIATIVE

For Terri Schiavo's parents, Robert and Mary Schindler. You beautifully demonstrated a parent's unconditional love for your disabled daughter.

For my parents, David and Glorianne Gibbs. You loved and trained me, and showed me by your lives how to find great joy and purpose in serving others. Dad, you have been a role model and hero to me as a legal missionary attorney helping hurting people and defending right causes across our land.

ACKNOWLEDGMENTS

David Gibbs would like to thank . . .

My wife, family, friends, and the entire team of outstanding professionals at Gibbs Law Firm for their support and advice while this book was being written.

Bob DeMoss for helping me tell the story.

Barbara Weller, Becky Wilson, and Dr. Robert and Dora DeMoss, for their many late nights of work to see this project through to completion.

Kyle Duncan, Gary Johnson, Julie Smith, and the wonderful team at Bethany House for their commitment to the heart and soul of this book.

Greg Johnson and WordServe Literary Group for finding us the perfect publishing home.

The millions of people who watched, prayed, and stood with us in spirit from around the world as we legally represented Bob and Mary Schindler in their valiant final efforts to save the life of their daughter Terri Schiavo.

The Creator of Life before whom every life has eternal worth.

ABOUT THE AUTHORS

DAVID C. GIBBS defends the rights of churches and Christians nationwide as a legal missionary through Gibbs Law Firm and the Christian Law Association. He's a graduate of Liberty University and received his law degree from Duke University. He co-hosts *The Legal Alert,* heard on more than one thousand radio stations daily, and he has appeared on many major news and talk shows, including *Larry King Live, FOX & Friends, Hannity & Colmes, Nancy Grace, The Michael Reagan Show,* and *Face the Nation.* David, his wife, and their four children make their home in Florida.

Attorney David Gibbs can be contacted at *dgibbs@fightingfordearlife.com.*

BOB DeMOSS served seven years as Youth Cultural Specialist for Dr. James Dobson and Focus on the Family. He has hosted his *Learn to Discern: Help for a Generation at Risk* seminar in more than three hundred cities worldwide and has appeared on numerous national radio and television shows, including *Good Morning America.* As a *New York Times* bestselling writer, he has coauthored books with Dennis Rainey, Tim LaHaye, and Point of Grace. A father of four, Bob lives with his family in Franklin, Tennessee.

CONTENTS

PART ONE: **THIS DAY WE FIGHT**

1. Fighting for Dear Life 13
2. Seeing Is Believing 19
3. Life on Trial 31
4. Terri's Law 39
5. Doctor's Orders 49
6. Is There a Doctor in the House? 59
7. In Sickness and In Health 69
8. Your Honor, I Object! 81
9. Let's Make a Deal 91

PART TWO: **TERRI'S FIGHT FOR LIFE**

10. Terri's Only Crime 103
11. Terri's Last Meal 117
12. The Big Lie 127
13. Washington Weighs In 139
14. Litigating at the Speed of Light 149
15. A Mother's Heart 159
16. Until We Meet Again 167

PART THREE: **FIGHTING FOR OUR FUTURE**

17. Supreme Denial 183
18. Examining the Medical Examiner's Report 191
19. The $64,000 Question 201
20. A Life Worth Living 205
21. Every Day's a Gift 215
22. The Least of These 227
23. If There's a Will There's a Way 237
24. Life Support in View of Eternity 247
25. Brave New World? 251
26. If My People 259

Appendix A: Frequently Asked Questions: Terri and the Case 267
Appendix B: Sample Form: Designation of Health Care Surrogate 271
Appendix C: Full Text of Terri's Law: October 2003 275
Appendix D: Text of the Act of Congress: March 2005 277
Notes 281

PART ONE

THIS DAY WE FIGHT

CHAPTER ONE

FIGHTING FOR
DEAR LIFE

The first duty of government is the protection of life, not its destruction. The chief purpose of government is to protect life. Abandon that and you have abandoned all.

—Thomas Jefferson[1]

Terri Schiavo is dead.

Nothing in this book will change that fact. The time for making motions and filing appeals is over. My clients, Bob and Mary Schindler, have no recourse. Terri, that precious daughter they carefully bundled up and carried home from a Philadelphia hospital back in December of 1963 was, on March 31, 2005, removed from their loving arms and reduced to ashes.

As much as I'd like to bring Terri back from the grave, I can't. You might be wondering why, then, would I write this book? What is the point of revisiting the painful details that have been rehashed a thousand times in the media? Let me offer three reasons why I feel compelled to tell Terri's story. The first is quite simple.

I was there.

I witnessed firsthand what transpired both in the courtroom and behind the scenes. I sat and visited with Terri on numerous occasions. I looked into her eyes. I spoke and laughed with her. I watched Terri's family interact with her in ways nobody in the media *ever* saw. And I was in her room the day her feeding tube was removed . . . as well as shortly before Terri took her final breath.

Not one reporter from ABC, CBS, NBC, CNN, FOX, the *New York Times*, or the international media community ever set foot in Terri's room. I can't blame them—they were denied entrance by Terri's husband, Michael Schiavo. For reasons known only to Michael, he did not want the world to see Terri as she was: a disabled, yet fully alive, spirited woman.

Perhaps more troubling was the behavior of Judge George Greer, who held the very heartbeat of Terri's life in his hands. For reasons I still do not understand, Judge Greer refused to go and meet Terri Schiavo, watch her interact with her mother, or call her as a witness in his courtroom—even though he was assigned the task of deciding Terri's ultimate fate.

In this regard, I had unmatched access to the truth of Terri's condition . . . the truth that has been withheld from you, the truth that we were not able to introduce as evidence in court. Indeed, I write because it's impossible for me to remain silent. As one of the few eye-witnesses, I have an obligation to you and to our country. I must confront the gross misrepresentations and outright fabrications that some are using to justify future abuses against thousands of those whose "quality of life" has been called into question.

What's more, the wall-to-wall media coverage during Terri's final days made her story one of the top media events of 2005. Yet a tremendous amount of confusion still lingers in the minds of most Americans as to what really happened. Everywhere I travel, people voice conflicting opinions about Terri's story.

Many people have told me they cannot understand why she had to die. They fear the judicial branch is unaccountable and out of control. They can't comprehend why Michael Schiavo paid hundreds of thousands of dollars to secure his wife's death—monies that should have been earmarked for her rehabilitation from a medical malpractice lawsuit. Others believe the Florida legislature, the U.S. Congress, and President George W. Bush had no business meddling in a "private" family affair. This confusion and division is especially evident in the legal, medical, and other professional communities.

I believe the reason our country is wrestling with these questions is because, at some deeper level, we instinctively realize something profoundly wrong has happened. The Terri Schiavo case is to our generation what *Roe v. Wade* was to our parents' generation.

Life itself was on trial.

I believe if "We the People" fail to stand for life in the wake of Terri's death, the intrinsic value of life for the infirm, the elderly, and the disabled will be severely diluted. Even the self-proclaimed atheist and well-known liberal journalist Nat Hentoff called the dehydration and starvation of Terri Schiavo "the longest public execution in American history,"[2] and he believes America has already lost her way.

There are some who say that our nation is simply unable or unwilling to appropriately face death as a culture. While I do agree that our nation is obsessed with youth and physical beauty, pro-euthanasia proponents claim that we are trying to run from death and avoid it at all costs. Their argument is that, although Terri wanted to die, her family and others simply did not want to face the ugly prospect of that fact. The Schindlers and I, and many millions of others who prayed that Terri's life might be spared, however, are not denying death's inevitability or suffering from some sense of cultural denial toward its prospect.

I understand that modern medicine has the technology to keep a flatline corpse "alive" indefinitely if so desired. It's entirely possible to keep the lungs working and the heart beating through machinery long after a person is dead. I'm not in favor of that. The Bible says there is "a time to be born, and a time to die" (Ecclesiastes 3:2). Sadly, the notion that Terri was already "dead and gone" was the most common misconception circulating about her.

We were not fighting against an inevitable or natural death; we were fighting against the *unnatural, premature death* of someone who did not deserve to die. There is a huge difference between fighting for legitimate life and being in denial when it's simply "someone's time to go."

Quite simply, it was not Terri's time to go.

Second, I write because I was raised to love and respect America and the rule of law. When I was a child, my parents encouraged me to memorize the Pledge of Allegiance. They taught me about the faith of our forefathers who founded the United States with their sacrifice and blood. I came to believe America was the greatest, kindest, and most generous nation in the world. But when the Supreme Court refused to grant our final appeal to rescue Terri from death, I thought, *Dear Lord, how, as a nation, have we reached this point?* For the first time in my life, I was embarrassed to be an American.

Here is what troubled me:

America has sent men and women overseas to fight the atrocities and human abuses in Afghanistan and Iraq. For decades we have had a rich history of opposing brutal dictators—Saddam Hussein, Slobodan Milosevic, Adolf Hitler, among others—for torturing and gassing to death their own people. Yet here at home on our soil, with the full blessing of our courts and under the alleged authority of American law, we were engaged in an equally barbaric act.

The third motivation for creating this eyewitness account flows from the tears of Mary Schindler, Terri's mother. There are some things law school cannot prepare you for. One such event was the afternoon Mary and I walked out of Terri's hospice room for what would be the last time Mary would see her daughter this side of heaven. Mary turned to me and said, "David, I'm no lawyer and I'm no doctor. But what I don't understand is why did they have to kill my little girl?"

That is *the* troubling moral dilemma.

When I first became involved with this case, Bob and Mary Schindler asked me to do anything that we could think of that was both legal and proper to save the life of their daughter. After Terri died, Bob and Mary asked me to tell what really happened—specifically the trial and error of this landmark case—so that many others would be spared from a similar fate.

I make no apology that, from my perspective, what happened to Terri was wrong. Very wrong. Maybe you agree. Then again, maybe you disagree, or the jury is still out in your mind. I believe if you will join me as I present my case, you will come to understand:

Why I fought for Terri.

Why I'd do it again.

And why I'd fight for you too.

CHAPTER TWO

SEEING IS BELIEVING

Theresa Schiavo didn't have a written living will. She didn't specify in writing what her wishes were, so we had to rely on oral statements.

—GEORGE FELOS, ATTORNEY FOR MICHAEL SCHIAVO[1]

In the predawn hours of February 25, 1990, twenty-six-year-old Terri Schiavo collapsed while home alone with her husband. Deprived of oxygen for several minutes, Terri was rendered a brain-injured woman and later was diagnosed as being in a persistent vegetative state (known as PVS). More than fifteen years later the cause of her trauma remains unknown.

On many occasions, through watching news reports as a concerned citizen, before I even knew the Schindlers or their daughter, I had heard various descriptions of Terri and her condition.

However, some things defy description.

Take the Grand Canyon. There are simply no words, pictures, or movies that can capture the magnitude of this 277-mile long, five-thousand-foot-deep breach in the earth's crust. A postcard from the gift shop will never take your breath away. But to linger at the edge of the Grand Canyon's North Rim—there's nothing like it. It's life changing.

How about gazing upward at the impossibly massive arms of a six-hundred-year-old California Redwood ... or swimming with the dolphins in the Florida Keys ... or bringing a newborn baby home from the hospital? To comprehend and appreciate these things, you just have to experience them for yourself. Nothing else will do.

Here's the connection to Terri Schiavo.

As an eyewitness, I can attest that there was a tremendous volume of misinformation circulated by some in the media about Terri. While many in the media genuinely understood and sympathized with Terri's fight for life, in general, the American public was—and continues to be—misled as to the true nature of Terri's medical condition prior to her death. Why? I particularly fault many in the mainstream press for their lack of due diligence. Rather than digging deep to authenticate her status—rather than pushing to *see Terri for themselves*—most chose to rehash secondhand, unverified information.

Published reports said Terri was "in a coma" ... she was on "life support" ... she was a "vegetable" ... she was "brain-dead" ... she was "unresponsive" ... she was on "the verge of death" ... she needed a "respirator to breathe." What's more, virtually every statement by Michael Schiavo and his attorney George Felos reinforced these descriptions that we found—as you'll see—to be completely false.

I am convinced Terri's life never would have been snuffed out if what I saw with my own eyes had been reported by more of those in the press. Granted, the short visitor list enforced by Michael Schiavo and the court restricted access to Terri. That would be an obstacle for the press, no question. But they should have gone deeper, pushed harder.

In this case the public was often misled to arrive at some erroneous conclusions. Probably like you, I had initially carried with me a number of wrong assumptions based on what was available through the media.

When I went to see Terri for the first time in late 2004, I didn't really know what to expect. Was she pale? Was she stretched out in a bed, immobile, a living corpse? Would she respond to me? Would she even know I was there? Or, as some had suggested, were her parents the problem? Were the Schindlers delusional and unwilling to acknowledge that Terri was, in fact, comatose? I decided to prepare myself for the possibility that the Schindlers may have loved their daughter so much that they were imagining signs of vitality.

But Terri was not terminal—or comatose.

Not even close.

INSIDE WOODSIDE HOSPICE

As I will relate in the next chapter, I became involved with the Schindlers' case to save Terri in October 2003, but it was not until September 2004 that the Gibbs Law Firm officially became lead counsel for the family. Then it took another few months before I was added to Terri's official visitors list by Michael Schiavo, her court-appointed guardian.

On Christmas Eve, 2004, my legal colleague Barbara Weller and I traveled with Bob and Mary Schindler the short distance from our office to the hospice. Woodside Hospice is a sprawling, seventy-two-bed, one-story red brick complex nestled in the shadows of groomed hedges, flowering fuchsia bushes, and tall trees. Hand-painted birdhouses and wrought-iron benches accent the winding walking trails, creating an otherwise tranquil setting for the patients.

To be candid, I fully expected Terri to be hooked up to a battery of tubes and monitors necessary to keep her alive. I've been in intensive care situations; I've known people who were teetering on the brink of death. Like the rest of the country (and the world), my mental picture had been shaped by the press, so I envisioned Terri in some kind of medically severe situation—you know, like an episode from a prime-time hospital drama with a doctor barking out orders to the nurses.

I was sorely mistaken. In fact, I was in for the shock of my life.

When we entered her room, I found Terri sitting in a recliner with a holiday blanket draped across her lap. She was dressed and washed, and her hair had been brushed. By all outward appearances, she could have been waiting for the morning paper to be delivered or her favorite radio program to begin. I almost gawked at the scene: Absolutely *nothing* was hooked up to her. No IV drip. No monitors. No ventilator. There was no indication whatsoever of any form of artificial life support in use. Even the feeding tube was unattached to the port in Terri's stomach since it wasn't lunchtime.

During our forty-five minute initial visit, it was clear Terri understood who the different people were in the room. Hands down, Mary was Terri's favorite. I'm convinced there's a bond between a mother and a child that is established at birth, one that lasts a lifetime. And in Terri's situation, even as a forty-one-year-old woman, I believe some of her strength and her will to live was derived from that mother-daughter bond. To watch the two of them interact was nothing short of incredible.

At the sound of her mother's voice, Terri squealed with delight, filling the air with a host of happy sounds. She had this excited animation about her that was part giggle and part sheer joy. In fact, Terri could move, and she almost jumped out of the chair. She was clearly animated and responsive, and very much alive. I was wishing some reporters could have been present to record the events of that day. If even one minute of this interchange had been seen by the public, there is no way Terri would have died. I saw an unmistakable inner light radiating from Terri as she and her mother "loved on" each other. I am told by neurologists that people in PVS do not react to external stimuli in a purposeful manner with such human emotion.

Mary was the first one to hug Terri. She cradled Terri's face with her hands. With soft, slow strokes, Mary caressed Terri on the cheek. She kissed her daughter, and much to my surprise, Terri attempted to offer a sloppy kiss back. Now, Terri never could maneuver her lips completely, but she did her best to return the affection. Between kisses Mary said, "Merry Christmas, sweetheart. We're here to visit."

Then it was Bob's turn to greet his daughter.

Interestingly, Terri responded very differently to her dad. Bob had developed this playful routine he'd go through with her each time they were together. I watched Bob announce, "Here comes the hug" as he wrapped her in a bearlike embrace. Then Bob said, "You know what's coming next—the kiss!" He moved in close for a smooch. Keep in mind that Bob sports a scratchy mustache. His chin was often unshaved too, which caused his facial hair to tickle Terri's face.

Over the years, as she did during our visit, Terri would scrunch up her whole face in preparation for the assault on her cheeks that she knew was coming with Bob's scratchy kiss. Her family called this Terri's "lemon face." With a giggle, she'd turn her head away as if toying with her dad. In the end, she'd laugh as his lips made contact with her cheek. She responded the exact same way every time to her father's auditory cues as he consistently initiated this playful routine.

After his kiss Mary said, "Terri, I brought with us some new friends I want you to meet. This is Mr. Gibbs. He's an attorney who is helping us help you."

After Mary's brief introduction, I said, "Hi, Terri. It's so good to meet you. Merry Christmas!" An interesting thing happened as I spoke. Terri's eyes widened like saucers as if to say, "What's that new sound I hear?" I confess I have a very deep, resonant voice. Terri obviously picked up on it. Even though I was quickly convinced Terri could understand much more than the outside world had been led to believe, I decided to keep my interaction with her very simple.

Standing in front of her, I said, "I want you to know we're gonna fight for you, Terri. We want to get you home for the Fourth of July if we can win this." Although she was watching me intently, I couldn't help but wonder, *Is she following any of this? Does she even recognize the fact that I'm standing right in front of her?*

As a test, I decided to walk around her recliner while talking to see if she would follow my booming voice. I'm not a medical doctor. My training is in law. But neurologists have told me that, by definition, vegetative patients are not aware of external stimuli. I was guessing if Terri was truly in a "persistent vegetative state" as the press had been told (since they weren't allowed to see for themselves—Michael had forbidden it), she'd be oblivious to my little experiment.

I started to move behind her chair, saying, "Boy, Terri, won't it be nice to have Thanksgiving at home next year?" At first Terri's head had been cocked to her left. As I walked around and stood directly behind her, I started talking again. I had just run in our local Thanksgiving race, called the Turkey Trot, and the legal team had been joking about how great it would be to push Terri the three-plus miles in her chair the next year as a sort of victory lap.

"Terri, maybe you and your parents could go to the Turkey Trot and see some of your old friends next Thanksgiving." You know what she did? She flipped around trying to follow me. Wherever I would stand and talk, Terri tracked my position. Clearly, she had some degree of comprehension.

Was Terri brain-injured? No question. The injuries she suffered that night in her apartment would be with her for the rest of her life. She was not, however, *brain-dead*. If Terri were truly brain-dead, she would be unresponsive to any stimuli and devoid of all muscle activity. She would not be capable of moving in her chair or even breathing on her own. Was she disabled? No question. We never disputed that. But was she aware of us on some level?

Absolutely.

I retraced my steps and stood in front of this special lady. Terri flipped around again to keep me in view. Just as I was about to share a few more thoughts, Mary astonished me with a little demonstration of her own.

I LOVE YOU

Mary Schindler was a stay-at-home mother. She had no formal college education and certainly no specialized background in speech therapy or training in medical rehabilitation. She did, however, have a mother's love and affection, which ran deep for Terri. Mary drew close to her daughter and started to softly rub her on the cheek.

Mary said, "Now, Terri, I want you to show Mr. Gibbs some things." She continued to stimulate Terri's cheek. After a moment, Mary said, "Terri, say 'I.'"

My heart started to pound. Was it possible Terri would respond? In court the "experts" had testified that she was unresponsive. I was also aware that back on October 27, 2003, Larry King had asked Michael Schiavo about her ability to speak.

KING: Did she ever speak since 1990?
SCHIAVO: Terri never has spoken a word.[2]

I braced myself. Would this woman, whom the court had ordered to die, begin to respond to basic verbal commands?

Terri obeyed her mom and said, "Ahhh."

I thought, *That's not even possible.* According to everything I'd read in the court documents and transcripts, as well as the numerous reports in the press, Terri was not aware of her environment and could not engage in voluntary behavioral responses, even when prompted. Yet here was Terri, verbalizing appropriate and different syllables at her mother's direction.

Mary stroked Terri's cheek some more and then said, "Good. Now, Terri, say 'love.'"

Terri got the "l" and said, "Laaa."

"Terri, say 'you.'"

We waited, but Terri couldn't get the "you."

Apparently certain letters were just too difficult for Terri to form with her mouth—at least without specialized instruction from a speech therapist. With more than a million-dollar malpractice award requested in 1992 for Terri's care and rehab, it was sad that her husband and guardian, Michael Schiavo, was spending that money on lawyers and not on Terri's rehabilitation, including speech therapy.

Undeterred, Mary said, "Here, let's do this again now." With great affection she said to her daughter, "Okay, Terri. Now come on and say 'I.'"

"Ahhh."

"Say 'love.'"

"Laaa."

"Say 'you.'"

Terri never managed to get the "you." Over the next ten or twelve minutes, I watched this woman obey her mom repeatedly as they worked on this one basic sentence. Throughout the exchange Terri searched Mary's face with a wonderment as if to say, "Did I do good?" As Mary offered affirmation, Terri's face literally shone as she basked in her mom's approval.

I found myself at a loss for words.

Here was a lady who was brain-injured and severely disabled, no question about that. Yet Terri recognized people, enjoyed the company of her family, and struggled to communicate. Interestingly, over the course of my future visits, Terri even warmed up to me. I'd walk in the room and start to talk to her as you would to a young child. She'd respond to my presence and appropriately jabber right back at me in her own way.

The time for our first visit was up.

As we said our good-byes and as her mother rose to leave, a remarkable thing happened: Tears began to roll down Terri's cheeks. I was told that almost every time Mary would visit and start to leave, Terri's great big tears would flow. No wonder the Schindlers thought there was no way the courts would ever buy the notion that Terri had no capacity to feel or that she should be ordered to die.

You might be wondering, *But, David, how can this be? Wasn't she in a "vegetative state"?*

Be careful when you hear the term "persistent vegetative state" (PVS). Don't allow yourself to think that PVS is a formal, fixed-in-stone medical diagnosis. It's not. I've learned that the PVS diagnosis is a gut-level guess at best. One 1996 *British Medical Journal* study suggested that doctors misdiagnose PVS approximately 43 percent of the time.[3] Another neurologist told me the number of false positive vegetative diagnoses is higher in patients who are motor or visually impaired. Terri had been visually impaired since childhood and was motor impaired as a result of her collapse in 1990. This neurologist estimated the possibility of a misdiagnosis for Terri at 40 percent. I am also told that patients can transition in and out of PVS over time, so unpredictability is also a factor in a PVS diagnosis.

Are you sitting down?

Dr. Ronald Cranford was one of the neurologists used by Michael Schiavo to certify to the court that Terri was in a persistent vegetative state. Cranford was so confident of his diagnosis that he claimed he was "105 percent sure" Terri was PVS. In 1980, however, according to news reports Dr. Cranford made a similar declaration about another one of his patients—Police Sergeant David Mack. David had been shot while serving a warrant.

Cranford told David's relatives, "Sergeant Mack will never regain cognitive, sapient functioning. He will never be aware of his condition nor resume any degree of meaningful voluntary conscious interaction with his family or friends."[4] Relying upon Dr. Cranford's prognosis, Mack's relatives made a life-and-death decision: They pulled the plug on his ventilator.

Guess what? Sergeant Mack didn't die. He continued to breathe and live on his own. Why? Dr. Cranford's unequivocal diagnosis of PVS was totally wrong. In fact, David Mack astonished his family by regaining his consciousness *and* communication skills.

You see, the American Academy of Neurology concedes that the PVS diagnosis is, "as with all clinical diagnoses in medicine, based on probabilities, not absolutes."[5] In other words, a PVS diagnosis is merely an educated guess. Even with the amazing advances in medicine, physicians do not fully comprehend how the brain operates.

In fact, medical journals continue to report rapid discoveries and changes in this area, even as recently as during the last twelve months of Terri's life. For example, neurologists are learning that the brain has an ability to almost re-create itself by reconnecting around the parts that have been damaged.

I'll use a computer example to illustrate this breakthrough. When Judge Greer ordered Terri's death back in 2000, the prevailing thought at that time was that the brain was like a computer hard drive. If it's no longer functioning, we have no option but to discard it.

But by 2005 leading doctors and neurologists were saying, in effect, "No, the brain is not like a hard drive. It's more like the Internet." In other words, when a portion of it is injured, the brain can reorganize and reroute itself (called neuronal plasticity) and still do some amazing things. God has designed our bodies and brains to be resilient and reparative in ways we may never fully understand.

By the way, if Dr. Cranford was wrong about David Mack, isn't it possible that he was also wrong about Terri? Tragically, we'll never know for sure. One thing is certain in my view: If the American public had seen Terri with their own eyes like I did, they never would have let her die.

Does that sound like an overstatement?

Let me give you a bit of corroborating evidence from another person who saw Terri that Christmas Eve day in 2004. My associate Barbara Weller admits that, like me, she anticipated seeing a sickly person with an unwholesome, grayish skin coloration. Instead, Barbara found Terri to be "a very pretty woman with a peaches-and-cream complexion and a lovely smile." After our initial visit, Barbara noted in her journal:

> I never imagined Terri would be so interactive, curious, and purposeful. I was truly taken aback by her beauty, particularly under the adverse circumstances in which she has found herself for so many years.

You see, for more than a decade Terri had not felt the warmth of the sun against her skin. Fresh air, the song of birds, and the rustling of squirrels scurrying about were simple pleasures she was not permitted to savor. Yet in spite of having existed in a warehouselike solitary confinement for many years, Terri appeared to be in remarkable shape to both Barbara and me.

And, though comfortable, Terri's living space where I visited her was not much wider than the width of two single beds and about as long as the average bedroom. A short hallway branching off the main corridor led to her room. In other words, the floor plan isolated Terri from the general population; Terri couldn't see out and there was no way for others to observe her from the hallway.

When pressed to give Terri some freedom, Michael repeatedly insisted that Terri be kept from mingling with the outside world. He refused to authorize the occasional stroll around the facility or across the parklike hospice grounds in her wheelchair.

Even for Christmas.

ALL I WANT FOR CHRISTMAS

Christmas Eve was always difficult for the Schindlers. They longed to bring Terri home to enjoy the holidays together as a family. Keep in mind there was no medical reason why Terri couldn't travel across town for the afternoon. Granted, the hospice had been tastefully decorated. Several lighted Christmas trees were tucked in various alcoves around the facility. The nurses' station had a splash of colorful lights too.

Terri would have enjoyed seeing those decorations, but as you recall her husband said she wasn't permitted out of her room. The only festive display Terri had was the holiday blanket on her lap and a small plastic tree on her bedside table—a stark contrast to what her family would have prepared had she been allowed home for a few hours.

As Bob shared with me later, he and Mary returned on Christmas day to sit with Terri. A number of carolers strolled through the hallways, stopping in the patients' rooms to spread some Christmas cheer. But when this group of minstrels approached Terri's door, the place went crazy. The nurses—fearful of defying Michael's wishes and concerned about losing their jobs—raced out of the woodwork to make sure no carolers went into Terri's room.

After some debate, a compromise was reached and the carolers were permitted to sing several songs outside Terri's door—and out of her view. Still, Bob reported that Terri was radiant. She obviously enjoyed every minute of that Christmas serenade. Christmas had always been her favorite time of the year. As it turns out, this was to be Terri's last taste of Christmas this side of eternity.

Here's what really bothers me.

The woman I saw was desperately trying to talk. She gave and received love. She exhibited joy and sadness. Like standing on the edge of the Grand Canyon, my life would be forever changed by what I saw. I can understand why people who never met Terri are confused. I wouldn't have believed all this myself if I hadn't seen Terri with my own eyes and personally interacted with her.

However, one judge—who never once saw Terri, who never once laid eyes on her, who never even once had her come to court—made the decision that Terri Schiavo's life didn't matter. Without the benefit of a jury, Judge Greer determined from the bench that Terri was in PVS and didn't have a "quality of life" worth living.

Make no mistake: Terri Schiavo was not terminally ill or near death. This case was not an end-of-life decision.

This was a decision to end a life.

As I came to know Bob and Mary Schindler and their lovely daughter Terri, little did I know that my experiences working with them would irrevocably change my life forever.

In the following pages, I will take you on my personal journey working with this remarkable family. I begin one year earlier, in October 2003, the first time my father and I met the Schindlers and heard their amazing story.

CHAPTER THREE

LIFE ON TRIAL

ORDERED AND ADJUDGED *that the Guardian, Michael Schiavo, shall cause the removal of the nutrition and hydration tube from the Ward, Theresa Marie Schiavo, at 2:00* P.M. *on the 15th day of October, 2003.*
—JUDGE GEORGE W. GREER, SEPTEMBER 17, 2003

It's human nature to speculate about what really happened that winter morning in February 1990 when Terri lost consciousness. If I were to record every accusation, conspiracy theory, or attempted murder theory I was presented by well-meaning folks during the case, I'd fill this book with an abundance of juicy speculation. However, to focus primarily on that aspect of the legal situation would be a mistake.

Why?

Doing so would sidetrack us from understanding the injustice that followed. Whatever really happened in their apartment that night, Terri never should have been put to death by order of an American court. You see, this entire case hinged upon two relatively simple legal questions: First, what was Terri's medical condition?

Was she brain-dead or brain-injured?

Was she comatose or alert?

Was she on life support, or did she just need a little extra help with basic necessities?

As I relayed in the last chapter, what I saw regarding her medical condition told me she was not brain-dead, she was certainly *not* on life support, and she was relatively aware of her surroundings. If I live to be a hundred years old, I'll never forget my time with Terri.

The second legal question the court had to answer was this: What were Terri's wishes about ending her life in the case of a medical emergency? And as I shall relate, Terri was ordered by a judge to die based upon conflicting evidence at best. Never had I witnessed such a tragic disregard for the due process rights, as I understood that concept, of a person, whether disabled or not, by our judicial system. Does that sound harsh? I'm not alone in that assessment.

Among the many famous voices who weighed in on the behavior of the court, actor and producer Mel Gibson got it right according to many who were watching when he described the court's order to starve Terri as a modern day crucifixion and "nothing more than state-sanctioned murder." On national radio while Terri was in the final days of her court-ordered dehydration and starvation, Gibson said, "I just sit here watching this whole scenario played out in front of me with my mouth hanging wide open. [I can't believe] that our country has come to this. I think it's really a dark, black day."[1]

There was, however, a golden thread running through the dark tapestry of this modern American tragedy. It's a part of the story overlooked by most of the media. I'm referring to the deep, unconditional love of two ordinary, middle-class parents and their unquenchable desire to rescue their innocent daughter from a court-ordered death.

THE THINGS WE DO FOR LOVE

When Bob and Mary Schindler first met with our legal team in mid-October 2003, they were exhausted, weary, and out of options. Terri was still very much alive, but her days were numbered after being rebuffed by the court system for more than a decade. Within days Terri's feeding tube would be removed for the second time.

In 2001, the first time the tube was removed, it was reinserted a few days later when new evidence surfaced questioning Michael's credibility in telling the court during the 2000 trial what Terri would want to do. After further litigation in 2002 to determine Terri's medical condition and prognosis, Judge Greer had again ordered the feeding tube to be removed. The Schindlers were told there was nothing more to be done this time, except to wrangle over where Terri would be buried. That view was unacceptable to this close-knit family.

Our first meeting with Bob and Mary was held at ten o'clock at night in our law firm conference room. Nearly a dozen lawyers from our firm were already assembled around the conference room table when the Schindlers took their seats. Although we had yet to make a commitment about representation, by the expression on their faces you'd think the cavalry had just arrived.

Without notes and for the better part of two hours, Bob recapped his family's all-consuming living nightmare. I remember his voice would occasionally catch as the sheer desperation of his situation bubbled to the surface. As I studied Bob's face, I saw the fear of a parent who knew his child was going to suffer and he was powerless to stop it.

These were parents frightened beyond words. They had already pursued all the legal avenues their previous attorneys thought might help them protect their daughter, but the court system was now insisting that she die—and die now. The date to begin the "death process," as Terri's husband's attorneys euphemistically called it, had been set to begin on October 15, 2003.

None of us had to say the obvious.

The Schindlers were outgunned and outfinanced.

They had nowhere else to turn and they had spent all of their money long ago. By contrast, their son-in-law, Michael Schiavo, had access to hundreds of thousands of dollars for his legal maneuvering— money that had been made available by a malpractice award for Terri's care and rehabilitation. But that's getting ahead of the story.

For her part, with a picture of Terri resting on the table in front of her, Mary's tears did most of her talking. At first she just sat back in her chair, dabbing her eyes with a crumpled tissue. She'd nod and occasionally clarify or underscore a point in her husband's narrative. Toward the end of our time together, Mary spoke. "You know what?" she said. "If Terri never improves, if Terri remains exactly as she is today, she is still a life worth saving. That's why Bob and I are praying for a miracle."

Mary expressed how stunned she was that so many lawyers from our firm had already cared enough to listen for hours while they bared their souls—especially since they were unable to pay us anything.

When Bob and Mary finished their summary of the case as they understood it, several troubling thoughts crossed my mind. If what I had heard was true, it was a bizarre tale of incredible conflicts of interest: a husband who was living with his girlfriend—with whom he had children—and who was trying to have his wife legally put to death . . . malpractice money, a lot of money, not being used for care and rehabilitation as intended but being used to kill the disabled person instead . . . distraught parents begging for the life of their child from a court system standing on the side of death rather than life. This contested civil court–ordered death of an innocent young woman was a story I might expect to find in a John Grisham novel. But if the Schindlers were to be believed, and I had no reason to doubt them, this was fact, not a work of fiction.

I was impressed, too, that the heart's desire of these parents was to save Terri—not to pinpoint blame or speculate about the events leading up to Terri's disability. And contrary to some members of the local press who had portrayed the Schindlers as selfish, delusional parents set on meddling in matters that were none of their business, I knew right then that nothing could be further from the truth. To this day there is no doubt in my mind that Bob and Mary would have traded places with Terri that very night if that would have prevented their daughter from dying.

I am not exaggerating.

After all the legal options had been exhausted, I know what their response would have been to the following offer: "Here's the deal. We're going to place you in a hospice bed. You'll receive no food or water. You will die slowly over thirteen days with not so much as an ice chip to ease your discomfort. In exchange, Terri gets to live." I'm convinced that these parents loved their daughter so much, they would have taken that deal in a heartbeat.

CASE CLOSED

I'm a realist. Even surrounded by a room filled with nearly a dozen very bright lawyers, including my father, my instincts told me that the Schindlers' legal options were close to nil. This was a case that had already been lost before it reached our office. I could see why most lawyers would advise these parents to cut their losses and get on with their lives.

First, the average lawyer wants to win cases and get paid for his work. In that respect, practicing law is no different from any other profession. If you're an accountant, dentist, teacher, or if you flip hamburgers, if you do your job, you'd like to get paid for your efforts. This couple had no cash to continue their fight. That's strike one.

Second, the average lawyer wants to get into a case from the ground floor so that he or she can be the architect of the situation. With the Schindlers, all of the judges that a new lawyer would have to approach had already ruled against them. All of the primary issues had been previously addressed.

In other words, if you were a lawyer about to take this case, you'd have to come before these judges and tell them that they had made a mistake and then ask them to change their minds. Trust me, judges don't like to be second-guessed. Why, I asked myself, would any lawyer in his right mind be willing to do that?

Furthermore, according to Bob, there had been a full trial and a number of appeals championed by hardworking, professional lawyers involved at various stages in the case. There had been a second trial and appeal, and the decision was the same from every single court. The decisions were clear: Bob and Mary Schindler had lost their case.

Their daughter would die in just a few days.

Any lawyer with even a few years of trial experience would have to at least wonder, *Why did all of those judges and so many rulings go against the Schindlers?*

Third, the average lawyer wants to protect his or her reputation; your reputation is what generates future business. Lawyers don't have a product to sell. Rather, they sell themselves, and they provide a service to people. Their reputation could well be ruined for the rest of their lives if attached to a case like this that was already lost.

That was the status of the Schindlers' situation when our office was asked to step into this case. To say yes to the Schindlers' request for help was to inherit all of that prior history. To be clear, there wasn't the slightest hint that maybe down the road the United States Congress, the president, or even the U.S. Supreme Court would get involved. Everybody around the conference table fully expected Terri to die in just a few short days unless something miraculous occurred to stop it.

I sensed that the Schindlers were looking for some sort of direction from my father and me and from our law firm that evening. Would we help with the case? Was there any hope to turn things around? Had they overlooked something? I adjusted my glasses and leaned forward to do one of the most difficult things a lawyer has to do: level with a client. On one hand, I didn't want to douse the last flames of hope that flickered within their hearts. On the other hand, I didn't want to mislead them into thinking we possessed the silver bullet for their defense.

After my father offered some personal counsel to the Schindlers, I said, "From what you've told us tonight and from the preliminary research we did in preparation for this meeting, we probably would have to concur with what you have already been told." I paused, not for effect but because of how difficult it was to actually say the words. "It appears that this case is over."

Bob nodded silently, as if he had fully expected this response. I looked at Mary and quickly added, "Just because rescuing Terri looks difficult and just because your prospects of winning appear impossible, we also acknowledge that we serve a God who can do the impossible."

With that, our team assured them we'd work through the night to see if there were any unexplored avenues that might be worthy of pursuit. Our offer was to lend a hand behind the scenes—at least for starters.

Just after midnight we held hands, prayed, and committed Terri into God's care. After bidding the Schindlers good-bye, our legal team rolled up their sleeves and headed for their desks. Then something amazing happened: Quite unexpectedly, the idea of taking a legislative approach instead of a direct frontal assault on the court system was planted that night.

Unknown to us, at the same time, others in Florida were also weighing this exact approach.

In the days that followed, our attorneys worked with longtime friends in the legislature to draft what widely became labeled "Terri's Law"—although she was not mentioned by name in the document. Our original version of Terri's Law called for a broad public policy change toward all patients whose medical wishes were not clearly spelled out in written living wills or advance care directives. Our intent was to craft a law that could withstand a constitutional challenge. I will talk about this incredible event in the next chapter.

WHY DO IT?

From time to time I'm asked why our legal team agreed to work with the Schindlers—especially given the pitfalls and incredible odds against us. In a word, I believe God called me to do this work. As my father taught me, having a servant's heart doesn't always mean you do what's *easy*; rather, you do what's *right*. I also couldn't escape the fact that Terri was in a hospice just six or seven miles from our office. You might say that Terri was a neighbor in need in our own backyard.

Talk about a divine appointment.

What's more, the issues at stake were huge. Every day of the week lawyers will go to court to try to keep people from going to jail, or try to win money in a malpractice suit, or to save people from having to pay money unjustly. But beyond directives, beyond incarceration, beyond money, there are cases that are of preeminent importance because they deal with life and death. Here was a life-and-death issue *not* involving a felon. With Terri, the life of an innocent woman was on the line.

How could the stakes be any higher?

In the last analysis, I looked at Bob and Mary and my heart went out to them. I had been blessed with legal training; they were in desperate need of legal assistance. After they approached us, I couldn't escape this question: Had the roles been reversed, what would I have wanted them to do for me? I was convinced we had an obligation to step in, no matter what the cost.

CHAPTER FOUR

TERRI'S LAW

The measure of a civilization is how we treat the weak, the
dependent, the helpless, and the ill.
—DR. LAURA SCHLESSINGER[1]

That Wednesday, October 15, 2003, just days after the initial meeting in which we agreed to try to help the Schindlers, Terri's feeding tube was removed for the second time. (The first time had been in 2001, when the Schindlers had been successful in having the tube reinserted.) Our window of time to save her life was narrow at best—and closing quickly.

We researched our options around the clock only to make a startling discovery: We could find no remaining judicial maneuvers that could protect Terri from the certain death imposed on her by the Pinellas County, Florida, Probate Court. Bob and Mary had already tried everything, and Judge Greer and the appellate courts—almost automatically it seemed to the Schindlers—had denied nearly every motion they filed.

After reviewing and discarding all of our court options, we determined that the only way Terri's life could be protected was through a *legislative approach* to counteract the judge's order to withdraw her food and water. Talk about an uphill battle.

As you might know, most state constitutions, like the federal consti-tution, establish a balance of power between the judicial, legislative, and executive branches, but the wheels of government move very slowly. Even if a new law could quickly be drafted, the legislature would have to be willing and able to act before it was too late. That could take months or possibly years—time we didn't have. For all we knew at that point, Terri had only a few more days to live.

Another challenge we faced was that the Florida legislature doesn't meet year-round. Even if it were possible to get a new law introduced, the legislature had to actually be in session to pass it—and they didn't meet in the fall. Of course, Governor Jeb Bush could call a special leg-islative session, but that couldn't be done in only a few days. As quickly as this improbable legislative solution came to mind, we dismissed it as not being a realistic option. Humanly speaking, we just didn't have enough time to pull it off.

But then the impossible happened.

On Friday we heard on the news that a special session of the legis-lature had, in fact, already been called and was scheduled to begin on Monday. The governor had called the special session to deal with some state economic development issues.

We thought this just might be our much-needed miracle.

Our office contacted Representative John Stargel, a Florida legisla-tor we had come to know and respect. Our first question was whether the special session could consider any other piece of legislation in addi-tion to the reason for which it had been called. Could a bill to save Terri's life be considered? Representative Stargel thought it could be and asked for our help to draft something that might work.

I called our office attorneys together to brainstorm the best lan-guage for a bill that might save Terri's life. Around the clock and throughout that weekend, our legal team pored over state statutes and drafted some proposed language. The legislative session would open on Monday, Day Five of Terri's "death process." The bill had to be ready to move quickly through the house and the senate.

Our office stayed in constant communication throughout that weekend with other legislators we knew who were also in contact with Governor Bush's legal advisors. Representative Stargel assured us that all of these key people appreciated the gravity of Terri's situation. Evidently, the lawmakers in Tallahassee had already been made aware through other channels that Terri's feeding tube had been withdrawn earlier that week and they were very concerned. They knew she was already dying. They, like us, didn't know how much longer she could hold on.

Legislators called our office over and over again that weekend, wanting more information on Terri's condition and more facts about the case and its procedural history to share with fellow lawmakers. Several allies were lining up supporters for the bill even as our office was drafting it. We made the final edits to our proposed legislation by the end of the weekend. At the crack of dawn on Monday, we rushed the document off to Representative Stargel just in time for it to be introduced a few hours later.

It was not until the bill was already on its way to the legislature that we informed the Schindlers we were working on what we hoped would produce a breakthrough for Terri. We had told the Schindlers on Friday that we were working on something but that we were not at liberty to provide them with any details at that point. We just told them not to turn off their cell phones for the next few days and that we would definitely need to be able to reach them on Monday.

You see, we were keeping our project very quiet because we didn't want the other side to learn of the pending legislation and, in turn, possibly build a strategy against it. But by Monday we felt we could finally encourage Bob and Mary not to give up—and to pray for the miracle legislation that just might still save their daughter's life.

ROADBLOCKS, DETOURS, AND ALLIES

Our hopes ran high as we worked that weekend, but we hit a snag on Monday. We received a troubling phone call informing us that we'd hit a brick wall in the legislature. A powerful state senator had made it known emphatically that, whatever the house did, he intended to personally block the bill from coming to the senate floor for a vote. We later learned why this noble effort had reached an impasse.

As it turned out, this powerful senator had been the chief architect of the 1997 Florida end-of-life legislation that had helped Michael's attorney George Felos get Michael into Judge Greer's courtroom. Therefore, the senator was opposed to *any* alteration to the law that he and several others had personally crafted for just this sort of situation. Keep in mind that Terri seemed to be the "test case" for this new law. As far as we were aware, George Felos used it for the first time at the 2000 trial to allow the court to condemn Terri to death.

It was this legislation, along with new interpretations of Florida's constitutional provisions regarding privacy rights, that now made it possible for a Florida court to determine that a disabled person without a living will, and who was "terminal" or in a "persistent vegetative state," could be ordered to die by a judge after a determination of that person's end-of-life wishes was made. The court could now hear oral testimony regarding whether that person would want to live or die in that circumstance.

All the court had to do was to determine whether there was clear and convincing evidence of the disabled person's wishes, and if the court found such evidence, a civil death sentence could be imposed. Under this new law, artificial life support now had a radically expanded definition and included the use of a feeding tube. Of course, removal of the tube for Terri would result in dehydration and starvation.

The senator who was opposing our proposed bill considered his earlier legislation to be a legacy to a family member whose dying was prolonged because there was no living will or other document that would have permitted doctors to unplug life support, food, and water. He wasn't about to let anybody tamper with his legacy.

Our law firm's original draft of what eventually became known as Terri's Law was intended to reverse the relatively new Florida public policy that permitted the unplugging of feeding tubes for people like Terri who had no written end-of-life directives. Our bill would have protected the disabled from having a feeding tube removed when there was a family disagreement regarding the disabled person's spoken end-of-life wishes. No wonder the senator was unwilling to agree to this change.

When we realized that the bill was going to be kept off the senate floor, a massive PR campaign was unleashed. The Schindlers had a small army of supporters who were watching the news eager to help. Within hours phone calls, faxes, and e-mails poured into the senate and into the governor's office as nearly two hundred thousand concerned citizens made their wishes known to the Florida legislators.

One reason there was such a tsunami of support for Terri is that the pump had already been primed by several talk radio hosts who had been following this case for years. In one particularly heated exchange, nationally syndicated radio host Glenn Beck grilled Steve Schiavo, Michael's brother, about the state of a country that would intentionally starve a person to death. I'm sure the fact that Glenn has a handicapped daughter weighed heavily on his heart upon hearing the news that Terri would be starved to death.

Steve asserted that Glenn and the public were being misled and misinformed by the Schindlers. Glenn took exception to that remark:

GLENN: I saw the videotape of his wife who is very much alive. I saw the videotape of a woman who is handicapped—not dead—that [Michael] is trying to kill. I don't get my truth from the Schindlers, I get my truth from the ultimate source: I see it with my own eyes.

STEVE: Excuse me, Glenn. When did you become a neurologist?

GLENN: I'm not a neurologist, sir. When someone is asked, "Open your eyes" and they lean up and open their eyes and follow commands, sir, I know the woman is alive. . . . She is handicapped, she is not terminally ill and we don't starve people to death that are handicapped.

STEVE: Okay. That's your opinion.

GLENN: Let me ask you a question: Do we, Steve, in America—or as people—starve handicapped people to death?

STEVE: That . . . that is . . .

GLENN: That's a simple question. It's a "yes" or "no" question, sir. In America—or as human beings—do we starve handicapped people to death? Yes or no?

STEVE: I would imagine so, yes. Yes.

GLENN: Hang on, Steve. I want to give you every opportunity to bail yourself out. Your statement is, as Michael Schiavo's brother, we do in America starve handicapped people to death.

STEVE: If that's what the courts call for, yes.[2]

Exchanges like these had exposed the truth of what was happening to Terri in Pinellas County. After the avalanche of faxes and e-mails supporting Terri, and at the urging of his fellow senators who were equally deluged with pleas from the public, the senator blocking the bill was persuaded to offer a compromise. He let it be known that he would agree to allow the bill to be heard and voted on in the senate on one condition: that he be permitted to rewrite the bill and introduce it on the senate floor as his bill.

Recognizing that, as the saying goes, half a loaf is better than none, our side agreed to the compromise. The version of the bill our office had drafted was designed to be broad in scope. The senate dramatically narrowed its version of the bill. They took out the general public policy language and inserted a more specific provision requiring action by the governor to reconsider Terri's case within a limited amount of time.

These changes substantially weakened the bill's constitutional viability. We had to wonder if this was a "poison pill" intended to permit the law to be passed but then to be struck down by a separation-of-powers argument. We couldn't be sure. All we knew was that we were being presented with a "take it or leave it" option. So we took it.

We also recognized that Terri had been without food or water for five days. No one knew how much longer she could survive. Worse, Terri had initially been dressed in warm clothing to cause her to sweat and dehydrate more rapidly. What choice did we have? We had to agree to this compromise to keep Terri alive for another round of legal battles, poison pill or not.

Even with this concession, the legislative struggle was not over. As the legislature was waging battle in debate, Representative Stargel's aides would call our office often, saying that some of the opposing representatives and senators were reading from a list of talking points that Stargel's aides did not believe were true. Each time they'd call, our attorneys would rush to pull together the accurate data and then fax the facts to Representative Stargel's office for him and other sympathetic representatives and senators to use to counter the misleading statements being made about Terri on the floor.

THE FINAL PUSH

While we worked to stamp out those fires, on Monday afternoon Michael's attorney, George Felos, called a press conference and declared that he would fight the proposed legislation as unconstitutional. Further, he threatened to sue any doctor who reinserted the feeding tube should the governor sign the bill.

When we heard about the press conference, our office jumped on the phone again to Tallahassee. We informed Representative Stargel about the press conference and that the joint committee (where the bill had now gone to resolve the differences in the house and senate versions) had to insert an immunity clause for the doctors. Otherwise, Terri might die despite passage of the legislation and an order by the governor.

At the same time that the bill was making its way through the legislature, our office had also begun a direct dialogue with the governor's office regarding how the measures permitted in the bill would be carried out. The new bill, as passed by the senate, gave the governor a onetime option to stay a judicial order and reinsert the feeding tube for a person in Terri's situation. This would give his office time to undertake a review of the circumstances. Our office, coordinating with the governor's legal counsel, hammered out how any order Governor Bush might sign would be carried out.

When it appeared that the redrafted bill would pass in both houses, our office began to look for the fastest way to rush the new law and a copy of the governor's order to the hospice facility immediately after the governor signed it. We called the governor's office and requested that as soon as the law passed, we would need a copy of the law and of the governor's order faxed to our office without delay. They agreed to help. Each time we spoke, the governor's legal team would ask how Terri was doing. We realized that they were genuinely concerned for her life.

As Day Five faded into evening, we called the county sheriff's office to request that their people be placed on standby. We politely asked for their help to serve the governor's order on the hospice as soon as it was signed and delivered. A few minutes later, a call came from the sheriff's office to inform us that they couldn't guarantee immediate service of the governor's order on the hospice.

That was a surprise. We asked (naïvely, perhaps) if the sheriff's office was at all familiar with the case and with the fact that a woman's life was hanging in the balance. The response we received continued to be both evasive and noncommittal regarding any assistance with speeding up the notification process.

We weren't about to let this lack of responsiveness deprive Terri of a chance to live. Within minutes we were back on the phone with the governor's office. We explained the potential problem we might face with the county sheriff's office. Without their willingness to guarantee immediate service of the governor's order, we needed some help from the Florida Department of Law Enforcement (FDLE). We asked if there was any way the governor could prearrange for a state trooper in the FDLE division in Pinellas County to serve his order on the hospice.

Once again, we found a desire to help at the highest levels. The governor's office agreed to use such a protocol. His legal team arranged for the governor's office to directly fax Governor Bush's signed order to our law firm. We, in turn, would work with a state trooper from FDLE to deliver it to the hospice without delay. With that settled, and the business of the day concluded, we waited and prayed into the night for the bill's final passage—and for Terri to hang on long enough for this help to arrive.

On October 21, 2003, six days after Terri's feeding tube had been removed, House Bill No. 35-E was passed by the Florida State Legislature and signed into law by Governor Jeb Bush. Representative Stargel called us with the wonderful news. He assured us that he was running to the governor's office to have an order signed immediately. As you can imagine, our staff burst into tears of joy.

Although it wasn't really necessary, we reminded Representative Stargel that every minute counted and that we would be hovering over the fax machine. After what felt like an eternity, but in reality was only a few minutes, our fax machine sprang to life. With eager hands outstretched, we watched as the machine began printing out what was to become the Life Certificate for Terri Schindler Schiavo. As we were about to learn, passing the law was the "easy" part. Getting it enforced would require three things:

A police escort.

A clash of wills at the hospital, and . . .

Another miracle.

CHAPTER FIVE

DOCTOR'S ORDERS

I'm very, very grateful to the Florida legislature and Jeb Bush. . . . They did the right thing.

—SEAN HANNITY ON THE PASSAGE OF TERRI'S LAW[1]

W e hovered close to the fax machine like doctors waiting to deliver a baby. As the pages emerged, our eager hands received the precious document before it ever touched the paper tray. With care, we quickly made several copies of Governor Jeb Bush's signed order. Rex Sparklin, one of our Gibbs Law Firm attorneys, jumped into his truck and made a beeline to Woodside Hospice.

As he turned onto the street where the facility was located, Rex slowed down as it took a long minute to absorb the surreal scene unfolding before him. Hundreds of Terri's supporters lined the street behind temporary orange barriers stretching the length of several blocks. Some held homemade signs protesting her starvation. Others were singing softly or openly weeping.

A number of the demonstrators were huddled in small groups of two or three to pray. The disabled, confined to their wheelchairs or leaning on their crutches, were scattered throughout the crowd pleading to save Terri's life.

In a clear show of force, police cars blocked access to the hospice's two entrances. Armed officers had been assigned to patrol the hospice grounds to prevent any unauthorized attempt to reach Terri with food or water. Rex also noticed that the media was out in full force. With a battery of cameras and microphones, they darted around looking for any scrap of news. If they had known what Rex held in his hand, he would have been stampeded by the press, of that he was sure.

Rex inched his truck forward. Progress was slow at best. The closer he got to the hospice, the more congested the road became as the crowd and the media swelled in numbers. Recognizing that getting through the masses with his vehicle was next to impossible, Rex quickly parked at the edge of the crowded area, hopped out, and made his way on foot. He just had to get those documents to the right authorities.

At the first police barricade, an officer approached and asked him to state his business. Rex informed the guard that he possessed a copy of the governor's order to reinsert Terri's feeding tube and that it needed to be delivered immediately to Terri's caregivers. As he handed the policeman a copy, Rex explained that he'd wait right there for confirmation of the delivery.

The officer scanned the paperwork and then told Rex to stay put while he walked the order into the hospice. With that, the policeman disappeared through the crowd. Sensing that something big was happening, members of the press started to drift in Rex's direction.

Just as Rex was about to be mobbed by journalists chasing the scent of a hot story, the officer returned to confirm the delivery. He also informed Rex that Terri would be taken by ambulance to the Morton Plant Hospital to have her feeding tube reinserted. As quickly as Rex had arrived, he slipped back to his truck. Making a U-turn, he started to drive away as a trail of cameras and news crews chased his vehicle.

He could hear the press shouting a barrage of questions. . . . *What's your name? What are you doing? Are you with the family? Did the governor sign the bill? Is the hospice cooperating? Is Terri still alive?*

Rex drove on, ignoring their endless questions. You see, at that point we were not planning to let the news media know about our involvement in the behind-the-scenes process. After Rex returned to the office, we were about to head home for some much needed rest, but we found ourselves fighting the clock once again. That evening, at about eight o'clock, we received a most disturbing phone call.

"We have a real problem," the caller said. "I have just received word that the Morton Plant Hospital doctors are refusing to reinsert Terri's feeding tube!" Our source wanted to know if we'd heard anything about that allegation. We hadn't. Nor could we understand why the hospital would disregard the governor's order. We knew that the immunity clause for the doctors had been inserted into the bill.

Having gone six days without food or water, if Terri didn't receive hydration very soon, her internal organs would begin to shut down—probably beginning with her kidneys. Certainly the doctors and nurses would know that Terri's situation was critical. Why, then, the delay? I dispatched Rex to be our eyes and ears on the ground yet again. Rex snatched another copy of the governor's order, jumped into his truck, and rushed to Morton Plant Hospital, located a few miles north of our office.

With Rex running to the hospital, we scoured our various news sources for any late-breaking developments. We quickly learned that George Felos had called another press conference. As Michael's attorney, he announced that he was immediately going to court to have Terri's Law and the governor's order declared unconstitutional and a violation of the separation of powers.

Another news source reported that Felos's hearing on this matter would be postponed until a later time. It seemed obvious to us what was happening. The other side intended to stall as long as possible in hopes that Terri would expire and make the whole issue moot.

As we were debating our options, we received another urgent phone call—this time from a friend at the hospital. We were told that Mr. Felos was already roaming the halls threatening to sue any doctor who reinserted the feeding tube—despite the immunity clause that was added at the last moment by the legislature. With Mr. Felos breathing threats, we were concerned that Rex might have no access upon his arrival. Just as the other side had managed to prevent unhindered access to Terri at the hospice, we believed Mr. Felos would be working to find a way to prevent Rex from helping Terri at the hospital.

Now what?

First, we called Rex on his cell phone to let him know he was about to walk into a hornet's nest of resistance; we wanted him mentally prepared for a possible confrontation. We told Rex to keep driving and that we'd have a plan in place by the time he arrived at the hospital. Second, we remembered that one of the people who had contacted us while we were drafting Terri's Law just happened to be the wife of the former chief of staff of Morton Plant Hospital, Dr. Jay Carpenter. We called the Carpenters' home, and although Dr. Carpenter was not there, his children gladly gave us his cell phone number.

A call to his cell was answered immediately. We gave Dr. Carpenter a quick rundown of what was happening at the hospital. Shocked, he said that he happened to be less than ten minutes from the hospital and would immediately go there to meet Rex. We gave him Rex's cell phone number. Dr. Carpenter called Rex and arranged to meet him at the front door of the hospital—which, we later learned, had been placed under police guard by the FDLE personnel after Terri had been moved there.

Rex arrived at the hospital and rushed to the front door. One of the guards blocked his path. Just as Rex began to explain that he was one of the attorneys from Gibbs Law Firm assisting Terri Schiavo's parents, a man emerged from behind the opening automatic doors. He told the guard, "I am Dr. Carpenter, and this man is with me." The two men had never met before and might not otherwise have been able to find each other so quickly.

The guard stepped aside, allowing them to enter. As Dr. Carpenter and Rex hustled through the lobby, Rex briefed the doctor with the information we had provided him from the office. Meanwhile, Dr. Carpenter steered Rex through the maze of hallways, stopping at the appropriate reception area of the hospital. After a few minutes a member of the hospital's administration team came into the room, introduced herself with a somewhat tentative handshake, and then escorted them into her office.

Rex advised her that our office had learned through various sources that Terri had been brought there under police escort to have her feeding tube reinserted. He asked whether she was aware that the governor had signed an order earlier that evening mandating that Terri's hydration and nutrition be reintroduced. Rex handed her a copy of the governor's order. When she finished perusing every word on the page, Rex told her that he had been dispatched by our office to ensure that the hospital would follow the governor's order to reinsert the feeding tube.

She responded with a certain cool detachment, Rex thought, as if unmoved by the urgency of Terri's situation. She claimed in no uncertain terms that the hospital did not make those decisions—the attending physician in the ER was the one who would have to make the call. Rex told her she had a duty to make certain the ER doctor was aware that the hospital had just received a copy of the governor's order; the doctor would now be under actual notice of his legal duty to reinsert the feeding tube.

His words appeared to fall on deaf ears.

The administrator folded her arms. She had been told by the doctor that Michael Schiavo's legal team had already instructed them *not* to reinsert the tube or they would be sued. Rex pressed the issue. He held an order from the governor to reinsert the tube. He reminded her that it was the governor's position—not Mr. Schiavo's wishes—that currently had the effect of law and that the hospital was now on official notice of that law. He didn't believe that anyone at the hospital would want to permit Terri to die on their watch—especially in violation of the governor's order.

Law or not, she apparently wasn't inclined to help Terri.

Running out of options, Rex called me at the office. While standing just a few feet away, within earshot of the woman, he loudly informed me that the hospital was not being cooperative and was refusing to follow the governor's order. In a firm tone and loud enough for her to hear, Rex began to discuss with me the whole issue of wrongful death liability and the lawsuit that was sure to be filed against the hospital and personally against any hospital personnel who allowed Terri to die in flagrant violation of the governor's order.

Now the hospital was in a real dilemma.

George Felos was threatening to sue if the doctors reinserted the tube; our office was threatening to sue if they didn't. The administrator was put in quite a bind. After some hesitation, she indicated that there was a judicial hearing coming up within the hour. Maybe we could resolve the matter there, she offered. Rex knew that was not accurate information. As I had previously told him, we knew that hearing had been postponed. Rex filled the woman in on that little detail, which took some of the wind out of her sails. Clearly, her predicament was not going to be resolved by any court order that night.

MIDNIGHT MIRACLE

With the tenacity of a bulldog, Rex demanded immediate compliance with Governor Bush's order, telling this staff member that if the hospital refused to comply with the governor's order, our office, on behalf of the Schindlers, would hold her, the doctor, and the hospital legally accountable if they allowed Terri to die. As Rex later reported to me, the tension in the room at that moment could only have been cut by a surgeon's knife.

Dr. Carpenter had been standing by Rex's side the whole time, watching the verbal clash of wills. Breaking his silence, he suggested that he go check on Terri and discuss her treatment with the doctor in charge in light of the order in hand. Whether it had been the threat of legal action, the realization that Rex refused to back down, or the weight of the words spoken by the former chief of staff of the hospital, the woman consented—with one condition.

She wanted to accompany him.

Twenty minutes later and just before midnight, Dr. Carpenter returned with the administrator. With the skill of a seasoned professional, he reported three things: He had talked with the attending physician, he had personally seen Terri, and she would be cared for immediately. Dr. Carpenter explained that they could not discuss the terms of the treatment without the guardian's permission, but that he and the administrator could confirm that Terri was receiving medical care consistent with the governor's order.

Rex, still in legal warrior mode, asked Dr. Carpenter one more time if he was certain that Terri was being fed. Dr. Carpenter explained that generally, when a patient has been without sustenance for such a long period of time, hydration and nutrition must be carefully monitored and only gradually restored. But yes, Terri's care was entirely appropriate for a person in her condition.

Exhausted from several hours of this intense face-off, yet encouraged by the breakthrough, Rex called the office with this fantastic news. While he went on to thank Dr. Carpenter for his life-saving role, I called the Schindlers. The Schindlers, who had been hearing news reports that Terri was not being fed, were elated beyond words that Terri's court-ordered date with death had passed and that she was still alive.

Indeed, we all rejoiced and gave thanks to God for this rare, albeit temporary, victory. In hindsight, the decision to move on a legislative front provided the Schindlers with almost two additional years to enjoy the company of their daughter.

TIME LINE OF EVENTS: 1990–2003

February 25, 1990: Terri's Collapse — Terri Schiavo, twenty-six, collapses while at home alone with Michael, her husband of six years. Oxygen flow to her brain is interrupted for several minutes, causing permanent brain damage.

May 9, 1990: Terri Improves — Terri has improved from her initial acute coma status and is taken to a Florida rehab center for a rehabilitation recovery program. Later Michael takes her to California for experimental surgery.

June 1990: Lawsuit Fails — Terri's medical coverage is terminated, and Michael Schiavo files an unsuccessful lawsuit against Terri's insurance company.

February 1991: Therapy Continues — Terri continues rehabilitation therapy. At this time the Schindlers report that Terri can still say words like "no" and "stop." She goes outdoors in a wheelchair and enjoys trips to the mall.

April 1991: Continued Progress — Terri's condition is improving. More advanced therapy is recommended.

September 1991: Moving On — Michael Schiavo reportedly has started dating again.

August 1992: First Award — Terri is awarded $250,000 in an out-of-court medical malpractice settlement with her general practitioner, who is later cleared by a Florida medical board.

November 1992: Second Award — A malpractice trial commences against Terri's gynecologist for $20 million, an amount calculated to provide care for Terri for her natural lifespan, which is estimated by actuaries to be at least fifty years. After attorney fees, the jury award and a previous settlement amount to $1.2 million, $700,000 of which is placed into a trust fund to pay for her medical care. The remainder is awarded to Michael for loss of companionship.

February 14, 1993: Disagreement Over Care — After Michael receives the money from the medical malpractice jury award, he and Terri's parents have a falling out when Michael refuses to use the money to move Terri from the nursing home where she is now residing to a premiere rehabilitation facility as the

Schindlers had expected him to do. Michael and Bob Schindler never speak again after that day. Terri receives no rehabilitative services, swallowing tests, or therapy of any kind from 1992 until her death in 2005.

June 1993: New Family — Michael Schiavo begins a romantic relationship with Jodi Centonze, a woman to whom he will subsequently become engaged and with whom he will have two children. Michael is still residing with Jodi and their children when Terri dies; Michael and Jodi marry in January 2006.

September 15, 1993: Contesting Legal Guardianship — The Schindlers fail in their legal bid to remove Michael as Terri's guardian.

1994 – 1998: The "Quiet Years" — Terri continues to live in a Florida nursing home and receives minimal medical care and no therapy. The Schindlers believe, and records appear to confirm, that during these "quiet" years Michael obtains the assistance of George Felos, a leading pro-euthanasia attorney in Florida, to find a way to have Terri's feeding tube removed.

1998: Michael Requests Court Permission to Have Terri Die — Using a newly-enacted Florida law, Michael Schiavo petitions the Pinellas County Probate Court to have his wife's feeding tube removed.

February 11, 2000: Court First Rules Terri Can Die — After a trial, Pinellas County Probate Court Judge George Greer issues an order for Terri's death, ruling that there is "clear and convincing" evidence of Terri's oral end-of-life wishes, that Terri is in PVS, and that she would not want to live with a feeding tube. Although Judge Greer has never seen Terri, he also rules that she is unconscious, unaware, and without cognition, conditions that Terri's family consistently deny.

February 20, 2000: Petition for Rehearing — Following the trial, the Schindlers obtain affidavits from three volunteer physicians who visit Terri and determine she is not in a PVS condition. They petition for a rehearing and ask Judge Greer to allow Terri to have medical testing to determine her swallowing capabilities and her true neurological condition. These motions are denied.

April 10, 2000: Terri Moved to Hospice — Michael moves Terri from her nursing home to the Woodside Hospice facility, where George Felos, his attorney, has served as chairman of the board, despite testimony at her malpractice trial of her anticipated longevity.

April 24, 2001: Terri's Feeding Tube Removed, First Time — Terri's feeding tube is removed for what will be the first of three times, but it is reinserted two days later by Florida Circuit Court Judge Frank Quesada after one of Michael's former girlfriends calls a radio talk show and claims that Michael had told her he had no idea what Terri would have wanted.

November 22, 2002: Court Again Rules That Terri Should Die — Judge Greer again rules that Terri is in a PVS condition and cannot be rehabilitated.

September 17, 2003: New Date for Removal of Tube — Judge Greer resets the date for the removal of Terri's feeding tube for 2 PM on October 15, 2003.

October 13, 2003: First Meeting — First meeting between Gibbs Law Firm staff and the Schindlers, in which the law firm agrees to help behind the scenes, on a pro bono basis.

October 15, 2003: Removal of Feeding Tube, Second Time — Terri's feeding tube is removed for the second time. Gibbs Law Firm attorneys draft an initial version of what will later become Terri's Law and submit it to Florida house members.

October 20, 2003: "Terri's Law" Passed in the State Senate — The Florida senate votes to pass a weakened version of Terri's Law, Public Law 03-418, authorizing Governor Bush to order Terri's feeding tube reinserted while he reviews her situation and all similar situations in Florida. A few hours later, the tube is reinserted and Terri is rehydrated, preserving her life for a second time.

IS THERE A DOCTOR IN THE HOUSE?

As I looked at Terri, and she gazed directly back at me, I asked myself whether, if I were her attending physician, I could in good conscience withdraw her feeding and hydration. No, I could not.

—Dr. William Cheshire Jr., MD, Board Certified Neurologist

I n early 2005 our law firm received sworn affidavits from more than forty medical professionals, including neurologists. None of these medical professionals were solicited. None were paid. They simply became aware of Terri's fight through various news accounts and decided to step forward. From all across the country, these brave men and women put their reputations and licenses on the line. How so?

By signing declarations for the court questioning the diagnosis that Terri was in a persistent vegetative state and recommending that she be reevaluated before her feeding tube was removed.

Each one felt compelled to offer Terri his or her professional help—especially if it might save her life. But how did they know this? Michael wouldn't permit any outside doctor into Terri's room without his consent. In order to make some level of an assessment without seeing the patient, these neurologists had to rely upon the available video clips, court files, and public documents. Without exception, these doctors, many at the top of their field, unanimously believed the evidence in the videotapes and reports of visits with her family contradicted a PVS diagnosis.

Of special interest was an affidavit submitted by Dr. Beatrice Engstrand, a fellow of the American Academy of Neurology and assistant professor of neurology at the New York Medical College. This recognized neurology expert advised caution. As with the other medical personnel, she based her opinion on a careful review of what was publicly available. She did not believe Terri met the PVS criteria and offered to personally examine Terri for the court.

Her opinion was shared by board certified neurologist Dr. Laurie Barclay. Dr. Barclay wrote:

> Terri Schiavo reacts with emotionally appropriate facial expressions, behaviors, and attempted vocalizations to her relatives, and she discriminates in these responses in that they are different toward beloved relatives than they are to strangers. These responses are not consistent with someone in a persistent vegetative state, and suggest a level of consciousness of at least "minimally conscious state" . . . if not even a higher level of consciousness.

Why should these two affidavits carry extra weight?

Both of these experts had personally studied under Dr. Fred Plum—the American neurologist who, along with Dr. Bryan Jennett, a Scottish neurosurgeon, originally coined the term *PVS syndrome.* The unique training afforded Drs. Barclay and Engstrand by Dr. Plum—the doctor whose contribution to science was the PVS diagnosis—is no small matter.

This begs a question. With these two as well as more than three dozen other experts weighing in and offering their services, why would

Judge Greer claim that all of the credible evidence pointed to a lack of cognitive activity? Furthermore, why would Judge Greer ignore the findings of two neurologists who *did* see Terri?

Take neurologist Dr. William Cheshire Jr., for example. Certified by the American Board of Psychiatry and Neurology, Dr. Cheshire was appointed by Florida's Adult Protection Services to offer his objective medical review for the Department of Children and Families during its investigation of abuse and neglect charges. Although neither he nor any other doctor was permitted by Michael and the court to actually examine Terri at that point, here are highlights from his seven-page sworn affidavit after an in-room, ninety-minute observation of Terri in March 2005:

> I came into this case with the belief that it can be ethically permissible to discontinue artificially provided nutrition and hydration for persons in a persistent vegetative state. Having now reviewed the relevant facts, having met and observed Ms. Schiavo in person, and having reflected deeply on the moral and ethical issues, I would like to explain why I have changed my mind in regard to this particular case. . . .
>
> Terri Schiavo demonstrates behaviors in a variety of cognitive domains that call into question the previous neurological diagnosis of a persistent vegetative state. Specifically, she has demonstrated behaviors that are context-specific, sustained, and indicative of cerebral cortical processing that, upon careful neurological consideration, would not be expected in a persistent vegetative state.
>
> Based on this evidence, I believe that, within a reasonable degree of medical certainty, there is a greater likelihood that Terri is in a minimally conscious state than a persistent vegetative state. This distinction makes an enormous difference in making ethical decisions on Terri's behalf.
>
> As I looked at Terri, and she gazed directly back at me, I asked myself whether, if I were her attending physician, I could in good conscience withdraw her feeding and hydration. No, I could

not. I could not withdraw life support if I were asked. I could not withhold life-sustaining nutrition and hydration from this beautiful lady whose face brightens in the presence of others.

Keep in mind, this observation was the *only* one permitted (due to a court order) in the last year of Terri's life. In that sense it is *critically important* and underscores the dubious rationale for putting Terri to death due to PVS, coupled with hearsay evidence that prior to her collapse she had made general comments when watching TV programs about people on life-support machines that she "would not want to live like that."

Notice Dr. Cheshire's observation, similar to mine and others', that Terri's face brightens in the company of other people. Patients in a PVS condition do not respond to such stimuli.

Some members of the press, however, have been critical of Dr. Cheshire's report. They argue that Dr. Cheshire failed to conduct a full neurological examination of Terri, and therefore, they dismiss his review as being invalid. It's true. Dr. Cheshire "observed" rather than "examined" Terri. Why? He was forbidden to do so by the court and by the guardian, Michael Schiavo.[1]

It's worth pointing out that Dr. Cheshire's observations were strikingly similar to what Dr. David Young noted in his affidavit. Dr. Young also personally observed Terri in 1998 when Michael first asked the court to have Terri's feeding tube removed. He writes:

I was there to determine several things, including if she could track moving objects, could she respond to verbal or physical stimuli, how did she respond, did she drool, and did she have any facial expressions. My findings were that she was not drooling, so she was handling secretions. . . . She did follow especially her mother across the room and focus on her.

The behaviors I observed from Terri Schiavo are not consistent with someone in PVS. . . . She can be taught to swallow and if she was worked with she could handle oral feedings, which is what I testified in court.

Let me summarize for you what several of the other doctors told me. Remember, these are not fringe doctors with outlandish theories. Many have been highly recognized in the field of neurology or have authored textbooks, while a number of these professionals have practiced at the finest hospitals and clinics around the world for more than thirty years.

THE ALL-STARS

In baseball terms, an all-star team of medical professionals volunteered to go to bat for Terri in early 2005, had Judge Greer welcomed their services. Take Dr. Ricardo G. Senno, who specializes in brain injury medicine. For years he served as the medical director of the Rehabilitation Institute of Chicago's Brain Injury Medicine and Rehabilitation Program. He "strongly" recommended a fresh round of testing for Terri using the latest technology.

Dr. Senno wrote, "Based on what I have seen, I believe that she is at least in a Minimally Conscious State; she does not appear to be in a persistent vegetative state." In his affidavit, Dr. Senno states,

> I have developed rehabilitation programs for patients just like Terri Schiavo. Because of continued advances in medical testing and treatment, even within the past several years, I believe, from a medical point of view, Ms. Schiavo deserves another evaluation, even if she was examined just a year ago. . . .
> Just because Ms. Terri Schiavo couldn't physically or mentally do something a year ago, doesn't mean she can't do it today, or tomorrow.
> Leaving all ethical, moral, and legal aspects aside, I believe it is a medical crime not to evaluate this person.

Consider Dr. Rodney Dunaway, a board certified neurologist who trained at Walter Reed hospital during the Vietnam War. In his capacity Dr. Dunaway saw "literally hundreds of brain-injured young men." He served as consultant in neurology to the NASA flight surgeon during a number of Apollo missions. In his professional opinion:

> The diagnostic studies upon which the decision to terminate her life have been based . . . were inadequate, and insufficient to allow a reasoned opinion by her physicians. In my opinion, further neurological studies are needed before a declaration of persistent vegetative state can be made.

Time and again, many of the doctors we heard from believed Terri was at worst in a minimally conscious state (MCS). Unlike those who are in PVS, patients who are in MCS have a much greater possibility of improving with therapy. What's more, modern advances in medical technology are such that brain function—not just brain anatomy—can be tested by using a brain SPECT, or imaging technology. So says Dr. J. Michael Uszler, an attending staff physician in nuclear medicine at the UCLA Medical Center. Dr. Uszler confirms my earlier point that the study of the human brain is constantly being refined.

Many physicians felt there was sufficient doubt over the diagnosis of PVS to warrant reevaluation. The American Association of Physicians and Surgeons, representing more than four thousand physicians, requested Terri be reevaluated. All appeals to the court, however, were denied.

The diagnosis of PVS had been made three years earlier in 2002. Much had changed since then. In particular, the minimally conscious state was just being recognized as a diagnostic entity. Before 2002, the minimally conscious state had never been formally defined. In addition, the full range of behavioral elements seen in the minimally conscious state was still being characterized. In the wake of these advances, Dr. James P. Kelly offered to reevaluate Terri so that her diagnosis would be based on up-to-date medical knowledge. Dr. Kelly is a highly acclaimed member in the neurology community. He is a diplomat in neurology in the American Board of Psychiatry and Neurology, a fellow of the American Academy of Neurology, on the board of governors for the International Brain Injury Association, and one of the authors of the seminal paper that defined the minimally conscious state. Despite his credentials, authority in the area, and expertise in rendering diagnoses concerning states of consciousness, his offer, as well as those from many other reputable neurologists, was flatly rejected.

How could the court refuse that offer?

Why didn't the media report this?

We also heard from speech pathologists who said Terri could be taught to swallow and speak using new techniques and advances in treatment. Dr. Jill Joyce, as both a psychotherapist and a speech/language pathologist, spent more than twenty years working with the severely brain-damaged. As with the other doctors who were not permitted by Michael to personally examine Terri, she studied the videotapes and related articles about Terri's condition. She wrote:

> It is my opinion that Ms. Schiavo would be able to learn how to swallow if given the proper therapy. I have personally treated stroke patients, and other patients with severe brain damage similar to Ms. Schiavo's that have regained their ability to swallow after being given the proper therapy . . . It is my opinion that Ms. Schiavo . . . would improve with aggressive swallowing therapy.

When these declarations from medical professionals of this caliber were put before Judge Greer, we asked the court for a reassessment of Terri's condition. The answer was always the same: No. All we were trying to do was to have the court allow Terri to be reevaluated in 2005 using the advances in medicine that had been made since 2000 and 2002. But we were rebuffed at every turn. I couldn't understand why there was such a rush to kill Terri.

I still don't.

Even though these compelling statements under oath by the aforementioned doctors and therapists—as well as many others we received—were ignored, I, for one, have had my confidence in the medical profession restored. This is, after all, a litigation-crazy world.

The willingness of these doctors to volunteer their time, resources, and expertise for free, and to take the side of Terri against a husband who had already sued and won a medical malpractice suit, was nothing short of a real inspiration for those of us trying to save Terri.

Why did they do it?

They believe life is sacred.

They believe life is worth preserving.

ENDING LIFE IS NOW
A LEGITIMATE MEDICAL PURPOSE?

When Florida legislators passed a law in the late 1990s that permitted Michael Schiavo to go to court and ask a judge to discontinue his wife's food and water, thereby causing her death, a line was crossed that had never been crossed before in America. This legislation declared that use of a "feeding tube" was a form of "medical treatment," which any person who is terminal or in a persistent vegetative state has a "right" to refuse.

But the law went even further in Florida.

If the person who is terminal or in PVS never had a living will or an advanced care directive, and can no longer speak for themselves, the guardian or other family members may go to court and convince a judge that death is what this patient would have wanted. The evidence used to support that claim is evidence that is generally not admissible in court because it is hearsay — no one can prove with absolute certainty what the patient's actual wishes would have been without a clear written directive.

Many were shocked that causing the death of a disabled person who cannot speak for herself had become so easy in Florida. But the slippery slope toward a death culture in America has become covered with a slick layer of ice ever since Terri's death.

Case in point.

In January 2006, the United States Supreme Court, in *Gonzales v. Oregon*, upheld a 1994 Oregon Death With Dignity Act that will potentially permit doctors all across America to dispense or prescribe a lethal dose of drugs upon the request of a terminally ill patient. While Oregon is currently the only state to have such a law (as of this writing), barring a federal law to the contrary, this new Supreme Court decision opens the door for other states to follow.

The main difference between the two pieces of legislation is that, in Florida, death is passive — the patient dies "naturally" over time, as any healthy person would do without food and water. In Oregon, on the other hand, death is actively induced instantaneously by the administration of a lethal dose of drugs.

Is this really what we want in America?

How soon will "permitting" patients to decline food and water or allowing them to ask for a lethal dose of drugs become an expectation placed upon them? The distance between those two positions is razor thin. Terri's case showed all America that judges are now free to order a patient's death at the request of a guardian or family member, even when the patient has no written directive requesting that end of life.

Many hospitals already permit doctors to refuse to treat patients, no matter what their expressed wishes are, if the doctor thinks treatment will be "futile." It's now legal for any state to enact these pro-death laws and cause the deaths of the elderly and disabled either passively (like Terri) or actively (in doctor-assisted "suicide").

Please let that sink in for a moment. We've crossed a line — a very dangerous one.

Terri's case and Oregon's assisted suicide law have now set a dangerous precedent for all vulnerable Americans, especially those who are disabled, those who have terminal illnesses, those who can no longer speak for themselves, and perhaps one day even those who are indigent and unable to pay for costly health care. I believe these patients may become increasingly pressured to make the choice to die and "get out of the way" no matter what their true wishes might be.

The Hippocratic Oath once required doctors to "cause no harm." Returning to the centerpiece of that oath is an important first step in keeping physicians in the healing business — to be ministers of life rather than enforcers of death under the veiled guise of "dignity."

CHAPTER SEVEN

IN SICKNESS
AND IN HEALTH

Michael claims he loves Terri and he has said it on numerous occasions, but he treats her in a way I don't think most of us would treat our own pets.

— BOBBY SCHINDLER, TERRI SCHIAVO'S BROTHER[1]

This might come as a surprise, but I was deeply troubled after my initial visit with Terri on Christmas Eve, 2004. You'd think I should have been encouraged by her healthy appearance, by her fully animated behavior, and by the glowing interaction Terri shared with her parents. No question about it, she'd surpassed any expectation I had of her vitality. I came away from her presence renewed in my resolve to fight for her life.

Still, as I headed for a Christmas Eve dinner with my family that evening, I felt agitated. I couldn't stop thinking about the numerous injustices surrounding Terri's case—from Terri's initial medical malpractice award in 1992 to the sheer unfairness that Terri was not permitted home for her favorite holiday. The lack of basic human kindness toward this disabled woman by her husband and the court gnawed at my spirit and trampled on my sense of fairness.

Come to think of it, one of my law professors at Duke University had cautioned me about getting too passionately involved in cases. Once, in my oral advocacy class, we were assigned to present arguments in a mock trial. When I was finished making my case, the professor said, "David, you're acting like this really matters. If tomorrow you had to go to court and argue for the other side, as a lawyer you should be able to do that."

He must have seen the look of surprise on my face. He continued, "Trust me, you need to disconnect yourself from the process. You cannot care—it's not your problem. You'll have a heart attack or an ulcer or a mental breakdown. Without a professional distance, the practice of law will destroy you." I'm sure he thought he was giving me sound advice. I respected his opinion, and in practical terms it's pretty good advice.

However, I've never been able to do that. I cannot distance myself from what I believe. To me, when I go to court, I have to believe I'm on the side of truth. I could never stand before God—or even look myself in the mirror—and say, "Sure, I fought for Terri, but it was just a job. I could just as easily have represented the other side."

These were several of the unsettling issues that grieved me as I left the hospice on Christmas Eve—concerns I still haven't fully come to terms with.

I SWEAR TO TELL THE TRUTH

Two years after his wife's disability occurred, Michael Schiavo sued Terri's general practitioner and gynecologist for malpractice, claiming they had failed to realize that Terri was bulimic (though her autopsy did not reveal signs of bulimia). At the time of the trial, Michael told the jury and Terri's family that he was committed to taking care of his wife for the rest of his life. Through what was at times an emotionally charged testimony, Michael made his intentions clear:

1. He was committed to getting Terri treatment.
2. He was committed to keeping her alive.
3. He was committed to doing everything he could to help improve the quality of her life.

On November 5, 1992, Michael Schiavo took the witness stand. Under oath and under direct examination by his own lawyer, Michael fought back tears as he affirmed his desire to care for his wife, Terri:

QUESTION: Why did you want to learn to be a nurse?

SCHIAVO: Because I enjoy it and I want to learn more how to take care of Terri.

QUESTION: You're a young man. Your life is ahead of you. When you look up the road, what do you see for yourself?

SCHIAVO: I see myself hopefully finishing school and taking care of my wife.

QUESTION: Where do you want to take care of your wife?

SCHIAVO: I want to bring her home.

QUESTION: If you had the resources available to you, if you had the equipment and the people, would you do that?

SCHIAVO: Yes, I would, in a heartbeat.

As you might expect, Bob and Mary Schindler were elated to know that their son-in-law was committed to caring for their daughter. They were especially heartened that Terri might finally have enough money to receive the professional rehabilitation and speech therapy she so badly needed. Naturally, the prospect of receiving funds to cover the mounting medical bills was a great relief too. No longer would the Schindlers have to initiate fund-raisers, hold bake sales, and scrape together money for Terri's treatment.

Originally, Michael sought $20 million in malpractice damages for Terri's future medical care and therapy. This figure was based on the prediction that Terri's life expectancy was another 51.27 years—a projection made by expert witnesses called by Michael's legal team. Part of the money requested was also for his loss of companionship.

Although Michael had already begun to move on in his personal life, during the malpractice trial his attorney asked specifically about Michael's relationship with Terri:

QUESTION: How do you feel about being married to Terri now?

SCHIAVO: I feel wonderful. She's my life and I wouldn't trade her for the world. I believe in my . . . I believe in my wedding vows.

QUESTION: You want to take a minute?

SCHIAVO: Yeah.

Michael's eyes brimmed with tears as he wrestled to keep his emotions under control. The jury watched in silence as Michael dabbed at the corners of his eyes and fought to compose himself.

QUESTION: You okay?

SCHIAVO: Yeah. I'm sorry.

QUESTION: Have—you said you believe in your wedding vows. What do you mean by that?

SCHIAVO: I believe in the vows that I took with my wife— through sickness, in health, for richer or poorer. I married my wife because I love her and I want to spend the rest of my life with her. I'm going to do that.

On November 10, 1992, the jury returned its verdict. Without going into all of the details, suffice it to say that the award was a fraction of the financial windfall Michael sought. After an appeal, on January 27, 1993, the court approved a final payment of $2 million.

Of the approximately $1.2 million left after paying attorney fees from the jury award and a previous settlement with Terri's personal doctor, 70 percent was designated for Terri's needs and 30 percent went to Michael. Not that the percentages were of much consequence. As Terri's guardian, Michael ultimately controlled the entire amount. Almost immediately following the jury award, a number of red flags surfaced in his behavior. The same month the malpractice award was approved by the court, Michael refused to honor his promise to the Schindlers (and to the jury) to use the money for Terri to begin receiving advanced rehabilitation therapy.

Indeed, the Schindlers' sense of euphoria was short-lived. On February 14, 1993, just two brief weeks after the malpractice award had been finalized, Bob and Mary had a heated falling-out with Michael. They had asked him to honor his agreement regarding the malpractice jury award for Terri and place her in a rehab facility. He, in turn, threatened a legal injunction forbidding family members to visit Terri at her nursing home. Furthermore, Michael instructed the nursing home staff not to release any medical information concerning Terri to her family.

The Schindlers were stunned beyond belief. But things would only get worse. Michael would later claim that a memory had suddenly surfaced: *Terri would not really want to live in a disabled condition.* In fact, although the money they needed was now there, Terri received absolutely no rehabilitative services, swallowing tests, or therapy of any kind between 1992 and her death in 2005.

You might want to read that again.

Absolutely nothing for more than a dozen years.

The timing of Michael's change of heart is deeply troubling. While you and I might question the way the mind works when remembering past details, the Schindlers could only wonder why Michael very much wanted Terri alive when he anticipated a jury awarding him more money than many people will see in their entire lifetime. Then, after the check arrived, Michael's story changed: Terri really wouldn't want to live anymore.

Why the sudden revision of his story?

As Bobby Schindler, Terri's brother, would later ask, "Which Michael are we to believe? The one who promised he would take care of his wife for the rest of his life, or the one who says these were Terri's death wishes?"[2] And so, for the Schindler family, a twelve-year battle over Terri's life was set in motion with that jury award.

For his part, Michael entered into a committed long-term relationship with Jodi Centonze. He and Jodi began living together in 1993 and subsequently became engaged. Michael started a new family and fathered two children with Jodi, while blocking the way for the Schindlers to bring Terri back into their own family. Michael continued to live with Jodi and their children after Terri's death in 2005; they were married in January of 2006.

SHUT IN AND SHUT OUT

That Christmas Eve afternoon in 2004 as I drove away from the Woodside Hospice in Pinellas Park, Florida, another aspect of Terri's case was bothering me. Back on April 10, 2000, Terri had been moved from her nursing home to a hospice; I couldn't figure out why. She wasn't terminal. She wasn't dying. She wasn't comatose.

She wasn't even sick.

To the contrary, Terri was very much alive. The Terri I saw was doing remarkably well, especially when you consider that this woman had only very minimal health care for over a decade.

Typically, patients with *incurable illnesses* are sent to a hospice to die, not to recover. In fact, generally, a person can only be admitted into hospice care if death is reasonably imminent—as a rule of thumb—within six months of admittance. Despite testimony at her malpractice trial of her anticipated longevity, Terri was admitted and confined to a hospice surrounded by death and the dying for *years* in violation of the practices generally governing such facilities.

What's more, Judge Greer's court was legally required to supervise guardianship cases like Terri's. Why didn't he intervene? Why wasn't Terri permitted to go home or to an appropriate extended care center?

In truth, Terri would *still* be in a hospice room today had she not been dehydrated and starved to death. Which, again, begs the question, why was Terri restricted to the walls of Woodside Hospice after 2000?

An even more disturbing thought was the fact that Michael Schiavo's pro-euthanasia attorney, George Felos, had served as chairman of the board of directors at the very hospice where Terri was sent. Judge Greer subsequently denied several petitions by the Schindlers to return Terri to the nursing home.

Another serious injustice from my perspective, having visited Terri many times, was Judge Greer's ruling on February 11, 2000, authorizing the first withdrawal of Terri's feeding tube. In his death order Judge Greer declared that Terri was "unconscious, unaware, and without cognition." But how could the judge fairly make that assessment? He never saw Terri—and she had never come to court even though she logically would be the star witness! Terri had the most to gain and the most to lose in this case. She was the person with the right to decide whether she received medical treatment or not, yet she never attended court and was never afforded a lawyer of her own throughout the entire court process.

Worse, even when hit by a tidal wave of controversy following his ruling, Judge Greer didn't make time to drive across town or to have Terri come to court to see her for himself—just to be sure.

Why not? Certainly Judge Greer's conduct and decisions were consistently upheld on appeal by other judges who also had never seen Terri in person.

But contrary to Judge Greer's arm's-length assessment, I know from personal observation that Terri went to bed at night, woke up in the morning, and functioned throughout the day without the aid of any special machinery or extraordinary care. She breathed on her own. She was not "unconscious," nor was she "unaware." She could have traveled across town—or across the country!—without jeopardizing her health. And though she was disabled, all of her bodily systems could have kept her alive for many years—with one exception:

She required assistance at mealtime.

I was also baffled that Terri was not allowed out of her room to socialize. What harm could there be in visiting with others or attending the occasional hospice function? Evidently, her guardian, Michael Schiavo, controlled Terri's life as a disabled woman much as he reportedly had done when they were living under the same roof.

I would later learn from Jackie Rhodes, Terri's friend from work, that "Michael was very controlling. [Terri] was not allowed to go anywhere after work. She had to go straight home after work. He would monitor the miles on her car."[3]

How the court could allow Terri's husband to isolate her from human companionship was beyond me. Was this really the same man whose tears had convinced a medical malpractice jury that his desire was to spend the rest of his life caring for Terri? I wondered what the jury's decision would have been if they'd known that Terri would remain deprived of medical therapy, rehabilitation, and human companionship, and that she would spend years in a hospice surrounded by a dying world—often with the blinds drawn on her windows by orders of her guardian/husband.

Where was the basic human kindness?

TERRI AND KAREN ANN QUINLAN

The Schindlers' legal team was contacted early in 2005 by an attorney affiliated with the Florida legislature regarding a mistake he noticed Judge Greer had made in his 2000 death order. Using that information, the Schindlers filed a new motion on March 2, 2005, alleging that during the 2000 trial to determine Terri's end-of-life wishes, Judge George Greer made an error in determining that clear and convincing evidence existed to support Terri's oral end-of-life wishes not to be kept alive with an artificial feeding tube.

Attorneys for the Schindlers pointed out that in his February 2000 order authorizing Terri's death, Judge Greer made a clear mistake in discounting the testimony of Terri's close friend Diane Meyer. Diane had testified that in 1982 Terri told her she did not agree with the decision by Karen Ann Quinlan's parents to take their daughter off life support.

Judge Greer stated in his 2000 order that he found Diane's testimony "believable" but concluded that this conversation could not have occurred in 1982, after Terri had reached the age of majority, but must have occurred when Terri was only eleven or twelve years old, in 1976, the year Judge Greer believed Karen Ann Quinlan had died. Terri's mother, Mary Schindler, also had testified that Terri did not approve of Karen Ann Quinlan's parents' decision to remove her artificial life support. But Mary became confused on cross-examination about what year it might have been when she and Terri talked about this situation.

Judge Greer's mistake was that Karen Ann Quinlan did not die in 1976, when she was taken off life support (but not her feeding tube, which was not then considered to be life support). Instead, she lived until 1985. Therefore, Diane's use of the present tense in court when describing her 1982 conversation with Terri was consistent with the facts. Mary Schindler's testimony that Terri was an adult when they conversed about the subject was also confirmed by this mistake in the date of Quinlan's death. The mistake in dates had apparently not been previously noticed. Was the evidence of Terri's death wish still "clear and convincing," we asked.

Judge Greer denied the Schindlers' motion to overturn his 2000 order. He ruled that this mistake was inconsequential because he had not been interested in Terri's views with regard to other people, but only with regard to what she would want for herself.

If Judge Greer's 2000 order to end Terri's life had been a criminal death sentence, this mistake might have entitled Terri to a new trial. But since Judge Greer's death order was a civil death order, the first of its kind in the nation, there was no precedent for a new civil trial and Judge Greer's original order was upheld, notwithstanding this critical mistake.

LARRY KING, BLOWN AWAY

During the late summer of 2004, a series of powerful hurricanes crisscrossed Florida, leaving massive devastation in their wake. In six short weeks four hurricanes hammered the Sunshine State: Charley (August 13), Frances (September 4), Ivan (September 16), and Jeanne (September 26). Floridians were stunned by the relentless barrage of severe weather and, tragically, suffered more than $50 billion in damages.

Nearly a year had flown by since October of 2003, when the Florida state legislature voted overwhelmingly in favor of Terri's Law. With its passage the Schindlers believed they had received the miracle we prayed for during our initial meeting. But Michael Schiavo and his legal team were relentless in their efforts to enforce the original death order and to oppose any action by the Florida legislature or the governor to keep Terri alive.

On September 23, 2004, just as Hurricane Jeanne was about to unleash her fury on Florida, we received tragic news: The Florida State Supreme Court had ruled that Terri's Law was unconstitutional.

Like watching precious property swept away by a hurricane, the Schindlers were stunned as they watched Terri's hard-fought legal protection evaporate before their eyes.

Just four days later, Bob, Mary, and I were scheduled to travel to California and tell the Schindlers' story on *Larry King Live* to millions of viewers. One problem: With Jeanne bearing down on us, the Tampa and Orlando airports had closed. Atlanta was in question because of the direction of the storm. In fact, most of Florida was under emergency or evacuation orders. Everybody either had left or had battened down the hatches.

The only airport that looked hopeful was Miami International— on the opposite coast and 250 miles away. Larry King's extremely helpful and kind staff in Washington, D.C., asked me the question, "Can you get to Miami?" Bob, Mary, and I decided that for Terri we needed to try.

Granted, residents were advised to stay home if at all possible— except in the case of an emergency. With Terri's life on the line and the opportunity to share the Schindlers' plight with the nation, we figured venturing out qualified as an emergency. On September 26, Bob,

Mary, a staff member, and I piled into a car and prepared for the ride of our lives. For about 250 miles, we navigated heavy downpours, high winds, and horrendous thunderstorms as Jeanne clobbered the state.

As we drove through the storm, we saw the devastation that Hurricane Charley had left in its wake. For a number of miles where the eye of the storm had passed, entire exits from the highway were completely leveled. For miles there were no gas stations, no mini-marts. Nothing. All that remained were the toppled carcasses of buildings picked over by Charley. We pressed on.

The farther we drove from Tampa Bay, the storm conditions, while harsh, appeared to ease. Thankfully, we arrived safely. We stayed at a hotel at the airport and grabbed a few hours of rest. Early the next day, although drained from the ride the night before, we escaped the hurricane and took off without further incident to Los Angeles.

Looking back, I believe God knew the Schindlers desperately needed to be encouraged. When the Florida State Supreme Court struck down Terri's Law, it was, needless to say, a huge blow to Bob and Mary and their family. With these recent court rulings and the details about the Schindlers' case starting to dominate the news, complete strangers would introduce themselves. This explained why the flight attendants and a number of passengers on the plane came up to encourage these parents throughout the trip. In some ways that flight to California turned into a pep rally at forty thousand feet!

After we touched down in Los Angeles, I received a phone call. A producer with the Larry King show had some bad news. She informed me that Larry had spent the night before in the hospital, suffering from a bad case of bronchitis. Larry may have to pass on conducting the interview personally. Whether they'd find a substitute host or just do something else was yet to be determined. She'd have to get back to me.

Talk about unfortunate.

We had come so far. . . .

That's when an amazing thing happened. Evidently, the producer shared with Larry King the incredible effort that the Schindlers had made to get there to tell their story. Larry King, clearly impressed by

Bob and Mary's depth of conviction, decided to leave the hospital and do the interview personally that night.

Although not feeling well, Larry was gracious, focused, and caring. His professionalism and interest allowed the Schindlers to effectively take their case to the world. At the end of the interview, Larry said, "Thank you very much for coming, for flying here across the country, out of hurricaneville in Florida and for making the presentation you made tonight. It's been extraordinary."[4]

Those weren't empty words. Privately, he extended his best wishes to the Schindlers for taking a stand for Terri. He shared that this case caused his family and him to discuss these issues on a personal level. Like many Americans were asking at this time, Larry asked why they just couldn't let the parents take care of their daughter.

Needless to say, Bob and Mary were wondering the exact same thing.

CHAPTER EIGHT

YOUR HONOR, I OBJECT!

This woman needs help, not a death sentence. She needs the warmth of a family that cares for her. She needs the help of doctors who want to treat her, instead of recommending that she die.

—REPRESENTATIVE JOSEPH PITTS, PENNSYLVANIA[1]

One court hearing is forever seared in my mind.

In many ways this court hearing was no different from the many others we had already experienced since taking over the Schindlers' case several months earlier. The air almost hummed with anticipation as I made my way to the front of the crowded room.

In a court case observers who support either the plaintiff or the defendant tend to sit on the same side of the courtroom as "their" side's legal counsel. This particular case was very different. I noticed that only Terri's supporters tended to come to court, and they filled both sides of the aisle.

During the entire time I represented the Schindlers, I don't ever remember seeing Michael in court. But I had always been pleasantly "accosted" by all of the wonderful people who faithfully showed up to support the Schindlers. They were always waiting by the courthouse steps, by the elevators, at the courtroom door—offering prayers and words of encouragement. We often joined hands with the Schindler family and their supporters to pray just before court began.

I took my seat at the petitioners' table. Like a boxer waiting for the bell to sound the start of round one, I mentally rehearsed the key points and objections I knew I had to register with the judge. My goal, as always, in addition to presenting the legal arguments was to attempt to enable this judge to see Terri in a new light—not as a worthless coma patient but as the beautiful, vibrant woman I had come to know and appreciate.

I prayed again for the grace to be able to make that seismic shift this case so desperately needed. I was the Johnny-come-lately to this legal battle; it had been a hard-fought legal contest for more than a dozen years before I ever met the Schindlers or Terri.

As always, with thoughts of the life-and-death issues at stake in this courtroom prominently in my mind, I placed my briefcase on the table and withdrew a yellow legal pad, a pen, and my documents. With a soft click, I closed the latch and then slipped my attaché case under the table. One lesson lawyers learn early in court is that most judges do not look kindly on them marring the shiny counsel tables with marks made by briefcases.

I couldn't help but sense the stare of the media's watchful eye. Media coverage of Terri's plight had been building steadily since the Florida legislature and the governor had gotten involved in this matter in October of 2003. And ever since September 2004, when Terri's Law was struck down and the Schindlers and I had appeared for the entire hour on Larry King's TV program, it seemed like the nation and the press had become even more aware of Terri's story. Millions were now aware of this family drama being played out amid the beaches and palm trees of Florida's Gulf Coast. As always, dozens of national and local reporters carrying their notebooks and shoulder cameras had arrived in force. They were seated behind me and to my left in what would have been the jury box in another sort of trial.

Like an array of unblinking glass eyes, the lenses of the television cameras were fixed on the center of the courtroom, ready to capture live every word uttered.

America would be watching. People all over the nation were forming opinions about Terri and about Michael, taking sides in this complicated family tragedy that was now anything but private.

But I was glad to see the press. One of our objectives in this case was to try to overcome the false impressions of Terri that had been planted in the media for years by Michael Schiavo and his legal team. They consistently referred to Terri as being in a coma, being a vegetable, unable to communicate, wanting to die. I had seen Terri, visited with her. I knew this portrayal of Terri was anything but accurate.

I glanced over at the table where George Felos, Michael Schiavo's attorney, sat. I imagined he was probably feeling some of the same prehearing pressure. Then again, Mr. Felos had been in this case for more than a decade, since the beginning, and the long string of favorable rulings he had been handed over the years in this same courtroom had surely bolstered his confidence. He was ready to defeat me in this ring too, just as he had defeated all the other attorneys who had tried to help the Schindlers save their daughter's life.

I glanced behind his counsel table again. Maybe Michael Schiavo would be here in court today. But as usual, I didn't see him. The only people sitting behind Mr. Felos's table were people I knew were there to support the Schindlers.

I never quite understood why Michael was always a no-show in court. He was the one who had started this litigation, yet he never showed up for the legal proceedings. It especially troubled me that for ten years Judge Greer had permitted this man, who was living with and having children with another woman, to remain as Terri's guardian. Michael had clearly moved on with his life. His priority now had to be with his children and their mother.

I couldn't understand why Michael's new status as a parent never seemed to increase his empathy or concern for the suffering he was causing Terri's parents in this matter.

I looked at my watch and then up at the empty bench. Judge Greer was running late. His tardiness could mean nothing—or it could mean that something was afoot. I wondered whether today's events might be more serious than usual. Could that be what was delaying the judge?

I knew my staff was praying for me every time we were in court. As I looked around the courtroom again, I saw that several of the spectators had their heads bowed. I knew Bob and Mary Schindler, three rows behind me in the gallery, were praying. And if the truth were known, millions of ordinary Americans were praying too. Without question, by now, the fifteenth year of the Schindlers' fight for their daughter, the case of Terri Schiavo had captured the attention of Americans everywhere. In fact, we had started to receive regular calls from the press, not only nationwide but around the globe. The world was intensely focused on this courtroom.

The fate of this one woman had raised the stakes of the life-and-death debate to an unprecedented level. And this was the first time in my career where I knew someone would die if I lost my case. The stakes here were very high.

In the last generation, the United States Supreme Court legalized abortion in *Roe v. Wade,* laying the groundwork for the proliferation of abortion in our society. Was our judicial system now set to approve the killing of disabled people hidden away in nursing homes and hospices?

But Terri wasn't hidden from me. I had come to know her during the last few weeks. I had to do my best, with God's help, to make this judge, the nation, indeed, the whole world, through those TV media eyes watching me from the jury box, understand that Terri had a life worth living. She had a family who loved her no matter what. Terri needed therapy, rehab, and good old-fashioned TLC, not a death sentence.

I was eager to get this hearing underway. Was Judge Greer's delay due to some threat against him? I was glad armed officers and security forces were on hand to worry about those things. It was enough for me to be thinking about my oral argument, the frayed emotions of the Schindler family, and the ever-present media. But was Judge Greer aware of something brewing?

As if reading my mind, one of the courtroom's law enforcement officers crossed the room and headed directly for my table. I offered a smile. I figured he was coming over to provide some sort of routine notification for the holdup. You know, something along the lines that someone was running late, or perhaps a transcript or key document needed to be dispatched to the courthouse before we could begin.

The officer appeared at my side. He placed his left hand on the table, palm down, and then leaned in close as if preparing to offer an insider stock tip. He cleared his throat. In a low, commanding tone he spoke three words.

"Don't turn around."

"Excuse me?" I said, matching his muted voice.

I noticed his eyes were focused somewhere over my shoulder on an unseen point of interest behind me. "Mr. Gibbs, I need to ask you to avoid making any sudden moves that would draw attention to us. Do you understand?"

I offered a slow nod, although in reality I was unsure where this conversation was headed.

"What's up?"

"We have a possible . . . *situation*," he said, as if struggling to find the right word.

I forced a smile as if to pretend we were just talking about the weather. A moment earlier I was busy arranging my notes and mentally cross-examining each aspect of the motion I was about to make. Out of habit I questioned everything. . . . Was there an oversight? A hidden insight? What about a potential weakness that my team had overlooked? I like to leave no flank uncovered.

So as you can imagine, I wasn't real excited about the interruption and I was having some difficulty discerning what the officer was driving at.

"We've identified what we fear is a potential threat," he said, adding, "to you."

"Me?"

"Yes, sir."

There had to be some mistake. Death threats against Judge Greer were well-known, which is why the judge held his hearings in four different courtrooms. Understandably, Judge Greer didn't want anyone getting too comfortable in any particular chamber. I had been told that the judge wore a bulletproof vest under his black robes. But why would anybody want to target me?

The first flicker of anxiety started to emerge.

Granted, I knew my staff was praying. Bob and Mary Schindler were praying, and millions of Americans were praying too.

But people were praying for *Terri's* life.

The officer leaned closer. "We're concerned about the conduct of a white male sitting in the last row. He appears to be intensely focused on every move you make. We've made the assessment that he could be a security risk."

This was the first time in my career where a member of the audience might be present not to observe but to cause harm for some unknown personal agenda. Then again, maybe I should have anticipated a stunt like this—if that's all it turned out to be. Now that Terri's struggle had acquired a national profile, surely some nut case with a desire to cash in his fifteen minutes of fame would surface.

I started to say something, but the officer cut me off. "Don't worry, Mr. Gibbs," he said, although the stiffness of his demeanor betrayed his unease. "The suspect entered through the security checkpoint so we assume he's not carrying a knife or a gun."

Assume? Even if this guy walked through the same security checkpoint as the rest of us, maybe he found a way around the safety measures. Did he manage to smuggle in a plastic bomb? Did he have an accomplice inside the court?

"As a precaution," the officer said, interrupting my thoughts, "we've stationed a number of armed, plainclothes marshals in the room. Two have taken up positions on either side of him."

Smart move. A smart *legal* move, that is. Doing so enabled the court to avoid a potential constitutional crisis by removing an individual just because he *looked* suspicious without proving an actual threat. Placing him under an immediate watch was a good start. I would have preferred to have heard that the SWAT team was on the way.

Suddenly, I found myself fighting not only for Terri's life but potentially for the lives of those around me. A thousand thoughts collided in my mind.

Where was my family?

Were they safe?

My wife hadn't planned to attend today's hearing. Had her plans changed? As a homeschooling mother, she sometimes brought the kids to court to further their education. I had to know if they were in the gallery. I wanted desperately to turn around and search for their precious faces. Right then and there I made a decision that my family would no longer tag along with me to these hearings. No way. I couldn't fathom what would happen if someone attempted to harm them.

That's when a new emotion pushed its way to the forefront of my mind: fear. Not a fear of dying *per se*. Rather, it was the inborn response that every father has when confronted with someone or some*thing* that threatens the safety of his family.

In a way, I was experiencing firsthand a taste of the sheer panic, indeed the living nightmare that the Schindlers had been battling for *years*. It was the fear of a parent knowing that their child is going to suffer—and they had no legal means to stop it. Like the Schindlers, I knew I would be compelled to move heaven and earth to keep someone from harming one of my own.

What sane parent wouldn't?

I felt a hand on my shoulder. "Uh, Mr. Gibbs? Are you all right?"

I blinked the room back into focus. The officer was speaking again. "We don't want to create a panic. However, I need for you to discreetly turn around and take a look. Tell me if you know this individual. Take your time. Be casual . . . and don't stare. Just scan the faces in the back row. Our man is the third guy from the doorway."

"I understand," I said, steeling myself.

I turned, slow and steady, hoping my face didn't betray the spike of anxiety within. I saw a guy, midthirties. His unshaven face and long, dark greasy hair came back to me, although I had never spoken with him. I remembered he was a somewhat unusual protestor; he was the sort of fellow who was kind of rough around the edges. I had no idea if he was a good guy or a bad guy.

Then again, he *was* wearing far too much clothing for a Florida afternoon. His heavy, black trench coat could easily conceal something strapped to his body. Now what? While thankful that I didn't find my family in the room, I still had a dilemma. Should I continue with the case, thereby becoming a lightning rod for every last person who disagreed with the outcome? After all, when I agreed to work with the Schindlers, I never dreamed that I'd become a target of someone's delusions—or rage.

Suddenly, the bailiff's voice broke through my thoughts.

"All rise."

The judge was entering the courtroom. It was time to get back to the business at hand. But in that moment of waiting, I had seen this case in a new light. I sensed even more that I was being called on not only to make legal arguments but to reach for something more fundamental about my convictions regarding the worth of every human life.

Come to think of it, that had always been the reason I was pouring myself into this cause, why my office staff thought this case was worth working long hours, indeed often without sleep, looking for any way to put Terri back into the loving arms of her mom and dad. I had to march forward, do the very best I could. Warehoused in a hospice room across town, an innocent woman condemned to die was counting on me.

Looking back on these events, I'm convinced that between the presence of the marshals and the power of prayer, the proceedings that afternoon went off without further incident.

Lawyers are not supposed to become too personally involved with their clients. But this case was different. And as I stood up to make my legal arguments before the judge, I realized that my few moments of prayer and reverie had given me something invaluable. I now carried in my heart an even more unshakable appreciation—indeed, a clearer understanding of why the Schindlers refused to give up on Terri. I prayed that if I were ever in Bob Schindler's shoes, someone would make an all-out effort for me and my family. I realized again that the effort to preserve life is always worth giving everything we have—no matter what the outcome.

I approached the podium. "Your Honor, my name is David Gibbs, and I have the privilege of representing Bob and Mary Schindler, the parents of Terri Schiavo."

OPEN TO A MIRACLE

While fighting for Terri's life within the court system was our primary avenue to save her from an unjust, premature death, a legal remedy wasn't the only potential solution. That's why behind the scenes my staff and I had worked around the clock to find some way—any way— to settle this tug-of-war outside of court. We knew that in just a couple of short months Terri's feeding tube was scheduled to be removed for the third and probably final time, and we were committed that no option to save her would be left unexplored.

For instance, with the single stroke of a pen, with a single decision, Michael Schiavo could have said, "You know what? I disagree with you that Terri has a quality of life worth maintaining. But she has a mother and father, a sister and brother who believe strongly that she can improve. All of her blood relatives want her to live. Maybe I should just walk away."

Now *that* would have been an unforgettable gift.

We wondered whether Michael might agree to some sort of compromise. Was there any set of terms under which he might consider releasing Terri to her family?

What about a million dollar offer to just walk away?

CHAPTER NINE

LET'S MAKE A DEAL

*Terri has parents whose unselfish desire is to simply love her,
care for her and let her live. . . . Terri may no longer be
perfect or complete but she has a fundamental right to life.*
—PATRICIA HEATON, ACTRESS[1]

I've always been of the opinion that this case should never have been taken to the courts. Long before George Felos or I or anybody else entered a courtroom, Michael and the Schindlers should have been able to hammer out an agreement between them. After all, this lawsuit involved a son-in-law who at one time was very close to Terri's parents— he and Terri lived with the Schindlers for a number of years.

In the context of this family tragedy, Michael could have said, "Look, I want a divorce. I want to get on with my life. I changed my mind about caring for her. She's a vegetable and nothing will ever change that. It's too bad what happened to her. . . . I just don't think she has any life and we should just let her go."

For their part, Bob and Mary could have said, "You know, we disagree, she is very much alive to us. She kisses us, she cries, she listens to the radio, she still loves music. We love our daughter and we will gladly take good care of her." At that point, I can't understand why Michael wouldn't have just said, "Look, if it means that much to you,

I'm going on with my life. Here, take your daughter. Dealing with her is your problem."

That's the way disputes and issues should be handled privately within a family. That's the way disputes and issues are often handled even after they are taken before a court and become a public matter. The two parties in a dispute often reach a settlement. Even in a criminal case, most criminals don't want to face the wrath of a jury or serve jail time. They certainly don't want to be sentenced to the fullest extent of the law, which is why they usually cut a deal with the prosecutor. They negotiate and then enter into a plea bargain.

Likewise, the vast majority of civil cases settle out of court. For example, when a business is sued, the officers of the company will evaluate several factors before going to court. They'll examine their odds of winning, and they'll calculate the cost to litigate against the cost of just paying an out-of-court settlement. They'll also factor in the reputation issue—in other words, would a trial negatively impact their reputation in the community?

Our system of justice places a premium on settlements. For a host of reasons, including the reality of a lengthy appeals process that could drag on for years, both sides in a dispute are encouraged to come to some mutually satisfactory agreement.

It's the classic give-and-take.

Why, then, couldn't Terri's family have settled her fate between themselves? Why couldn't there have been a private family agreement long ago? As I studied the family dynamic, I concluded the reason they had reached an impasse and had to take the case to a public court was that the Schindlers were willing to give up everything *except* the life of their daughter. For Michael's part, the only option he was willing to consider was some plan by which Bob and Mary would at least potentially agree to Terri's death.

Of course, that was the deal breaker.

But even though it was late in the game, and even though we appeared to be dealing publicly now with irreconcilable differences, I felt an agreement might still be reached privately within the family. And if there were even the slightest possibility, we had to try. Which is why, behind the scenes, we had taken steps toward mending fences, hoping to arrive at what we believed might be a win-win solution.

HERE'S THE DEAL

On October 26, 2004, I drafted a letter of compromise and gave it to Michael's attorneys on behalf of the Schindlers. Contrary to the media's portrayal of Bob and Mary, this was not a grudge match on their part. They would have agreed to *anything* that would have somehow allowed Terri to continue living so they could take care of her and get her the therapy and rehabilitation they believed would help her.

I invite you to read the actual letter we sent, which is reprinted at the end of this chapter. Briefly summarized, the Schindlers were very nondemanding. Michael could keep all the money from the malpractice settlement. He could remain married to Terri, or get a divorce and move on. Michael could still inherit Terri's estate. He could have as much or as little contact with Terri as he desired. He could visit her if he so wished, or he could walk away and never turn back. That would be Michael's call to make.

As long as he wouldn't take steps to end her life, Michael could remain as involved as he liked. Or, if he wanted to be released from all responsibilities, that was fine too. If he had an insurance policy on Terri, he could keep the funds upon her natural death. If there was ever money to be made later telling Terri's story, he'd be welcome to keep those funds. *Anything* was fine with Bob and Mary—just as long as he allowed them to keep their daughter alive.

For their part, as you'll find in the letter, Bob and Mary and their two other adult children, Bobby and Suzanne, would agree to care for Terri at their own expense. They promised never to pursue any legal action against Michael concerning anything that had transpired from the time of her collapse to the present. As far as we were concerned, we had found the makings of a peaceful and private resolution to this dispute.

What grounds for objection could Michael possibly raise?

We delivered the offer to George Felos and then waited . . . and prayed really hard.

When I called George for a reaction, he simply rejected our offer out of hand. He stressed that the only deal Michael would consider would be for the Schindlers to agree to allow a doctor to go in and examine Terri; if the doctor thought she was in a persistent vegetative state, then Michael wanted the Schindlers to agree she would die. If, however, the doctor said she had the possibility of being rehabilitated, then she could live.

At that point in the conversation, I said, "George, you and I both know Terri is alive and nonterminal. Regardless of her prospects for recovery, this family loves her and wants to take care of her." In my heart I could tell we were miles apart with little hope of spanning the distance between us.

The hard reality was this: I knew both parties never would be able to agree on the same doctor. Remember that a PVS diagnosis is extremely subjective. Yet as the saying goes, "Nothing ventured, nothing gained." I told George that if *we* could pick the doctor, we'd take the deal. He laughed. We both knew that if Felos picked the doctor, Terri would be dead for certain. The Schindlers had no confidence that an impartial doctor could be selected by the court since the court had demonstrated for years that it was leaning toward death in this matter.

Though our offer of compromise had been rejected, I refused to give up trying to find a private solution. There just had to be another way to bring these two parties together. The absolute core, haunting question that drove me to seek common ground was this: *When you have a mom and a dad who are begging to care for their daughter, why not err on the side of life?*

What possible reason was preventing Michael from agreeing to a compromise that would allow Terri to live and receive therapy? There had to be a way to unlock this deadlock. With the New Year just around the corner and with time running out on our options, a new avenue to reconcile the differences presented itself: mediation by former president Jimmy Carter.

PRESIDENTIAL APPEAL

Throughout our involvement in the case, we received hundreds of thousands of offers to help. They came from every imaginable direction, and even a few you couldn't imagine. Of each "hot tip" or "surefire solution" we had to ask two questions:

1. Was it legitimate?
2. Was it potentially helpful?

One of the more promising phone calls came from a news producer in our state capital, Tallahassee. He had first made contact with us right about the time Terri's Law had been struck down. He had followed the legislature closely as they voted on Terri's Law, and he had strong pro-Terri feelings. When he approached us, he asked if we had ever thought about getting former president Jimmy Carter involved. I told him we hadn't considered that avenue, but if President Carter would help us, why not? We were open to any legitimate approach that might mend the rift in this family. Of course I told him it would help if he had an "in" with the Carters.

As the producer described his connection to the Carter family, it triggered a memory of a story Bob Schindler had told me. At the time, thousands of supporters were trying to reach Bob. Due to the overwhelming number of phone calls he'd receive (sometimes upward of a hundred calls in a single night), Bob occasionally forgot who had called.

Keep in mind, Bob Schindler is a semiretired man with no staff, no secretary, and no press handler. He and Mary and the family had to juggle everything on their own. So when he received a call from a "Rosalynn Carter from Georgia," the name didn't automatically ring any bells. Bob didn't put two and two together, you know, that this was *the* Rosalynn Carter, wife of former president Jimmy Carter. Afterward, Mary read him the riot act much like my wife would if I had done the same thing. I laughed.

The point is that Rosalynn Carter apparently had contacted Bob in the past, and now we had somebody offering to connect us with the Carter Center for mediation. President Carter has a long track record of dealing with difficult situations, including mediating with dictators, heads of state, and warring nations. The former president had been a recent recipient of the Nobel Peace Prize. His well-known mediation skills might be exactly what we needed to bridge the gap.

I told the producer that if President Carter would step forward and work with us, we'd be all for it. But before I could propose this to Mr. Felos, I had to have Mr. Carter's assurances that he and his team would meet with us. Without that, we'd look pretty ridiculous securing Michael's consent only to have the Carter Center then refuse to help.

The producer graciously understood. He approached his mother, who had the primary contact with the Carters, and asked her to inquire about this option. As a Democratic Party supporter, the producer's mother had been to a number of fund-raising events with Jimmy Carter. And as a mother with her own handicapped child, she believed that the disabled should be treated with dignity. She also felt strongly that to kill Terri through dehydration and starvation was unconscionable.

I hesitated telling too many people because I didn't want to raise false hopes. After all, there were hundreds of behind-the-scenes options we at the Gibbs Law Firm were chasing down; most never came to fruition. Still, as with this promising lead, we had to be ready for any and all contingencies. There wasn't time to sit around and assume we could work out the details next month—Terri might not be alive that long. In that respect this case always had that constant life-and-death pressure.

Every day, every hour was precious.

We soon learned that the Carter Center had declined involvement in the case. Both this mother and her producer son in Tallahassee were heartbroken. Whatever level of interest Rosalynn had exhibited earlier by trying to contact the Schindlers, the Carter Center had now deter-

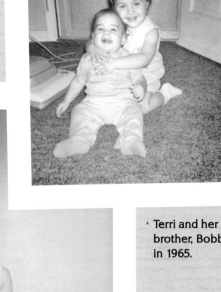

Schindler family photo

Schindler family photo

Schindler family photo

◄ Terri at eleven months old, 1964.

▼ Bob, Mary, Terri, and Bobby Schindler celebrate Terri's third birthday, December 3, 1966.

▲ Terri and her brother, Bobby, in 1965.

Schindler family photo

Schindler family photo

▴ A teenaged Terri with her Labrador, Bucky.

▴ Terri's senior class picture, 1981.

Schindler family photo

▴ Terri on her wedding day, November 10, 1984.

▲ Bobby, Terri, Bob, Mary, and Suzanne Schindler on Terri's wedding day, November 10, 1984.

▲ A 1987 Christmas photo of Terri, taken twenty-six months before her collapse.

▲ Michael visits with Terri at St. Petersburg's College Harbor Nursing Home in November 1990, about nine months after her collapse.

▲ The sign outside of Woodside Hospice. Michael had Terri moved to Woodside on April 10, 2000.

AP Images

▲ Bob Schindler, left, with his
wife, Mary, daughter
Suzanne, and son, Bobby,
at a hearing December 13,
2002, at the Pinellas County
Courthouse. On November
22 the court had ruled that
Michael Schiavo could have
Terri's feeding stopped on
January 3, 2003, but the
Schindlers won a stay to
continue Terri's feeding until
an appellate court could
rule on the case.

AP Images

▲ On October 23, 2003,
Florida Governor Jeb
Bush signed Terri's Law,
the order that allowed
her feeding tube to be
reinserted. (Pictured
here in June 2005.)

AP Images

▲ Michael Schiavo, left, answers questions at a news
conference following oral arguments in the Florida
Supreme Court case concerning Terri's Law, on August
31, 2004. With Michael are his brother Bryan, center,
and his attorney George Felos, right.

St. Petersburg Times

Florida's Best Newspaper

WEATHER: High 86, low 74
60% chance of rain.

SUNDAY, September 26, 2004

$1

Powerful Jeanne lashes east coast

EAST COAST: More than 2-million were urged to evacuate before the Category 3 storm closed in.

By MATTHEW WAITE,
JAMIE THOMPSON, STEVE
BOUSQUET and CARRIE JOHNSON
Times Staff Writers

STUART — A strengthening Hurricane Jeanne battered Florida's east coast this morning and began its dangerous trek across the state's midsection, bringing damaging winds and driving rain that storm-weary residents find all too familiar.

From Florida City to the Georgia border, more than 2-million residents were urged to evacuate. But after four such orders in the past six weeks, state officials worried

many were too tired or jaded to heed the warning.

"I know people are fatigued and some are still recovering who were hit by Frances, and I know they are tired," said Max Mayfield, director of the National Hurricane Center in Miami. "However, they must treat this hurricane as if it's the only hurricane they've ever been through."

As southeast Florida endured the outer bands of rain and wind, Jeanne was a Category 3 hurricane with 115-mph winds extending more than 70 miles from the eye

Please see **EAST** 13A

INSIDE

DEVASTATION IN HAITI

Jeanne was the latest hardship to befall the impoverished island nation. A story and photographs. **14A–16A**

WHAT DO YOU DO NOW?

If you've lost power, are worried about flooding or have insurance concerns, check out the hurricane Q&A. **13A**

COSTLY CHALLENGES

Everything from the state's electrical grid to building codes to beach restoration will be under review. **1B**

AREA BRIDGES STURDY

They are meant to endure high winds, but storm surge can threaten. **1B**

FEW BLUES IN THE BAY: Residents' moods range from weary resignation to self-assured preparation.

By JANET ZINK
and ABBIE VANSICKLE
Times Staff Writers

TAMPA — Residents in the Tampa Bay area expected to sit this one out, but Hurricane Jeanne had other plans and shifted course just enough to trigger evacuation orders for thousands before the storm's expected arrival this morning.

From Crystal River to River-view, people in mobile homes and low-lying areas were encouraged or outright ordered to evacuate for yet another hurricane.

Forecasters predicted Jeanne

would head northwest across the state instead of turning, bringing hurricane-force wind gusts across Polk, Pasco, Hernando and Citrus counties before turning north. Expected storm surges ranged from 9 feet in Citrus County to a foot in Hillsborough.

Citrus, Hernando, Pasco and Hillsborough counties ordered mandatory evacuations of thousands of mobile homes. Citrus officials also closed schools for Monday and ordered mandatory evacuation of low-lying areas and homes west of U.S. 19. More than 500

Please see **JEANNE** 15A

St. Petersburg Times

◄ Bob and Mary Schindler, along with David Gibbs, raced Hurricane Jeanne across Florida to catch a flight to California to tell their story on *Larry King Live* just days after the Florida Supreme Court ruled Terri's Law unconstitutional.

Tampa Tribune

▲ David Gibbs with the Schindlers at a press conference on February 25, 2005 — the day Judge Greer issued his third and final death order to remove Terri's feeding tube on March 18, 2005.

◄ George Felos and David Gibbs talk before the start of a hearing in the Pinellas County Circuit Court on September 30, 2004.

AP Images

▾ Twelve pro-family organizations stage the Rose Rally for Terri on March 13, 2005. Supporters gather in Tallahassee's Old Capitol courtyard, holding one thousand long-stemmed roses to be delivered the following morning to Florida legislators as a reminder of the urgency at hand in the fight for Terri's life.

▴ Bobby Schindler meets with Senate Majority Leader Bill Frist (R-TN) at the Capitol in March 2005. Bobby was in Washington meeting with every member of Congress who would see him during the legislative push to protect Terri's life.

◂ Pinellas Park police block the entrance to Woodside Hospice on March 16, 2005, two days before Terri's feeding tube was to be removed.

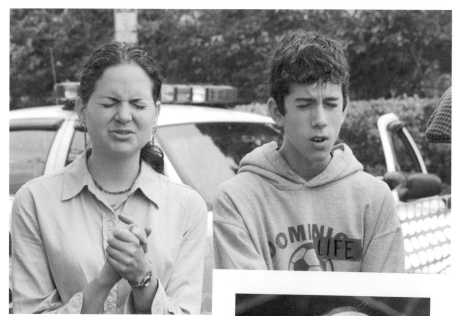

Tim Boyles/Getty Images

^ Supporters gather and pray outside Woodside Hospice on March 16, 2005.

˅ Pinellas Park police maintain a presence as supporters gather on March 18, 2005, the day Terri's feeding tube was removed for the last time.

AP Images

^ Pinellas County Circuit Judge George Greer listens to arguments during a hearing on March 17, 2005.

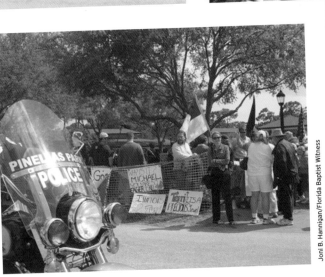

Joni B. Hannigan/Florida Baptist Witness

mined that Terri's situation fell outside its scope of mediation. You can imagine Bob and Mary's disappointment when we later discussed this missed opportunity.

I can't say whether or not Michael Schiavo and his attorney would have agreed to meet with President Carter. We never got that far. But I'm sure his presence would have helped us jump-start the exchange. I don't fault President Carter. I never learned whether the president had made the decision or whether someone on the Center's staff had done it, perhaps without actually consulting him.

In the end, all we really knew was that another door had closed.

When it became clear that the aid of the Carter Center was no longer an option, I decided to propose our own confidential, face-to-face meeting at a neutral location. I invited Michael, his brother Brian, his lawyer, and anyone else he desired to be present for a private meeting with Mary Schindler and Bobby Jr., the two family members we believed had the best chance of reaching Michael's heart, with our representation. I had hopes that, through dialogue, a mutually agreeable outcome might be reached.

The details of the meeting could not be hammered out, so unfortunately, it never took place.

Even more, I was about to discover the hard way that Terri would have had more legal protection if she had been a terrorist, a mass murderer . . . or an animal.

Offer to Settle Out of Court

October 26, 2004
Ms. Debbie Bushnell, Esq.
204 Scotland Street
Dunedin, FL 34698

Mr. George Felos
Felos & Felos
595 Main Street
Dunedin, FL 34698

IN RE: THE GUARDIANSHIP OF THERESA MARIE SCHIAVO
File No. 90-2908GD-003

Dear Ms. Bushnell and Mr. Felos:

As the new lead counsel to the cases surrounding Terri Schiavo, we are not aware of any recent attempt to resolve this matter among the family members without continued court intervention. In order to make certain that this avenue of potential resolution is not overlooked, we are providing you with the following proposal from the Schindler family. We would ask that you apprise your client of this proposed settlement offer, provide him with a copy of this letter, and respond to us on his behalf within five days of your receipt of this letter.

The Schindlers' sole desire in making this proposal is that they be permitted to take their daughter and sister home to care for her within their family. The Schindler family members would take on this responsibility at their own expense. In consideration of your client permitting them to take Terri home with them, they would be willing to provide him with any legal guarantees he would desire, including the following:

1) The Schindlers would never seek any money from Michael. He could retain any monies or other assets that might remain to him, either from their married life together, from the malpractice awards for himself or for Terri, or any other assets he might have received in the past. They would not seek any financial help from him for any care, therapy, or rehabilitation for Terri.

2) The Schindlers fully understand and appreciate that Michael now has a new life with Jodi and their two children. If he would desire to divorce Terri, the family would sign any necessary legal documents to assure Michael that, upon Terri's natural death, he would receive any of Terri's estate that he would inherit were he to remain her husband. Whether or not Michael would choose to pursue a divorce from Terri, the Schindlers would guarantee that he could retain whatever visiting rights he might desire with Terri for the rest of her life.

3) The Schindlers would agree to forego any and all future legal claims or actions against Michael or against any of his agents in this matter for any reason.

4) The Schindlers would permit Michael's attorneys to draft any agreement regarding this matter that Michael would desire, including the above referenced terms and any other terms he and his attorneys would find appropriate, excluding payment of Michael's previous legal fees or costs.

Now that Michael is a father himself, the Schindlers are pleading with him to consider their love for their daughter and sister and to permit them to take over Terri's care, with their blessings on Michael as he continues to live his own life with his new family.

Please provide a copy of this letter to Michael and respond to us within five days.

Sincerely,

Gibbs Law Firm, P.A.
David C. Gibbs III
ADMITTED IN FLORIDA, TEXAS, NORTH DAKOTA, COLORADO, MINNESOTA, AND THE DISTRICT OF COLUMBIA

PART TWO

TERRI'S FIGHT FOR LIFE

CHAPTER TEN

TERRI'S ONLY CRIME

If you [starved] condemned criminals, how far would you get? It would take about two seconds for the court to strike it down as cruel and unusual.

—JACK KEVORKIAN[1]

When Alice falls down the rabbit hole in Lewis Carroll's classic tale *Alice in Wonderland,* she encounters a twisted reality where nothing makes sense. And when the White Rabbit and the Mad Hatter cross her path, she starts to question her own sanity. Logic and reason are relative concepts in Wonderland. In the bizarre finale, Alice finds herself on trial accused of stealing tarts. Justice, she discovers as the trial unfolds, is dangerously rooted in the whims of the eccentric creatures she has met.

In some ways Alice and Terri Schiavo shared a similar predicament. Both were ensnared by a court in which the law seemed to be standing on its head to accommodate an illogical and unfounded verdict. While Alice fought for her life in this fable, Terri battled for her life in a real-life case replete with legal problems, misconceptions, and contradictions.

You see, Michael Schiavo was confronted with a serious dilemma after he decided (following the 1992 malpractice verdict) that Terri wouldn't want to live and should therefore be permitted to die. How could she legally be put to death? It's against the law in Florida to kill either people or pets with the exception of the death penalty in criminal convictions. But Terri wasn't a convicted felon, and she hadn't committed any crimes worthy of death, so the death penalty option was off the table. Michael needed help from the Florida legislature and the courts before he could legally carry out his plan to have his wife put to death.

Likewise, Judge Greer must have known that euthanasia, mercy killing, assisted suicide, and other variations of helping people die are all forbidden by the state of Florida. Furthermore, Florida has a law prohibiting the mistreatment and starvation of disabled persons.

So how could Michael legally end Terri's life? That's where this case and the 2000 trial come in.

Michael had help in ending his wife's life from a few sources:

- his pro-euthanasia attorney, George Felos
- the Florida legislature, which by 1998 had enacted the law that permitted Michael to take his dilemma to the courts
- the Florida appellate courts, which upheld the vast majority of lower court rulings in this case.

In fact, that is why the U.S. Congress in the end tried to have a federal court take another look at the facts and the testimony, in the same way that a federal court would review the decision of a state court in a criminal death penalty case—just to be absolutely sure the state court got it right. By determining that Terri would have wanted to die, state court Judge Greer used two main sources to authorize the withholding of Terri's food and water so that nature would take its course:

- a previous Florida right-to-die case, in which George Felos succeeded in having Florida courts authorize the removal of another woman's feeding tube in 1990 (a woman, in that case, however, who had a written living will asking not to receive artificial feeding)
- the recent 1997 Florida end-of-life law intended to make it easier to

remove feeding tubes from patients no longer able to speak for themselves

Thus, with the help of George Felos and the new Florida law that for the first time defined a feeding tube as artificial life support (on the same order as heart/lung machines), Michael Schiavo could use the new public policy of the state of Florida to argue that it was lawful to remove his wife's food and water in order to cause her death. It seemed to me that this argument contradicted other public policy in Florida that required care to be provided for the disabled and prohibited euthanasia. And with a bewildering leap of logic worthy of the Mad Hatter, Terri's husband, Michael, later told *Nightline* viewers:

> Terri will not be starved to death. Her nutrition and hydration will be taken away.[2]

You might want to read that statement again.

Whether you call it death by starvation, death by dehydration, cessation of nutrition and water, or give it some other illogical name, this interpretation of the law wouldn't have worked if Terri had been a prisoner of war; the Geneva Convention prohibits starvation. It wouldn't have worked if Terri had been a convicted mass murderer on death row anywhere in America, even in Florida, because the Eighth Amendment to the United States Constitution would then have protected her from "cruel and unusual punishment."

Such as starvation or dehydration.

What's more, had Terri been an animal, she also would have been protected under Florida law. It's a crime to starve or even mistreat pets or other animals in Florida; that is a crime punishable by a fine and up to a year in jail. You see, the Department of Agriculture takes the well-being and treatment of animals very seriously; their protection has generated a complicated set of rules and regulations governing animal welfare that is more than four hundred pages in length—that's roughly the size of a Tom Clancy novel.

But with Terri Schiavo we didn't have an animal, we had a beautiful human being. We didn't have a convicted mass murderer, we just had an innocent, disabled woman. And we didn't have an international prisoner or terrorist detainee housed in Guantanamo, we had a law-abiding American citizen and a resident of the state of Florida. How, then, did Terri fall into this unbelievably horrific crack in American law?

Frankly, I don't have a good answer for that.

All I know is that Terri would have had more legal protection if she had been a cow, a horse, a dog, or even a laboratory rat. That's not an exaggeration. There are laws on the books in Florida prescribing the humane and acceptable methods of euthanizing rodents. What's more, transferring personal property such as a sofa, a desk, or a refrigerator requires more legal certainty in Florida than killing Terri did.

REASONABLE DOUBT

With less due process than it would take to give away a refrigerator in the Sunshine State, Judge Greer determined whether Terri should live or die. Let me illustrate in simple terms what I mean when I say that, despite all the court decisions to the contrary, I still believe Terri was denied "due process of law" as afforded by the Fifth and Fourteenth Amendments.

Let's say I went on *Oprah* or *Good Morning America* to announce how I wanted my earthly possessions dispersed upon my death. Let's say I got very specific and said, for example, "I, David Gibbs III, am of sound mind and do hereby declare my last will and testament. With you as my witnesses, I swear that I want my co-worker Barbara Weller to have my refrigerator when I die."

Do you know what I just did?

Absolutely nothing.

If Barbara went to claim my refrigerator upon my death, the probate judge would refuse her request. Why? Because unless I *wrote down* that my wishes were to bequeath my refrigerator to Barbara, she gets nothing. That's crazy, you say? What about the millions of people watching TV that day who could attest that they actually heard me express my desire to give Barbara my refrigerator on national TV? What if Oprah herself was willing to fly in and testify?

Nope, neither action would help.

Unless I have a will *in writing*, my comments to the media—or to my spouse while watching TV—are nothing more than hearsay evidence. Florida law clearly states my wishes to dispose of my refrigerator must be written down. That's "due process" or, if you will, the established legal course of action governing the distribution of my assets at death.

Barbara won't get the fridge. Period.

Consider, then, the insanity of this case. On the one hand, my legal associate would be prevented from receiving a thousand-dollar appliance for lack of a written will, despite anything I said publicly on national TV. But on the other hand, when Terri's husband wanted to terminate his wife's life—a woman with no living will, no written document of any kind, and no physical proof spelling out her wishes regarding medical treatment—the judge granted his request, deciding that casual conversations more than a decade earlier while watching TV or having casual conversations with family about heart/lung machines provided the court with "clear and convincing" evidence of Terri's wishes regarding the removal of her feeding tube.

Judge Greer decided that Terri must die despite evidence that it seemed to me was just as strong, if not stronger, in the other direction. Others and I continue to believe that, in making his decision, Judge Greer violated part of the due-process test for life-and-death cases. Writing for the *National Review*, attorney Andrew C. McCarthy observed, "Due process mandates that no person may be deprived of life by state action unless every factual predicate legally necessary to validate the state action has been proved beyond a reasonable doubt."[3]

Reasonable doubt is a higher legal standard of proof than the clear and convincing standard set by the Florida legislature and used by the judge in Terri's case. But without written instructions, how could the state know *for certain* what Terri's wishes really were any more than my oral statements about my refrigerator could legally prove in court that I really wanted Barbara to have it?

McCarthy concludes, "An American [was killed] by a court order based on fact-finding so palpably unreliable there cannot even be the pretense that the due-process yardstick our country has long demanded in death cases was used."[4] Rather than stepping forward in the proud history of our nation to protect Terri's right to life, the court said, in effect, *We don't think Terri's life is one worth living.* Then, without reviewing any new evidence, other state and federal courts upheld Judge Greer's civil death order.

If you think sentencing a person to die without clear evidence of his or her wishes doesn't really happen in America, let me direct you to Judge Greer's own admission that Terri never spelled out her wishes in writing. This is taken from his February 11, 2000, authorization to discontinue her life:

> There are no written declarations by Terri Schiavo as to her intention with regard to this issue. Therefore, the court is left with oral declarations *allegedly* made to parties and non-parties as to her feelings on this subject. (emphasis added)

The court relied on Michael's word and on the sudden recollections of his brother and a sister-in-law, made a full nine years after Terri's collapse, and just one year before the 2000 trial. Let's set aside the unusual timing of these belated collective family memories. After hearing the testimony of the Schiavo family on which Terri's fate was to be determined, Judge Greer characterized their statements as "oral declarations *allegedly* made" by Terri (emphasis added). Another judge just as easily could have dismissed Michael's and his family's memories as failing the "clear and convincing evidence" standard.

What also bothers me is that for nearly ten years both Michael and these members of his family had remained silent about Terri's alleged wishes. *If* Terri had really mentioned something about her end-of-life wishes during casual conversations as Michael and his family members claimed, why didn't Michael's family remind him that Terri wouldn't want to "live that way" when she was first injured?

Why didn't Michael himself do the honorable thing and step forward to declare Terri's wishes during the malpractice trial before a jury awarded more than a million dollars for her care if both he and his family believed that Terri wouldn't want to have that care?

YOU DECIDE

Terri Schiavo might still be alive today if she had either had a different husband or a different judge. Terri had no jury at the 2000 trial to weigh the evidence regarding what her end-of-life wishes would have been regarding use of a feeding tube. Florida law requires clear and convincing evidence at trial if a person who can no longer speak for himself does not have a living will or some other written document stating their end-of-life wishes. Since Terri had no such written document, testimony had to be presented and evidence evaluated in court to determine what those wishes might have been in the circumstances in which she found herself.

Since there was no jury to hear this testimony, the judge himself weighed the evidence presented by Michael Schiavo and his brother and sister-in-law (that Terri would want to die) against the evidence presented by Terri's parents, her siblings, and friends (that she would want to live). Appellate courts would most likely have upheld the judge's decision, whichever way he decided the case. The trial court is the only judicial body concerned with weighing evidence and determining facts. Appellate courts only review the procedure used and any legal questions. In Terri's case, the judge weighed the evidence and erred on the side of death rather than on the side of life. Another judge might just as easily have taken the opposite approach. What would you have done if you were the judge? Let's see how you would have weighed the evidence.

First of all, it is important to point out that Michael never mentioned Terri would not have wanted to live with a feeding tube until

several years after her collapse in 1990. In fact, during the medical malpractice trial in 1992, Michael assumed that Terri would live a long life.
He told the jury in that trial that he needed millions of dollars so he
could take care of Terri for the rest of his life. But after receiving a jury
verdict of more than a million dollars, Michael reassessed his situation
during the mid-1990s, and by 2000 he testified in Judge George Greer's
courtroom that Terri had told him she would not want to live "like
that."

Michael Schiavo testified before Judge Greer that, in her early twen-
ties, Terri had expressed an oral declaration while watching various
nonspecified television programs about disabled people that she would
not want to live "like that"—i.e., presumably on artificial life support,
which prior to 1990, when Terri allegedly made these statements, con-
sisted only of artificial heart and lung machines and did not include
feeding tubes. Michael also testified that Terri had told him she would
not want to live "like that" when talking about her uncle who had been
injured in a car accident and was semiparalyzed although he lived at
home, traveled to the beach, and had a job.

To back up Michael's version of Terri's wishes, his brother and sister-in-law testified that Terri had made similar end-of-life statements in
casual conversations with them, including a discussion about "life-support machines" at a family funeral and a discussion about friends who
had removed their severely disabled newborn from a breathing
machine. Both of Michael's relatives testified on cross-examination that
they had never told Michael about these conversations with Terri and
didn't "remember" them until 1999 when they were preparing for their
court testimony.

This was the entirety of the pro-death testimony regarding Terri's
wishes.

On the other hand, Terri's family and friends testified that Terri
had great compassion for the sick and disabled, often visited her grandmother at a nursing home, and had never made any end-of-life statements, except to disapprove of the actions of Karen Ann Quinlan's par-

ents when they removed their daughter from life support (but did not remove her feeding tube).

Terri's family and friends always stressed to me that Terri had great compassion for sick animals and elderly people and that her favorite saying was, "Where there's life, there's hope."

Judge George Greer, who conducted the trial in 2000, also heard testimony from a sociologist who stated that most people would not want to live after becoming severely disabled. The court approved payment of Michael's legal bills for this trial using Terri's medical malpractice trust fund. The Schindlers, who had no money for legal expenses and who were denied use of Terri's malpractice funds to defend her life, offered no expert testimony to contradict this evidence.

If Judge Greer had determined that the evidence he heard was not clear and convincing in favor of removing Terri's feeding tube, she might still be alive today, receiving therapy and interacting socially with her family and friends. Would she be able to eat on her own? Could she have recovered? These are questions we can no longer answer. Even Dr. Jon Thogmartin, the medical examiner who conducted Terri's autopsy, said it is impossible to make such determinations by viewing a corpse. Such a diagnosis can only be made by examining a live patient.

But there is one thing we can know for sure. If Terri were still alive today, she would be basking in the love and care of her devoted family and her many friends, no matter what her condition or the degree of her recovery. One thing Terri's family and friends fully agreed with her on was that "where there's life, there's hope."

The lack of a paper trail detailing Terri's wishes wasn't missed by ABC News' Chris Bury. In a *Nightline* interview, Bury quizzed Michael about this missing link of indisputable evidence:

BURY: Michael, did Terri, your wife, leave any kind of written instructions about her wishes?

SCHIAVO: She didn't leave any written instructions. She has verbally expressed her wishes to me and other people.

BURY: She had verbally expressed them in what context exactly?

SCHIAVO: Through watching some TV program, a conversation that happened regarding her uncle that was very ill.

BURY: And how long ago was that?

SCHIAVO: Oh, we're talking—it's now been fifteen years. We're talking a couple of years, three years before this happened to Terri.

BURY: So there's no kind of written record at all? It's basically your recollection and those of other family members?

SCHIAVO: Yes, it is.[5]

Why would Judge Greer permit hearsay testimony, suddenly remembered by Michael and his family years after the fact, as the basis for a life-and-death pronouncement? Since Terri could no longer speak for herself, she had no way to correct or clarify what she was alleged to have said. At the very least, the Schindlers argued, the court should have provided Terri with a lawyer to represent *her* own interests, since they might not have been the same interests her husband had.

Unbelievable as it sounded to me, that never happened. Throughout the many years of this intrafamily legal wrestling match, Terri never had any legal representation of her own. The court's unfortunate assumption apparently was that Michael's attorney was also representing Terri since Michael was Terri's legal guardian. (Keep in mind we were representing her parents, Bob and Mary Schindler, while George Felos was representing Michael Schiavo.)

As it turned out, a probate court judge was able to overrule the will of the governor, the Florida legislature, the U.S. Congress, and the president by ordering Terri to die.

This is why I maintain that the fate of an ordinary kitchen appliance would have had greater legal protection than did the life of Terri Schiavo.

THE DEATH PENALTY

Much like Alice struggling to make sense of Wonderland, I still cannot comprehend how the people who were entrusted with protecting Terri—namely, her guardian/husband and the guardianship court—were so in favor of ending her life. I'm also amazed when I meet people in my travels who fail to grasp the fact that starvation/dehydration is an act of brutality so severe and so heartless that fellow Americans would never permit such a death, even in a case where death was warranted, as with Ted Bundy, the Florida mass murderer.

Imagine this scenario.

As of this writing, thirty-eight states permit the execution of men and women who have done horrible crimes against humanity. What do you think would happen if, in one of those states, the legislature were to say, "Here's an idea that will save money and take some of the strain off our budgets. Instead of using the electric chair or spending funds on lethal injections, we hereby authorize the wardens to lock all condemned inmates in their cells, with a police guard to make sure no one attempts to feed them, and then let them starve to death 'naturally' when their appeals have expired. A couple of weeks later, send in the guards and haul out the corpses."

The lawmakers could contend that these inmates are already sentenced to die, and as reported by the *New York Times*, "experts say ending feeding can lead to a gentle death."[6] Sure, such a proposal sounds farfetched. But why not explore the starvation of death row inmates for efficiency and cost savings? Answer: The Eighth Amendment's cruel and unusual punishment clause covers *all* people, including hard-core prisoners.

The courts have ruled that states must execute their capital punishment sentences as painlessly and as swiftly as possible. Understandably, electric chairs have fallen into disfavor because of their unreliability. For instance, Florida used to use an electric chair that became known as "Old Sparky"—it killed the condemned *most* of the time on the first jolt. But sometimes it didn't and a second try was attempted. That was completely unacceptable. So given the desire to treat criminals humanely, we've gone to lethal injections.

Clearly, our system of justice bends over backward to minimize pain during the death process of convicts. Which is why *Terri's only crime was that she committed no crime worthy of the death penalty.* Think about what I just said. If Terri had broken the law, she never would have been dehydrated and starved to death anywhere in America. How did we get to such a low point in our nation's history where there are better protections in place for people incarcerated against their will than there were for Terri as a ward of the state?

I believe what happened to Terri is a reflection of our culture at large. We're a disposable nation with an insatiable appetite for what's newer, brighter, bigger, and better. Take mobile communications. What do we do when our cell phones and pagers become out-of-date? We toss them, right? What do we do when a computer is old? We buy a new one and trash the old workhorse. Appliances, clothing, gadgets—you name it, we toss 'em and run to Wal-Mart for a new one at the first signs of wear.

If we're not careful, that disposable consumer view will regularly find its way into the courtroom setting. In fact, that's what happened with Terri. The Pinellas County Probate Court had no problem lumping Terri in the "damaged goods" bin even after many excellent doctors, neurologists, speech therapists, and others gifted with rehabilitation training and skills stepped forward to testify that Terri might be rehabilitated.

The court said, in effect, that no matter what condition Terri was in or might be in—even if we could teach her to swallow, to drink on her own—nothing the Schindlers might be able to demonstrate to the court could prove that any treatment would raise her quality of life to the level where the judge would believe Terri would want to stay alive.

Is that difficult to believe?

Consider Judge Greer's second order to withdraw Terri's nutrition and hydration on November 22, 2002 (the first was on February 11, 2000). He wrote, "The real issue in this case, however, deals with treatment options for Terry [*sic*] Schiavo and whether or not they will have any positive affect [*sic*] so as to 'significantly improve her quality of life.'"

Do you see the dangerous slope we have just stepped onto with that line of reasoning?

It's as if we, as a nation, have collectively fallen down the rabbit hole and entered Wonderland. Here we discover that the disabled, the handicapped, the sickly, the elderly, and potentially, people suffering from terminal HIV/AIDS are being told by the courts: Your life is not worth living if it doesn't meet our own minimal quality standard.

At least in Lewis Carroll's fable, Alice awakened to learn that her topsy-turvy courtroom drama and her visit to Wonderland was simply a fantastical dream. If only we could do the same. Instead, Terri's tragic story finished as a nightmare.

CHAPTER ELEVEN

TERRI'S LAST MEAL

ORDERED AND ADJUDGED *that absent a stay from the appellate courts, the guardian, MICHAEL SCHIAVO, shall cause the removal of nutrition and hydration from the ward, THERESA SCHIAVO, at 1:00 P.M. on Friday, March 18, 2005.*

—JUDGE GEORGE W. GREER, FEBRUARY 25, 2005

For weeks on end our attorneys scaled a mountain of case law searching for any crevice that could be pried open into a legal foothold to save Terri. We prepared briefs by night and presented arguments by day. Press conferences were wedged in between meetings. Sleep was grabbed in meager bundles of adjacent minutes: at the desk, on the couch, or in a parked car before appointments. We squeezed every precious minute out of the day trying to find a reprieve.

Most of all, we prayed—a lot.

But as we saw, even the prospect of a million-dollar offer to give Terri back to her parents could not get Michael to budge from his position.

As the eyes of the world were glued to the television for the latest minute-by-minute developments, a California businessman upped the ante by depositing $1 million dollars in a trust. The money was

Michael's for the taking—if he would just agree to release the guardianship of Terri to her parents.

Speaking for Robert Herring Sr., founder of both HERCO Technology and a firm called WEALTHTV, attorney Gloria Allred said Herring "retained my law firm to convey the following offer to Terri's husband. If Mike Schiavo agrees to transfer the legal right to decide all of Terri's current and future medical decisions to Terri's parents, then Mr. Herring will pay Mr. Schiavo the amount of $1 million."[1]

What motivated this most incredible offer?

Herring said, "After viewing a video of Terri on television, I came to the belief that there was hope for her." He added, "I believe very strongly that there are medical advances happening around the globe that very shortly could have a positive impact on Terri's condition."[2] We held the same position and wondered why Michael Schiavo and the courts would deny Terri the chance to benefit from such medical treatment.

The reaction from Michael's attorney was as swift as it was abrupt. Calling the offer "offensive," in a huff Felos said, "Michael has said over and over again that this case is not about money for him. It's about carrying out his wife's wishes. There is no amount of money anyone can offer that will cause him to turn his back on his wife."[3]

The truth is, we could only speculate what Michael's true reasons were for refusing to settle privately outside of court and for refusing cash offers to save Terri. What we did know was that if an agreement outside of court wasn't going to materialize, then we had to aggressively advocate every possible appeal that might reverse Terri's civil death sentence.

BLACK FRIDAY ARRIVES

I was up by five-thirty that Friday morning, March 18, 2005, after two hours of rest, and hit the floor running. We had a little more than seven short hours before Terri's nutrition and water would be cut off at 1:00 PM—the deadline set by the court to begin her "death process." I held my wife and prayed with her that God would work a miracle. Looking at my sleeping kids, I kissed them each on the forehead with fresh appreciation for their lives, and then I hustled out the door. My first stop would be Woodside Hospice to see Terri. A number of pressing issues were on the table, each with its own set of ramifications.

Number one, I wanted to encourage her with some wonderful news: The U.S. Congress had now gotten involved. Several lawyers from Congress had flown into town with a subpoena for Terri to appear before a health subcommittee of the House of Representatives. There was a razor thin chance the feeding tube would be allowed to stay in place for her to travel to Washington, D.C. Of course, we also had to be prepared for the possibility that it might still be removed.

A second issue in the works was the possibility that the Florida Department of Children and Families (DCF) might arrive at the hospice to take Terri into their protective custody. If marshals sent by DCF were dispatched to secure her, a confrontation between the concerned parties would most likely occur. The Schindlers would need us by their side to represent their interests.

RESTRICTED AREA

I was about to turn down 102nd Avenue to access the front entrance of the hospice when I hit the brakes.

For a split second it appeared that I had been somehow transported to a checkpoint at one of the world's war-torn hotspots. An uninformed pedestrian might think he was about to enter Iraq, Gaza, or Israel. For starters, a newly erected police barricade prevented vehicular traffic to the street. Armed officers patrolled the grounds with dogs as if engaged in a prison lockdown. A number of police sharpshooters were positioned on the hospice rooftop to survey the crowd for any signs of trouble.

I would later learn that the initial estimates for this Pinellas Park police protection totaled $98,162, a sum that was being paid for by the hospice facility.[4] And this wasn't the first time Woodside had requested and paid for a police presence during Terri Schiavo's stay. In 2003 the hospice had paid a tab in excess of $125,000 for police security.[5] Neither of these figures takes into account the nonovertime use of police officers to direct traffic, or the expenses to the public works department to erect barricades and to remove the daily trash and litter associated with the media and the crowds.

Granted, I fully expected some level of law enforcement involvement. For many months, and at the request of Michael Schiavo, an armed guard had been posted outside Terri's room. Typically, off-duty officers from the Clearwater Police Department were hired to provide an around-the-clock presence at a cost of twenty-five dollars an hour.[6] With this level of security, you'd think the Secret Service was on hand working to protect the president or a visiting head of state. The no-trespassing perimeter around the hospice was being strictly enforced.

After stating my business and presenting my ID, I was waved past the first set of police patrol cars. Even this early in the day, the crowd—some of whom had spent the night camped out on the sidewalk—numbered in the hundreds. In addition to those who prayed, sang, or carried protest signs, I noticed a group of teenagers sporting bright red tape over their mouths signifying that Terri couldn't speak for herself. They'd returned for another day of silent prayer and protest.

Just beyond them, another group of disability advocates, many of them in wheelchairs, chanted, "We're not dead yet!" As disabled persons, they had the most to lose if Terri's death was permitted to be carried out.

The media encampment across the street buzzed with activity like a hornet's nest. Members of the press from around the world patrolled the sidewalks waiting for late-breaking news. Would Terri be saved? How was she doing? How was the family holding up? Virtually overnight, an electronic forest of satellite towers had sprouted and now pierced the morning sky. This was, after all, to be Day One of Terri's death watch. Occasionally, a TV news helicopter hovered overhead, capturing the commotion below for the viewers at home, many of whom were praying fervently for Terri—a woman they had never known except through the round-the-clock press coverage. We thanked God for them.

I parked alongside a media tower truck, grabbed my cell phone, and worked my way quickly through the sea of people to the second police checkpoint in the hospice driveway. Even though my face was on almost every major network and the guards knew who I was, I still had to present my ID and explain my reason for seeking admittance to the building. My name was compared to an official list of authorized visitors before I was directed to proceed to the main doors.

At that point all guests were subjected to a physical pat down and wand treatment. Everything had to come out of our pockets no matter how innocuous: breath mints, wallets, gum, combs, paper, pens, cell phones, keys, watches—only the clothing on my back was permitted in. The guard placed these personal effects into a tray and held them until I exited. This would come to be the routine every time I visited Terri during her final days.

Inside, the mood was extremely tense. The receptionist and staff were on edge; I don't fault them for being agitated. They were there to provide services and comfort to upward of seventy terminal patients against the backdrop of a circus of activity outside. Adding to the tension was the presence of one of Michael's attorneys, who was on hand to enforce her client's wishes. Like a hawk, every move was watched.

I made my way down the corridor and was checked again outside of Terri's room. The officer standing in front of her door had another list of approved visitor names, which was consulted to make sure there hadn't been a last-minute court order or legal directive preventing me from going inside. The same drill was required of all of Terri's visitors. In spite of these hassles, I did my best to maintain an upbeat spirit for Terri's sake and for her family.

I knew the attorneys from the House of Representatives had flown down from Washington, D.C., to conduct last-minute filings with the court on Terri's behalf; they'd be arriving at my office shortly. I had to make my morning visit with Terri quick. Thankfully, Barbara Weller, my legal associate, planned to stay by her side while I rushed back to the office to meet with the attorneys from Congress; that is, after I shared the encouraging news with Terri first.

I WANT TO LIVE

Terri was in great spirits that morning. Her eyes had a brightness that seemed to complement the light pink glow in her complexion. She sat in her reclining chair clutching her favorite stuffed cat under her arm. Her hair was brushed, she was wearing a pink robe, and a light brown blanket covered her lap. Her feet, poking out from underneath the blanket, sported velveteen ballerina slippers, the kind little girls like my own daughters like to wear around the house.

Barbara Weller and Terri's sister, Suzanne Vitadamo, sat on the edge of her bed, visiting and laughing with Terri, along with several other extended family members. I hated to interrupt but I knew time was of the essence. I came alongside Terri and told her that we were working with Congress and even the president to allow her to go to Washington, D.C., to testify before a congressional committee. She seemed pleased that I was there, even though I'm sure she did not totally comprehend that news. Suzanne and Barbara interjected that Michael would finally have to get her wheelchair fixed for the trip, not to mention that they'd be able to take Terri shopping in the mall while they were in the nation's capital. That news seemed to visibly excite her.

Terri appeared to be enjoying her interaction with Suzanne and Barbara. She laughed at all the right times and was paying close attention to what was going on in her room. I could see that this was one of Terri's "good" days, as the family often rated them.

After a number of minutes of encouraging Terri not to lose hope, that we were doing everything in our power to prevent the feeding tube from being removed, and that millions of people around the world were praying for her, her spiritual advisor of many years arrived for what I sincerely hoped would not be his last visit. Satisfied that he had been able to gain entry, I moved into the hallway to confer with other arriving family members and with Michael's attorney. I promptly retraced my steps through security and the crowds to my car and then raced back to the office.

When I arrived, the attorneys from Congress were waiting for me in our conference room. With the morning rapidly slipping away, we pored over last-minute preparations to present the congressional subpoenas in what we had hoped would be a hearing with Judge Greer. One problem: Nobody could locate the judge. The best we could figure was that he was out of town for his own safety and security. Someone suggested that we conduct the hearing by phone rather than in court. But that still required us to find Judge Greer.

Rather than risk not being able to discover his whereabouts in time, we contacted Chief Judge David Demers of the Sixth Judicial Circuit Court. We explained our predicament. Judge Demers, in turn, ruled that Terri's food and water could not be removed until we had a hearing on the matter in light of the congressional subpoenas. For the moment, it appeared that we had a much needed late-morning victory with this new judge. The feeding tube would stay in—for now.

Lunch was brought in for our guests. As we talked, ate, and worked, the phone rang. Judge Greer was on the line. Clearly, he didn't sound happy. I couldn't tell if he was upset that Judge Demers had temporarily blocked his orders to remove Terri's food and water or if he was merely displeased about the need for another hearing.

Whatever the reason for his unsettled demeanor, he allowed the attorneys from the House of Representatives to argue their case. As they presented the subpoenas and the basis and rationale for a stay, I prayed. We needed a break and we needed it right then. I thought they did a fantastic job laying out the facts. I believed we might just have a shot at protecting Terri.

After this hearing I later heard rumors that Judge Greer had been encouraged to take his time with this hearing and to go along with the congressional subpoenas. After all, there were big issues on the table, not the least of which was the matter of states' rights versus federal rights. With the entire world watching, what would be wrong with taking a few more days? But Judge Greer was not inclined to allow anyone else to take charge of his case; instead, he called us and conducted the hearing by telephone himself.

When the Washington, D.C., attorneys had finished making their legal presentation, Judge Greer unloaded both barrels: He rendered a scathing judgment against them. He made it absolutely clear that he would not wait another day, let alone a week, before her feeding tube was removed just for Terri to go to the nation's capital for a hearing. Judge Greer was insistent. He said, "My order will be upheld. The feeding tube will be removed at one PM," and then he abruptly hung up.

My heart sank.

As if that setback wasn't damaging enough, we also received devastating news on another front: The DCF was not going to send marshals to take Terri into protective custody. That meant the D.C. attorneys sitting across from me now had an urgent decision to make: Would they hold Judge Greer in contempt of Congress for ignoring their subpoenas? Could he, in fact, go to jail for ignoring a legitimate congressional subpoena?

As we were starting to discuss those issues, my phone rang. It was Barbara Weller at the hospice. To say she was excited would be an understatement. Her words ran together as if she couldn't spit them out fast enough. She said, "David, you've got to hear this—you won't believe what just happened!"

"Sure, Barbara. What's up?"

"Not long after you left, I went over to Terri's chair and—"

Noticing the time, I interrupted her. "Is she being fed right now?"

"Yes, they started feeding her around eleven. But listen, David," she said. "I leaned over and took Terri's arms in both of my hands and said to her, 'Terri, if you could only say *I want to live*, this whole thing could be over today.' "

Barbara continued. "I pleaded with Terri to just try to say those words. You'll never believe what happened. Terri's eyes opened real wide. She looked me square in the face. She had this look of intense concentration—"

I found myself inching toward the edge of my seat.

"David, Terri actually said, 'Ahhhhhhh.' And then, seeming to summon up all of the strength that she had, she virtually screamed, 'Waaaaaaaa' . . . She yelled so loudly that we all heard her—even Suzanne's husband and the police officer standing outside of Terri's door heard her."

Was this the breakthrough we had been praying for? I found myself gripping the phone in my hand. "Barbara, did she finish the sentence?"

Barbara took a moment to collect her thoughts. "All I can say, David, is that she had this terrible look of anguish on her face. I can't say I've ever seen her appear so troubled. She seemed to be struggling to form the next word, but the word wouldn't come out. It was a consonant. You know Terri can't say consonants."

My head pounded with the implications. I removed my glasses and massaged my temples. I could imagine the scene back in Terri's room. A fully alive, spirited yet handicapped woman, who had been thrust into the center of the world's attention, was trying to speak. Yes, there was no doubt in my mind that what Barbara had just witnessed was Terri's last-ditch effort to communicate her own wishes. But given the tone of the conversation with Judge Greer, I was convinced even this event wouldn't change his heart.

"What happened next?"

Barbara fought to control her emotions. "Terri became very frustrated and started to cry. I didn't mean to cause her such anxiety—I just thought . . ."

Her words drifted off. "Look, Barbara, you did the right thing." At this point, the others in the conference room searched my face for some clue as to what was transpiring.

"While Suzanne and I comforted Terri," Barbara continued, "I promised Terri I'd tell the world that she did her best to say, 'I want to live.'" Barbara then asked if I thought it would be okay for her to hold an impromptu press conference with the hundreds of reporters waiting outside the hospice. She thought retelling her encounter with Terri might do some good. I couldn't see a downside, so I encouraged her to do whatever seemed best at her end.

In fact, a few days before Terri died, we even presented this information to Judge Greer in one last hearing, arguing that Terri had been trying to express her own wishes about her feeding tube. George Felos argued that Terri was in PVS and, therefore, incapable of that sort of purposeful interaction. Judge Greer bought his argument and denied our motion.

After Barbara and I had finished our phone conversation, heaviness settled on my spirit. Doors were being closed faster than we could find new ones to open. While I knew Barbara would be holding a press conference to share what had just happened, I turned my efforts to what I felt was our best bet: getting the lawyers to agree to hold Judge Greer's feet to the fire. In my view, for a judge to ignore the wishes of the federal government demanded a firm response. They asked me to give them some privacy while they called Washington, D.C., for direction.

I stepped outside the conference room and attempted to catch up with the endless stream of phone messages. Ten minutes later the attorneys waved me back to the table. Even before they spoke I could tell by their body language that the news wasn't going to be good. It wasn't. Rather than initiating a contempt process, they had been instructed to go through the regular appeals process.

I argued that the appeals pathway would be slow and most likely not effective in saving Terri's life.

I argued in vain.

With all of our current options exhausted, Terri's feeding tube was removed at 1:45 PM.

CHAPTER TWELVE

THE BIG LIE

*When I close my eyes at night, all I can see is Terri's face in
front of me dying, starving to death. Please, someone out
there, stop this cruelty. Stop the insanity. Please let my
daughter live.*

—MARY SCHINDLER[1]

A curious thing happened the moment Terri's feeding tube was
withdrawn: I call it *starvation spin control.* As they had done twice
before when Terri's feeding tube had been removed, Michael Schiavo
and George Felos worked overtime to put a happy face on this uncivilized practice. Eight days after Terri had been without food or water,
Mr. Felos emerged from the hospice and gushed, "In all the years I've
seen Mrs. Schiavo, I have never seen such a look of peace and beauty
upon her."[2]

What was his implication? That Terri was better off being starved
than being fed?

Michael, during an appearance on *Nightline,* glibly dismissed the
notion that starvation is painful, saying, "That's one of [the Schindlers'] soapboxes they've been on for a long time."

Soapboxes?

Then, in what can only be viewed as a desperate rationalization,

Michael claimed, "This happens across the country every day." Unfortunately, that is true. But what Mr. Schiavo and those who use that excuse fail to grasp is that medical treatment decisions made for patients do not make the practice of dehydrating and starving an otherwise healthy but disabled woman morally right. He quickly added, "Death through removing somebody's nutrition is very painless."[3]

Anxious to lend their endorsement of this highly controversial, public starvation, the *New York Times* sided with Michael Schiavo's efforts. Two "medical experts" were lined up to bolster their editorial position, namely, that withholding food and water "is relatively straightforward, and can cause little discomfort."[4]

How can the *Times* be so sure starvation is pain free? They cited a Dr. Linda Emanuel, who founded something called the Education for Physicians in End-of-Life Care Project at Northwestern University. Dr. Emanuel made a vague reference to "the data that is available" and concluded that starvation "is not a horrific thing at all."[5]

Really?

It might be interesting to test out her theory in Rwanda, Ethiopia, Sri Lanka, Uganda, or any one of the world's impoverished lands ravaged by drought and famine. I'm sure those suffering with empty stomachs and parched lips would be astonished to hear that anyone could think their daily plight is not "horrific."

Adding insult to injury, the *Times* quoted a professor from Mount Sinai School of Medicine in New York as saying, "They generally slip into a peaceful coma. It's very quiet, it's very dignified—it's very gentle." Again, I'm fairly confident most compassionate persons would not call the photos of starving people around the globe—nor what we saw of Terri as her body shriveled away—"dignified" or a "gentle" way to die.

Why, then, apply such disingenuous adjectives?

I believe there are dual purposes at work here.

First, the *Times* wanted to assuage our social conscience for what was being inflicted upon this disabled woman. In other words, if Americans could be convinced that Terri felt no discomfort, we might be willing to accept the barbaric method of her death. Which plays perfectly into one of their frightening positions: advancing the pro-euthanasia, or so-called "death with dignity" movement.

Whatever their motivation for running a "news" story that failed to introduce an opposing point of view, the question remains: Does starvation lead to a "painless" or "gentle death" as argued by the *Times*?

Dr. James H. Barnhill would think so. He's the neurologist and "expert witness" used by attorney George Felos in this and other "right-to-die" cases. The first time Terri's feeding tube was removed in 2001, Dr. Barnhill explained his belief that Terri felt no pain to Greta Van Susteren on CNN's *Burden of Proof*.

VAN SUSTEREN: To the best of your medical knowledge, can she feel pain?

BARNHILL: Not feel pain in the sense that she has con-sciousness of it, but react to pain in the sense that there are reflexes that will be provoked in response to pain. Similarly, if you step on a nail, you will move your foot before you have awareness that you have pain.

VAN SUSTEREN: If you remove this feeding tube, in essence, she will starve to death. Is that a kind of pain that she could feel in her state?

BARNHILL: Actually, she won't starve to death. What will happen is there will be initially dehydration. There will be chemical changes in the elec-trolytes—the sodium, the potassium. And generally, death will ensue from complica-tions related to the dehydration and the chemical imbalances before someone starves to death.

VAN SUSTEREN: Okay, *dehydration*, I assume, is some level of
                   pain to someone who is—I mean, unless
                   you're in a particular state. Is she likely to
                   feel the discomfort from that?

BARNHILL: No. As people dehydrate—and unfortu-
                   nately I've seen this many times—they just
                   kind of go to sleep. They become less con-
                   scious—or since she's not conscious, that's
                   maybe not the right [word]—they're less
                   alert and gradually become unresponsive.[6]

You can almost feel Greta's exhaustion from Dr. Barnhill's verbal gymnastics after three attempts to get a direct answer. Perhaps a more credible—and certainly a more compelling—viewpoint would be to hear from someone who, like Terri, was once diagnosed as being without hope of recovery and who, like Terri, had experienced eight days without sustenance, but who differs from Terri in that she lived to tell about it.

I'm referring to the incredible testimony of Kate Adamson.

NOTHING BUT SHEER TORTURE

At age thirty-three, Kate Adamson, a remarkable, healthy young mother of two, was in the prime of her life. Without warning, a near-fatal and massive stroke left her categorically unresponsive. She was rushed to the hospital, placed on life support, a feeding tube, and a ventilator. After performing an emergency tracheotomy, her doctors gave Kate no hope of surviving. Her husband, Steven, disagreed. He insisted that his bride would recover despite seemingly impossible odds. In fact, a notation was made in Kate's medical records suggesting Steven was delusional. Why?

Because he wouldn't give up on Kate.

Completely paralyzed, Kate remained in the intensive care unit for approximately seventy days. Each day initially brought with it a contest of wills: Husband Steven valiantly fought for medical treatment. The hospital and the insurance company pushed to cut their losses. After all, she was nonresponsive, unable to communicate. Nothing would change that. Ever. But Steven refused to walk away and, instead, literally set aside his successful legal practice to remain at her side. Likewise, their church rallied behind them, providing an around-the-clock prayer vigil in the hospital waiting room as well as sacrificial help with meals and other obligations at home.

Several months passed.

Still no progress.

The doctors initially pressured Steven to let Kate die. They predicted—on the off chance that Kate should beat the one in a million odds of survival—she'd remain a vegetable hooked up to machinery for the next fifty years. Steven wasn't buying what they were selling. His faith was unwavering. As he hovered close to pray over his comatose wife, something happened.

She wiggled the tip of one finger.

At first the nursing staff and doctors insisted Steven was just seeing what he wanted to see. Kate was incapable of responding, her doctors maintained. Incidentally, doctors told Terri Schiavo's parents the same thing—that they were only imagining Terri's responsiveness. (I saw it with my own eyes, and I *know* she was responsive, as did my colleague Barbara Weller.)

The medical team was completely baffled when, in time, Kate regained the ability to eat, speak, and walk. Today, Kate travels widely to address crowds of thousands with her inspirational message of hope. One of her opening statements is this: "The only difference between me and Terri Schiavo is I had a husband who loved me and wouldn't give up on me."

As you might expect, Kate has deep feelings about the tug-of-war over Terri Schiavo. She should. Like Terri, Kate had been diagnosed as having no chance of recovery—let alone a meaningful life as a nationally acclaimed public speaker. Like Terri, at one point in her ordeal Kate had her feeding tube removed for eight days. What's more, Kate reports that not only did she endure unspeakable pain, she was totally aware of everything going on around her.

In her book, *Kate's Journey: Triumph Over Adversity*, Kate reveals what went through her mind while her doctors discussed her fate with husband, Steven:

> I'm treated as if I'm a dead person already. Why are people talking in front of me as if I'm not here? I can hear and understand everything being said.[7]

Unfortunately, like Terri, Kate had no means of vocalizing her thoughts or wishes. Come to think of it, at least Terri was able to make her "lemon face" when anticipating the tickle of her dad's mustache and cry when her mother left the room. Kate was paralyzed and had no outward contact with her world. She was "locked in," utterly alone with her thoughts, her feelings, and her fears.

What about the question of pain?

Did Kate feel anything after the doctors suspended her nutrition? Was she thirsty? Did she crave food? Or are Michael Schiavo, George Felos, and the *New York Times* right when they claim starvation is a "painless," "gentle" way to die? Here's Kate's exchange with Bill O'Reilly, host of *The O'Reilly Factor*.

O'REILLY: When they took the feeding tube out, what went through your mind?

ADAMSON: When the feeding tube was turned off for eight days, I thought I was going insane. I was screaming out in my mind, "Don't you know I need to eat?" And even up until that point, I had been having a bagful of Ensure as my nourishment that was going through the feeding tube. At that point, it sounded pretty good. I just wanted something. The fact that I had nothing, the hunger pains overrode every thought I had.

O'REILLY: So you were feeling pain when they removed your tube?

ADAMSON: Yes. Oh, absolutely. Absolutely. To say that—especially when Michael [Schiavo] on national TV mentioned last week that it's a pretty painless thing to have the feeding tube removed—it is the exact opposite. It was sheer torture, Bill.

O'REILLY: It's just amazing.

ADAMSON: Sheer torture. . . .[8]

Why didn't the *New York Times* invite Kate Adamson to weigh in on their article before perpetuating a myth? Why did Michael Schiavo feel compelled to discount the concerns and feelings of his in-laws about the inhumane treatment of their daughter—calling it one of their "little soapboxes"? And why does George Felos, who is a learned man, continue to this day to misrepresent the reality of Terri's suffering?

FELOS: "SHE LOOKS BEAUTIFUL"

To say that attorney George Felos has some unusual ideas about life, death, and making the transition from one world to the other would be an understatement. His cold, clinical view of Terri's slow, torturous death and his ongoing efforts to put a positive spin on her unbearable pain can be traced back to his first right-to-die case, that of Estelle Browning.

Like Kate, Mrs. Browning suffered a stroke. In her case, she remained comatose or, as Mr. Felos described her, a "total care" patient for eighteen months. Here's the complication. Although Mrs. Browning left an advance instruction *declining* a feeding tube, both the nursing home and the doctors in charge of her care insisted that the tube remain in place. The year was 1990. The Florida legislature had not yet declared that a feeding tube was "medical treatment," which a patient could refuse. Removing the tube would have been illegal in 1990.

At that juncture a cousin of Mrs. Browning sought legal assistance from George Felos to use the courts to remove the feeding tube in a first-ever state "right to privacy" case to decline food and water. Felos agreed to take the case, with one condition: He wanted to visit Mrs. Browning first. In his book, *Litigation As Spiritual Practice*, Mr. Felos described his quest to understand what Mrs. Browning's true wishes were in the matter. He writes:

> I stared as far into her eyes as I could, hoping to sense some glimmer of understanding, some hint of awareness. The deeper I dove, the darker became the blue, until the blue became the black of some bottomless lake. "Mrs. Browning, do you want to die? . . . Do you want to die?"—I near shouted as I continued to peer into her pools of strikingly beautiful but incognizant blue. It felt so eerie. Her eyes were wide open . . . but instead of the warmth of lucidity, they burned with the ice of expressionlessness.[9]

Oddly, he interrupted the poetic, trancelike narrative in order to spend almost an entire chapter vilifying the feeding tube as if it were a living, monstrous thing. He described this medically essential tool as nothing more than "a plastic sack half filled with sickly beige-looking fluid" that "snaked down" into Mrs. Browning's stomach.

With great passion, he railed against the feeding tube as "an instrument to cruelly perpetuate, a painful, degrading, and horrific existence." In his view, it was nothing more than "an unwelcome agent" artificially prolonging "the natural process of her death."

Mr. Felos then moved on to describe what he calls "soul speak"— that's the moment when his soul allegedly communicated through some mystical union with the soul of Mrs. Browning on an unseen, higher dimension. That encounter would forever change his life's work. He writes at length about his unexpected brush with the spiritual realm:

> As I continued to stay beside Mrs. Browning at her nursing

home bed, I felt my mind relax and my weight sink into the ground. I began to feel lightheaded as I became more reposed. Although feeling like I could drift into sleep, I also experienced a sense of heightened awareness. As Mrs. Browning lay motionless before my gaze, I suddenly heard a loud, deep moan and scream and wondered if the nursing home personnel heard it and would respond to the unfortunate resident. In the next moment, as this cry of pain and torment continued, I realized it was Mrs. Browning.

I felt the midsection of my body open and noticed a strange quality to the light in the room. I sensed her soul in agony. As she screamed I heard her say, in confusion, "Why am I still here . . . Why am I here?" My soul touched hers and in some way I communicated that she was still locked in her body. I promised I would do everything in my power to gain the release her soul cried for.

With that, the screaming immediately stopped. I felt like I was back in my head again, the room resumed its normal appearance, and Mrs. Browning, as she had throughout this experience, lay silent.[10]

In case there might be any who find such a narrative a tad eccentric if not difficult to embrace, Mr. Felos adds:

My first thought shouted, *Did this happen . . . did I imagine it?* Quite typical for the rational mind, wouldn't you say? I knew without a doubt what had transpired was real.[11]

Are you beginning to understand where Mr. Felos is coming from? His belief system, which enables him to engage in such "soul speak," is, by his own admission, rooted in an unorthodox blend of mysticism, Buddhism, Christianity, Hinduism, and a heavy sprinkling of yoga. Based upon this personal construct, he asserts that in "reality you have never been born and never can die."[12]

That view might explain why he is able to exhibit such a skilled, otherworldly detachment for the very real-world suffering and death of Terri.

It might also explain why he is now on a crusade to advance the right-to-die movement and views the death of Terri Schiavo as a satisfying accomplishment. As he would comment later in an address to fellow lawyers and judges in West Palm Beach, Florida, "She died a dignified and peaceful death. To the extent that the law was ultimately able to provide that for her, I'm very proud."[13]

Challenging Mr. Felos's assessment that she didn't suffer and that she died peacefully, Terri's brother, Bobby Schindler, hit the nail on the head when he said, "This is heinous what's happening . . . absolutely barbaric. If she is in fact dying so peacefully and easily, why not allow a camera in there to videotape it?"[14] I'll tell you why. If the networks had broadcast even sixty seconds of Terri's suffering, the public outcry would still be ringing in our ears today.

After a valiant fight against death, Terri's body finally shut down on March 31, 2005, after thirteen days of dehydration and starvation. At that point George Felos displayed an amazing exercise in illogic. Approaching the swarm of cameras just outside the hospice, he spoke with a mortician's unflappable monotone: "Patients don't starve to death by removal of artificial nutrition and hydration."[15] That's true. They dehydrate first.

Now who's on a soapbox?

Unshaken by Terri's loss, Mr. Felos turned a corner in his thinking. He actually believes what was done to Terri has the support of the American people. He said, "In a world of conflict people crave peace and understanding. I'm gratified to receive the overwhelming support and heart-felt response to my message of healing."[16]

Let me ask you a question: How is depriving a person of food and water until they die a form of "healing"?

Thankfully, his view isn't very widely shared—yet.

FORCE-FEEDING FELONS

In the fall of 2002, the nation was gripped by a series of random, yet deadly, sniper attacks against innocent civilians in Washington, D.C.,

Maryland, and Virginia. With ten dead and three wounded, residents in the area held their breath wondering when the next senseless shots would claim another life.

A break in the case led to the capture and conviction of John Allen Muhammad, who had converted the trunk of a 1990 Chevrolet Caprice into a private shooting arcade. Each of his victims was murdered by a single .223-caliber bullet fired from a Bushmaster rifle. Muhammad, an expert marksman, pulled the trigger while his younger partner in terror, Lee Malvo, drove the car.

In 2003 Muhammad was convicted and sentenced to die for one of the shootings in Manassas, Virginia. He was then transferred to the Montgomery County jail in Maryland, where he remains incarcerated to face six additional murder charges. The case took an interesting turn, however, when Muhammad decided to stop eating.

Upset about the rules governing access to his legal files as well as his disapproval over the food served, Muhammad refused to eat or drink. That is, until Montgomery County Circuit Court Judge James L. Ryan stepped in and ordered the convicted sniper to be force-fed. Corrections officials warned that their prisoner was "in imminent danger of very serious bodily harm, including death, if he does not begin to receive nourishment within the next several days."[17]

Let's not miss the irony.

In Florida, a judge ordered the *starvation* of Terri Schiavo, an innocent woman, who left no written instructions that she wanted to die that way. Meanwhile, a Maryland judge ordered the *forced feeding* of John Muhammad, a convicted murderer who had been sentenced to die, even though he was in full control of his faculties and had made it perfectly clear that he *wanted* to starve. Why didn't the legal system protect his "right to die" in the same way that judges imposed this "right" on Terri?

Let's set aside the absurdity of a legal system that permits this inexcusable paradox. Even if we really knew what Terri wanted, Florida law makes aiding and abetting a suicide a criminal action. Rather than starve Terri Schiavo, the state of Florida should have examined how

New Jersey dealt with the intentional starvation of fellow humans. What would they have learned?

Read on.

HUNGRY FOR JUSTICE

In October of 2003 Bruce Jackson was nineteen years old but had the body weight of a seven-year-old child; he weighed just forty-five pounds. Measuring just four feet tall when authorities from New Jersey's social services spotted him, Bruce was rummaging through a neighbor's trash can for something to eat. Bruce and his three younger brothers had been adopted by a family who allegedly refused to feed them properly.

Bone thin and suffering from severe malnutrition, Michael, nine, weighed a mere twenty-three pounds. Brother Tyrone, ten, fared slightly better, weighing twenty-eight pounds. Their fourteen-year-old sibling Keith weighed forty pounds.[18] All four children were taken into protective custody while the adoptive parents were charged with twenty-eight counts of aggravated assault and child endangerment. Published reports indicate that the children had frequently relied on a diet of uncooked pancake batter and discarded gypsum wallboard.

While the physical and mental damage is possibly irreversible, the state of New Jersey wants to make sure the Jackson brothers receive a fighting chance at survival. In September 2005 the state agreed to award $12.5 million[19] out of the treasury for their rehabilitation, education, and care; Bruce Jackson will receive $5 million since he suffered the most damage. His brothers will net $2.5 million each.

Clearly, the state of New Jersey takes a dim view of starving people. If Terri had been abused by her parents in New Jersey, or if she had been a felon in Maryland, she never would have been allowed to be dehydrated and starved. This inconsistency demonstrates for me the uncomfortable irony of Terri's case.

CHAPTER THIRTEEN

WASHINGTON WEIGHS IN

The diagnostic studies upon which the decision to terminate [Terri Schiavo's] life have been based . . . were inadequate, and insufficient to allow a reasoned opinion by her physicians.

— Dr. Rodney Dunaway, MD, Board Certified Neurologist

For Christians around the world, Palm Sunday marks the beginning of the traditional Easter Holy Week. In 2005, however, millions of believers carried an extra burden with them into their houses of worship: The fate of Terri Schiavo was weighing heavy upon their hearts. While the faithful were praying, they knew that the United States Senate and, in turn, the House of Representatives were deliberating if and how to protect Terri's life.

As you'll see in this chapter, the courageous decision by our representatives to act on Terri's behalf was ultimately a costly one. That's a shame. I am firmly convinced that the Congress was simply fulfilling what Thomas Jefferson called the chief purpose of government: *to protect life.*

Briefly, Terri's feeding tube had been removed by a state court order on Friday, March 18. The Schindlers were devastated. Their daughter was now suffering from hunger and thirst and was going to die without a miracle. In an extraordinary move, the U.S. Senate worked on legislation that would empower the Schindlers to take their case to a federal judge for a fresh review.

To be candid, I thought getting an Act of Congress passed was a rather long shot. After all, moving legislation through both houses of Congress usually takes weeks or months—certainly not three days, especially over a holiday weekend. We were in for a surprise.

First, these public servants delayed their Easter recess to finalize the bill. On Palm Sunday afternoon, the Senate assembled on Capitol Hill and, in what was a unanimous bipartisan vote of those present, passed Senate Bill S.686. The measure immediately moved to the House of Representatives for debate and then a vote.

Meanwhile, President Bush, who was at his home in Crawford, Texas, rearranged his schedule and flew back to the White House. Rather than wait for the bill to be flown to Texas—a delay that could impact Terri's viability—President Bush sacrificially put forth the effort to be available to add his signature immediately over the holiday. If President Bush was at the White House, he could sign the bill into law within minutes of its passage.

Sunday evening, with the president en route to Washington, D.C., lawmakers gathered at nine PM in the House of Representatives for what would be three hours of televised debate followed by a vote. The Schindlers were spending time with Terri at the hospice while we were back at the Gibbs Law Firm office drafting documents and monitoring C-SPAN on the Internet. Terri's brother, Bobby, was on Capitol Hill visiting with every Congress member who would see him.

As we watched the House deliberate, we worked the phones to clarify any questions lawmakers on the Hill might have during the overnight session. We were in touch with dozens of senators and representatives and literally hundreds of staffers throughout the process.

Let me give you a flavor of this historic debate.

Speaking in favor of the bill, Representative Jim Sensenbrenner (R-WI) made an opening statement to frame what was at stake. He said:

Mr. Speaker, I rise in support of S.686, for the relief of the parents of Theresa Marie Schiavo. As the House convenes this Palm Sunday, the Florida courts are enforcing a merciless directive to deprive Terri Schiavo of her right to life.

Terri Schiavo, a person whose humanity is as undeniable as her emotional responses to her family's tender care-giving, has committed no crime and has done nothing wrong. Yet the Florida courts have brought Terri and the Nation to an ugly crossroads by commanding medical professionals sworn to protect life to end Terri's life. This Congress must reinforce the laws and compassion for all Americans, particularly the most vulnerable.[1]

As you might imagine, the debate became testy at times. For example, believing that the entire effort to pass S.686 was nothing more than an appeal to conservative voters, Representative John Lewis (D-GA), a leader in the civil rights movement, said, "We are playing with a young woman's life for the sake of politics. This is not about values. This is not about religion. It is pandering for political gain with the next election in mind."

Echoing that assessment, Representative Barney Frank (D-MA) quipped, "The caption tonight ought to be 'We are not doctors. We just play them on C-SPAN.'" Representative Phil Gingrey (R-GA), however, took exception to that dim view of their motives. In what was one of the more poignant rebuttals, he said:

Mr. Speaker, in response to the remarks a few minutes ago from the gentleman from Massachusetts, I want to say that I am not sure whether or not I am on C-SPAN, but I am absolutely sure that I am not playing doctor, for indeed I am one.

Florida law prohibits the starvation of dogs, yet will allow the starvation of Terri Schiavo. Florida law does not allow for physician assisted suicide or euthanasia, nor does my compassionate, God-fearing state of Georgia.

Although I am not a neurologist by specialty, my basic courses in medical school taught me that dehydration is a horrific process. It is a process that only the cruelest tyrants in history have used to "cleanse" populations. The patient's skin cracks, their nose bleeds, they vomit as the stomach lining dries out, and they have pangs of hunger and thirst. Starvation is a very painful death to which no one should be deliberately exposed.

Evidently unmoved by Representative Gingrey's assessment, Representative Julia Carson (D-IN) appeared exasperated that she had to "run to Washington" after having left for home for the Easter recess. She said, "For the life of me, I cannot understand why we are here. . . . We have no business being here. . . . It is none of our business. This is called meddling." Perhaps she also missed the comments of Representative Trent Franks (R-AZ), who said:

> Mr. Speaker, protecting the lives of our innocent citizens and their constitutional rights is why we are all here. The phrase in the 14th amendment encapsulates our entire Constitution. It says: "No State shall deprive any person of life, liberty or property without due process of law." . . .
>
> If we as a Nation subject Terri to death while her brother, her mother and her father are forced to watch, we will scar our own souls. And we will be allowing those judges who have lost their way to drag us all one more ominous step into a darkness where the light of human compassion has gone out and the predatory survival of the fittest prevails over humanity.

Nevertheless, an irritated Representative Michael Capuano (D-MA) stood before the assembly and urged the members to vote down the measure:

> I have a living will that I wrote years ago, and I will check it myself as many Americans will. The bottom line is: I do not want you interfering with my wife and me. Leave us alone. . . . Stay out of my family. If you can do it here, you can do it to me. You can do it to every one of my constituents. Leave us alone!

Mr. Capuano's impassioned comments completely missed the larger issue. While he and his wife had a living will, Terri did not. Her wishes were not so precisely known. Which is why Representative Jeff Miller (R-FL) urged caution. He said:

> Before an irreversible decision is made, [Terri's] country must afford her process to which she is entitled under the 14th Amendment of our Constitution. Whether you're using morality, or religion, or the Golden Rule, or legal analysis to guide your decision, at the root of all this is a living, breathing American citizen who has been deprived of her rights.

In the opinion of Representative Debbie Wasserman-Schultz (D-FL), however, this was not the government's business. She argued:

> Do we really want to set the precedent of this great body, the United States Congress, to insert ourselves in the middle of a family's private matters all across America? . . .
> When I ran for Congress, I didn't ask my constituents for the right to insert myself in their private, personal family decisions and they don't want me to make those for them. They don't want you to make those for them either. That's the bottom line.

Representative Wasserman-Schultz was joined by Representative David Wu (D-OR), who added, "The Republican leadership has transformed a profound tragedy for the Schiavo family into a tragedy for the entire Nation." Not so fast. How was this a private family matter when Michael used a newly enacted Florida law to take Terri's life out of her family's hands and put it into the hands of judges? Also, the bill under consideration by the House of Representatives had been crafted and was unanimously passed by the Senate with full bipartisan support.

In fact, Democrat Senate Minority Leader Harry Reid worked closely with Republican Majority Leader Bill Frist, who is also a medical doctor, to draft the wording of the measure. Likewise, Senator Tom

Harkin (D-IA), always an advocate for the disabled, said in a press release, "Over the last week, I have been working hard . . . to come up with legislation that would allow federal review of the Terri Schiavo case. Yesterday afternoon, we came up with a bipartisan measure that did just that and many of my Senate Republican and Democratic colleagues deserve praise for their hard and swift work."[2]

Clearly, the preservation of life should not be a Republican-versus-Democrat issue.

A FAMILY AFFAIR?

What about the notion that the government had inserted itself into a private family affair? Believe it or not, that is simply false. Attorney Ken Conner, chairman of the Center for a Just Society, who served as Governor Jeb Bush's attorney in defending Florida's Terri's Law, put it this way:

> Critics of government intrusion into the acrimonious battle between Terri Schiavo's husband and her family seem to have overlooked the fact that it was Michael Schiavo who first petitioned the Circuit Court of Pinellas County to authorize the starvation and dehydration death of his disabled wife. In doing so, Mr. Schiavo is the one who injected government into the controversy.[3]

You see, Michael Schiavo could have just allowed Terri to starve to death in the privacy of his own home. Of course, had he done that, Michael could have been charged with a crime under Florida statutes. Rather than take that chance, Michael sought the protection of the courts by enlisting them to sanction the action. By taking the matter to court, Michael invited the government into his "private family affair."

There were some who objected to Congress's involvement because they felt that Terri had had her day in court and the matter had been settled numerous times before in front of a long parade of judges.

While not attending the hearing, House Democratic Leader Nancy Pelosi issued a statement decrying the effort to protect Terri's due process rights. She wrote, "Congressional leaders have no business substituting their judgment for that of multiple state courts that have extensively considered the issues."[4] I had to wonder if she would have held the same position when state courts were permitting the lynching of blacks in the South during the civil rights era.

Let's be very careful here.

While a number of judges did review Terri's case, all of them relied on the prior factual findings made by Judge Greer. Appellate courts do not call additional witnesses or determine facts. They determine legal questions. No appeals court judge would have requested Terri's presence in court to see her for themselves.

This new bill, if passed, wouldn't substitute the judgment of Congress over the courts as Ms. Pelosi claimed. All it was intended to do was to provide an opportunity for a federal court to start with a clean slate, new witnesses, proper depositions, and new up-to-date medical tests before carrying out the state court's order. And for the first time Terri might have her own lawyer.

Regarding the question of what were Terri's wishes, Representative Marilyn Musgrave (R-CO) raised this question:

> Tonight in this gallery my daughter sits. I think of my daughter, I think of my other three children, and I think of the day they were born. I think of the milestones in their lives and the love that I have for them. I think of the lengths that I would go to protect my children as adults even if they had an injury. . . . I would die for my children. I would do anything for them.
>
> My heart is raw when I hear the things about Terri Schiavo and her mother and her father and her siblings. . . . We talk about a family decision. What about Terri's mom and dad? What about her siblings? What about the people who cared for her and nurtured her as she was growing up? Do you not think they know what Terri wants?

The passionate appeals from both sides of the issue continued for the better part of three hours. The debate raged while we watched, prayed, and prepared for what we hoped would be a favorable outcome.

LIFE IN THE BALANCE

At one point Representative Tom Cole (R-OK) reminded the members that while debating states' rights, worrying about setting precedents, and wrestling over separation of powers are all important and legitimate issues, "a life is in the balance, and that is really the only immediate and compelling issue." He added, "If we do not act, Terri Schiavo will die. Great questions often are raised by individual cases, inconvenient cases, cases that break precedent, cases that confront us when we prefer not to be confronted."

I, too, respected the heartfelt issues raised by those who dissented. Yet in my mind I kept going back to the core question: What was the urgency to end Terri's life? Why shouldn't she be given the same review in federal court afforded to convicted felons on death row? Indeed, what harm would have been done to wait while the case received a final review by a federal judge?

I also continued to be troubled by the seeming lack of human kindness that accompanied Judge Greer's order to remove Terri's provision of sustenance. Speaking as if he had read my thoughts, Representative Todd Akin (R-MO) said:

> As we stand here in Washington, Terri is being starved to death. We refer to the "removal of feeding tubes," but let's talk about what is really happening. Not only has a tube delivering food and water been removed, but her parents have been barred from even putting ice chips on her tongue. . . . To bar parents and relatives from offering the most basic of comforts to a dying loved one is not only an egregious overreach of judicial powers, it is cruel and morally wrong.

I must share one last comment made during the debate. In what was a profoundly moving, personal story, Representative Bob Beauprez (R-CO) captured the heart of why so many senators and representatives worked through the Palm Sunday weekend to fight for Terri's life. He said:

> I believe fairly deeply that life does have a purpose. I lost my father 6 months and 6 days ago tonight. And in his very final days, he too needed to be fed by a tube. He needed help with his basic bodily functions, could not get out of his bed, and could not take care of himself.
>
> But in the 56 years of life I have been granted, Mr. Speaker, I shared the most intimate, the most profound moment I ever had with my father about 36 hours before he passed away, after he could no longer speak, after he could no longer feed himself or care for himself in almost any manner at all. He communicated with his eyes, and he communicated with a hand on my forehead in the most profound way imaginable.
>
> I would have regretted deeply had I been denied that moment, and I am absolutely convinced, Mr. Speaker, that my father would have regretted having been denied that moment as well.

With time running out on Terri's life, Representative Tom DeLay, then Republican majority leader from Texas, said, "Terri Schiavo has survived her Passion weekend and she has not been forsaken. No more words, Mr. Speaker. She is waiting. The Members are here. The hour has come. Mr. Speaker, call the vote."

The vote was called shortly after midnight.

At 12:34 Monday morning at the beginning of the Easter Holy Week, the House overwhelmingly passed S.686: *Terri Schiavo Incapacitated Protection Bill* with more than a two-thirds majority (203 to 58 votes). Almost half of the Democrats present joined the Republicans in a bipartisan victory for Terri's life. While 174 representatives didn't vote on the legislation, many of them simply couldn't make the trip back to

Washington, D.C., in time to place their vote. Others may not have wanted to put themselves on the record about this issue. But we thank God for those who were willing to stand up for Terri.

PARTY BREAKDOWN

VOTE TOTALS	DEMOCRAT	REPUBLICAN	INDEPEND-ENT
Aye 203 (47%)	47	156	0
Nay 58 (13%)	53	5	0
Absent 174 (40%)	102	71	1

At 1:11 AM, President Bush was awakened and promptly signed S.686 into law. With his signature, the jurisdiction of Terri's case moved from the state court to a federal judge for a de novo review—that is, to basically retry the case. As President Bush would explain later that day, "This is a complex case with serious issues. But in extraordinary circumstances like this, it is wise to always err on the side of life."[5]

Predictably, Michael Schiavo was outraged by this turn of events. He told CNN, "I think that the Congress has more important things to discuss,"[6] adding, "They're thumbing their nose up to the American people and the Constitution. This is a sad day for Terri."[7]

The Schindlers were elated beyond words. We had actually secured an Act of Congress. Terri would now have a fighting chance; we promptly filed a middle-of-the-night injunction in the federal district court in Tampa to have Terri's feeding tube reinserted. That afternoon, an excited Bob Schindler asked Terri "if she was ready to take a little ride . . . and get her some breakfast. I got a big smile out of her face. She seemed to be very pleased."[8]

We were deeply thankful for the breakneck pace at which both legislative bodies in Washington, D.C., had worked over the Easter recess and grateful for a president who supported this emergency measure in the dead of night. Bolstered by this much needed burst of wind in our sails, we charted a course that would take the fight for Terri's life all the way to the United States Supreme Court—twice.

CHAPTER FOURTEEN

LITIGATING AT THE
SPEED OF LIGHT

If prisoners on death row are guaranteed federal review of their cases, Terri Schiavo deserves at least as much consideration.

— REPRESENTATIVE JOSEPH PITTS, PENNSYLVANIA[1]

W hen President Bush signed S.686 into law, our legal team began one final, incredible run through the federal courts in an effort to save Terri. I've been told we set a record in legal history: We had the only case that worked its way through the federal court system, to the United States Supreme Court, and back—*twice*—in just ten days.

Clutching a faxed copy of the congressional bill with the president's signature, as well as the documents we intended to file in federal court, I rushed to the hospice to meet Bob and Mary. The Schindlers reviewed and signed the paperwork, blinking back tears of hope. For the first time in years, it seemed to us all that victory just might be within our reach.

With signed documents in hand, I left the hospice and headed to my vehicle. Even though this was the dead of night, the media was still out in full force. They quickly caught up with me and pressed me for details about the breaking news. They asked whether they could follow us to the federal courthouse. No problem. This was a big break in the case—or so we were praying.

As I raced to the federal courthouse in Tampa, I maintained phone communication with the court clerk. It was about two o'clock in the morning and, naturally, at that time the court building was closed. Once again, we were granted exceptional treatment from those within the system who were sympathetic to the urgency of the matter. The court clerk had agreed to open up the building just for us. Small kindnesses like this went a long way in encouraging our spirits.

When I arrived, the media was already gathered on the sidewalk. The clerk politely but firmly informed the press that I was the only one permitted inside the building. As soon as I entered, the clerk locked the door behind us. The jangle of her keys reverberated in the empty lobby. Under the watchful eye of the security guards, the clerk, an extra staffer, and I moved through the darkened hallways.

The moment was surreal. It was difficult for my mind to grasp this swirl of activity. Had the Congress actually pushed through legislation to help Terri? Was that really the signature of the leader of the free world in my hand? Would Terri finally have what we thought she deserved: an additional review of her case in federal court? The echoing of our heels against the polished marble floor provided evidence that this was not a dream. With a ping, the elevator doors opened. Arriving at the third floor, we exited and hustled through the dimly lit maze of cubicles until we reached the clerk's office.

As we walked, I reflected on my immediate goal. I needed to ask the federal judge—who still had to be picked from a random pool of judges—to stabilize Terri. We needed the judge to immediately order a reinsertion of Terri's feeding tube and the resumption of her food and water. This would give us time to proceed in an orderly manner to have her case reviewed from the ground up. I had high hopes the judge might even rule on the Schindlers' initial pleadings almost immediately, which would not be out of the ordinary.

When the three of us arrived at the clerk's office, my heart sank when we learned that the computers weren't functioning properly. The clerk needed her computer to randomly assign the judge for the federal review. We were losing valuable time trying to get the system to work. After what felt like an eternity—but in reality may have been only minutes—a decision was made to handle this selection the old-fashioned way: I would draw the name of a judge by hand. While drawing names might sound like a fun thing to do at a birthday party, this process in court was cumbersome at best.

First, the available judges had to be individually identified, a process that, when done manually and without the aid of a computer, took what seemed to be an immense amount of time. We then had to create little slips of paper and toss them into the "hat"—in reality, a bowl-shaped object without a brim. At that point I reached in and pulled out a slip of paper: Federal District Court Judge James D. Whittemore, Middle District of Florida.

With the judge appropriately selected, the clerk had a decision to make. She was supposed to call and notify Judge Whittemore that he had been assigned the Terri Schiavo case. But when? Should the clerk wait until normal business hours to place the call, or should she wake the judge up at three AM? Knowing that every hour was precious to Terri, she decided to awaken the sleeping judge.

After faxing the congressional bill and the various legal documents to Judge Whittemore at home, we waited. And waited. My plan was to wait with the clerk and her associate until we received some direction from the judge. I thought it would be wise to be available to answer any questions. I also thought that any judge who looked at this Act of Congress and knew our well-publicized situation would surely respond favorably and expeditiously—at least by ordering the feeding tube to be reinserted to maintain Terri's health while further decisions were made.

I was wrong.

When the judge finally called the courthouse about an hour later, we had our first hint that this particular judge might not be exactly warm to our cause. Judge Whittemore indicated that he intended to deliberate the matter and then call a hearing sometime later that day. He told us to go home, assuring us he wouldn't rule on the matter before coming to his office in the morning. What would he do about Terri in the meantime?

Nothing.

And so there was nothing more for us to do at that moment either. I'm not sure if my head was spinning from what I had just heard or from the fact that we had really stepped onto the fast track and had covered an amazing amount of ground in just the last twenty-four hours.

We exited the building around four AM, and the media converged upon us. As I would quickly learn, the buzz on the pavement was that we had won—which, of course, wasn't even close to the facts. The bill passed by Congress had only opened the door to the possibility of a full federal review—but that assumed the judge, whose sleep we had just interrupted, would agree to undertake that review.

We still had a long, long road ahead. And that road had just gotten a lot bumpier. In order to pass the bill, the Senate had removed a specific directive to the federal court to reinsert Terri's feeding tube before beginning a fresh review of the case. In the version of the bill that was actually passed, that decision was left to the discretion of the judge. And this judge had not chosen to relieve Terri's suffering that night.

THREE DAYS AND COUNTING

Monday's predawn sky was a thick blanket of gray clouds, a product of Sunday's rainstorm. The streets were largely empty as I made my way home for some breakfast, a change of clothes, and a much-needed hour of sleep. In the stillness of those early morning hours, I poured my heart out to God. Without His blessing, these efforts wouldn't amount to anything of lasting value.

I prayed for Terri as she entered her third day without so much as a drop of moisture on her lips. I knew if she were not hydrated and nourished quickly, she might experience lasting mental and physical damage. I prayed for Bob and Mary too. They had been through so much suffering for so many years. And though their hopes had been bolstered by the courageous action of Congress on behalf of their daughter, they knew Terri still might not make it. In fact, at that point they might have been more realistic about the outcome than I was.

Even though I was physically spent, I knew we had to press on. For Terri. For disabled people everywhere. For life. And so I prayed for wisdom and strength for what lay ahead. Sometime after eight in the morning, I received a call notifying me that Judge Whittemore, rather than deciding to rule on the pleadings we had submitted, would hold a hearing that afternoon at three o'clock—a full twelve hours after we had filed our paperwork.

That seemed odd.

Over two hundred members of the House of Representatives had weighed, debated, and decided on a piece of legislation in a mere three hours. Why did this judge want four times as much time just to schedule a hearing? Granted, the world was watching every step closely. Yet congressmen and women had returned from their holiday recess, traveling hundreds—even thousands—of miles in order to respond when needed. A sitting president had flown back to the White House to be available. All had gone to great lengths to act in a timely fashion knowing Terri's life was on the line. Judge Whittemore's twelve-hour delay in scheduling a hearing and his refusal to immediately reinsert Terri's feeding tube were not good signs.

Minutes before three o'clock that afternoon, having cleared the ultratight security, I headed to the courtroom. In the hallway just outside the rather small and now crowded chamber, I bumped into Michael Schiavo's attorney, George Felos. With a wry grin, he said, "Mr. Gibbs, if I ever need to get something passed by the United States Congress, I'll know who to call."

I'll take that as a compliment.

We took our places inside the courtroom. This federal judge literally had the power to decide whether Terri Schiavo would live or die. Organizing my notes, I continued to believe there was no way the judge would ignore the obvious intent of Congress to keep Terri alive while he conducted a full review of the facts in this case. We needed time to bring in witnesses, perhaps even conduct new depositions or arrange new medical tests for Terri.

I anticipated that getting this job done right could take weeks, perhaps even months. But Terri had to be fed and hydrated in order to provide the time needed for a proper review. I glanced over at the opposing legal team and was stunned to see something like twenty-five attorneys hovering around George Felos. I didn't realize so many lawyers could be mobilized so quickly.

They were ready and loaded for anything.

With the crack of his gavel, Judge Whittemore called the hearing to order. It didn't take long before it was painfully evident to me that this judge was not happy about being told what to do by the United States Congress. No question about it in my mind: The judge wanted to make me answer for this last-minute rush by Congress to have Terri's case reviewed.

Another point of annoyance for him seemed to me to center around the very structure of our lawsuit. As these things go, the party filing a complaint is required to name the people they are suing. And one of the parties we happened to be suing was the state court judge George Greer. That is common procedure in a criminal habeas death penalty proceeding—you must name the state court and name the parties. But Judge Whittemore was clearly bothered by the fact that Judge Greer, a state court judge, was named in this civil death case.

After a particularly grueling exchange between us about this matter, Judge Whittemore—a former state court judge himself—decided that Judge Greer's death sentence would stand without further review. He had already examined the state court records. And he made it perfectly clear he had no intention of hearing evidence de novo (all over again).

Tragically, just like that, all the valiant efforts of Congress and even the president himself, both coequal branches of government with the courts, were thwarted. It was clear this federal court would not step up and do for Terri what federal courts nationwide routinely do for convicted felons on death row—not even at the specific request of Congress and the president.

I'm not naïve. I realize there's always the potential for a political side whenever politicians are involved. However, many of them told me, "David, we'll get politically creamed over this. People will want to know why would the Congress get involved in just one woman's life?" None of those with whom I spoke had ulterior motives that I picked up on. None felt that this was going to be politically popular.

And while I didn't speak with, and only once had the privilege of meeting President George W. Bush (when he was governor of Texas), if I ever get the opportunity, I will personally thank him for his commitment, sacrifice, and leadership in preserving life.

Speaking to an audience in January of 2006, the president said, "You believe, as I do, that every human life has value, that the strong have a duty to protect the weak, and that the self-evident truths of the Declaration of Independence apply to everyone, not just to those considered healthy or wanted or convenient. These principles call us to defend the sick and the dying, persons with disabilities and birth defects, all who are weak and vulnerable."[2]

While President Bush was immediately castigated for his involvement in trying to save Terri's life, I believe future generations will look back at the actions of this Congress and this president and will record their actions as a hallmark of their commitment to life over political expediency. I also trust that Bob and Mary Schindler will one day be recognized for their unswerving commitment to have and to hold, in sickness and in health, their disabled daughter.

POLLS, POLITICIANS, AND POSITIONS

I realize it's easy to be cynical whenever politicians get involved in anything. Almost daily we hear about another misuse of governmental power, personal pockets enriched with funds from special interest groups, or influence peddling by lobbyists. So I wasn't entirely surprised when a number of polls taken in the wake of this historic effort suggested the public wasn't all that pleased with Congress's involvement in this life-and-death matter. Americans generally have a jaded and suspicious view of politics.

Polls, however, are highly influenced by how the specific questions are phrased. For example, in a nationwide Zogby International survey of 1,019 likely voters taken between March 30 and April 2, 2005, pollsters asked: "If a disabled person is not terminally ill, not in a coma, and not being kept alive on life support, and they have no written directive, should or should they not be denied food and water?"

Guess what?

An astounding 79 percent said the patient should *not* have food and water taken away. And guess what else? That was exactly the way Congress had framed the question. When the same poll asked about Congress's involvement in the Terri Schiavo case, the results were statistically deadlocked: 44 percent favored it, 43 percent opposed the action.[3]

That's radically different from what other pollsters found by asking the question in a very different way. Rather than focusing the question on a person's quality of life, they focused it on family privacy.

For instance, a CBS News poll conducted with 737 adults March 21–22, 2005, found that an overwhelming majority of Americans—82 percent—believed Congress and the president should have stayed out of the Schindler-Schiavo "family" matter. Except that this "family" matter had become a publicly disputed court case nearly ten years earlier. I was a little surprised, however, to note that 68 percent of evangelical Christians concurred with that assessment. When asked why Congress had gotten involved, 74 percent of those surveyed believed Congress was using the case to advance a political agenda and not just because it was the right thing to do.[4]

Those results are similar to a CNN/*USA Today*/Gallup Poll taken April 1–2, 2005, of 1,040 Americans that found 76 percent disapproved of Congress's involvement in a so-called "private family matter."[5] This matter hadn't been private for years. Likewise, the Pew Research Center discovered in a nationwide poll conducted by Princeton Survey Associates November 9–27, 2005, that of 1,500 adults surveyed, 72 percent believed Congress should have stayed out of the case and left the matter entirely to the courts.[6]

There's no question that Congress took a beating for defending Terri's rights and for wanting to give her the same shot at life that a convicted murderer would have in federal court.

That's unfortunate. I happen to applaud them. Having spoken with so many of the legislators myself—both Democrat and Republican—during the heat of the floor debate, I could tell this was one of those decisions where political ambitions, in most cases, took a backseat to trying to do the right thing just because it was the right thing. Perhaps the most troubling question that prompted many of the Congress members to act on Terri's behalf was this: *The state of Florida prohibits mercy killing, assisted suicide, and euthanasia. Florida has strict penalties for starving pets. How, then, could a Florida judge using Florida law permit—in fact, order—Terri Schiavo to be starved to death?*

That's exactly the right question to ask. Frankly, I have yet to come up with a good answer for it. That's not the question that most of the public polls were asking. Yet it's the question we, as a nation, ought to ask. Why? So that what happened to Terri never happens again in a country that is supposed to protect life, liberty, and justice for all.

CHAPTER FIFTEEN

A MOTHER'S HEART

Removing somebody's feeding is very painless. It is a very easy way to die. . . . And it doesn't bother me at all. I've seen it happen. I had to do it with my own parents.
—MICHAEL SCHIAVO[1]

No mother should ever have to endure the kind of heartache and agony that Mary Schindler experienced watching her daughter starve to death. No parents should be forced to stand by helplessly as their daughter struggles for her next breath. As long as I live, I'll never forget the last time Mary saw Terri alive.

Eight days into Terri's dehydration and starvation "process," as Michael and his attorneys were fond of calling it, Mary turned to me and said, "David, I'd like to go see Terri." We had been going to the hospice about once a day to encourage Terri. With her condition deteriorating by the moment, however, these visits became increasingly difficult for the family to bear.

While I wanted to be supportive of Mary's wishes, I could tell she was weary. I said, "Mary, are you sure you're up to that?" She nodded and said, "Yes, but can you go with me?" I knew what she was driving at. Mary wanted my help navigating the pandemonium on the street. She also wanted me nearby just in case someone attempted to deny her access to Terri.

During these final days, a kind thrift store owner had closed his store, which was located just across the street from Woodside Hospice. He wanted to provide a place where the Schindlers could relax and meet with supporters. The building was surrounded outside by a sea of media trucks, journalists, protestors, and police, so the store was our one oasis in the midst of the storm. The moment we stepped outside, the media swirled around us. The fact that we were going to the hospice was always news. Cameras were focused on our faces. Microphones on long boom stands were pointed in our direction. Yet despite this blitz, the media was the source of much support for the Schindler family, and the Schindlers appreciated it—most of the time.

"Is Terri still alive?"

"How much longer can she hold on?"

"What does she look like?"

Several police officers came to our aid and cleared a pathway for us. With the press at our heels—calling out questions, snapping photos, and rolling video to catch the Schindlers' profound grief—we reached the security area. After presenting our IDs and going through the now routine search for anything that might be used to feed or hydrate Terri, we made our way to the building.

Just beyond this security zone, the circular driveway led to a covered carport where patients and visitors would normally arrive and depart. As I approached the front doors, an American flag waved in the evening breeze from its pole. In the shadow of Old Glory, our national symbol of freedom, a decorative fountain sprayed a gentle stream of water four feet into the air. The irony would come to me later: The water Terri's parched lips craved flowed freely out here under the flag. But just inside those doors, I'd have been arrested on the spot for bringing her one drop.

Mary and I passed through the next security checkpoints and then walked down the hallway to Terri's room. Standing just outside her door while the guard double-checked our names on his approved visitor's list, I was startled to *hear* Terri before I could *see* her. When a healthy person breathes, they take in air and exhale air naturally. But when a person starts to die, they move into what is called the death pant. It's a rapid, short gasp for air similar to an animal panting after running around on a hot day.

Terri's breathing was severely labored. We assumed she didn't have a lot of time left. Frankly, standing at the threshold of her life-and-death struggle was more than a little unsettling. With an armed guard never more than several feet from us, we walked in. Mary immediately went to Terri's bedside, and as was her habit, she cradled Terri's head and started to kiss her face.

This time, however, Mary started to sob.

As Mary cried, her words tumbled out in a half-prayer, half-confession plea: "Oh, God, help Terri. . . . Terri, don't fight it . . . oh, sweet Terri. . . . Jesus, please help my girl. . . . Terri, it's too late, there's nothing we can do. . . . Don't fight it. You'll be at peace soon. . . . I love you, honey."

Not wanting to get in the way, I remained at the foot of the bed. As I watched Mary cry and talk and pray, my heart hurt so bad. I wanted to cry. I wanted to yell. There are no words to describe what it's like to witness a mother weeping over her dying daughter.

A PAINLESS DEATH?

Several days before Mary's final visit, Michael Schiavo appeared on ABC's *Nightline* and told the world that Terri "doesn't feel pain. She doesn't feel hunger." Speaking as if he had researched the topic of dehydration and starvation, he added in clinical tones, "So what's going to happen is slowly, her potassium and her electrolytes will slowly diminish and she will drift off to a nice little sleep and eventually pass on to be with God." Michael added, "Death through removing somebody's nutrition is very painless. . . . It is a very painless procedure."[2] Really?

Why, then, was the hospice administering morphine?

Why should a "vegetable" require pain-killers?

Furthermore, there was nothing "peaceful" about Terri's appearance—an adjective frequently used by George Felos in radical contrast to the suffering I witnessed in person. Speaking at a press conference during her final days, here's how Mr. Felos characterized Terri's condition: "She is calm, she is peaceful, and she is resting comfortably. When I saw her . . . she looked beautiful. In all the years I've seen Mrs. Schiavo, I've never seen such a look of peace and beauty upon her."[3]

Frankly, I could not disagree more.

Join me for a moment, if you will, at Terri's bedside. The most disturbing aspect of seeing Terri was her face. Dehydration has a way of taking all the flesh and fat out of the body. A healthy body craves nourishment—contrary to her husband's assurances. The best way to describe Terri's countenance is to picture a photo from a concentration camp. Incredible dark circles from extreme fatigue radiated from the skin around her eyes down to her nose. Her teeth protruded outward against cracked, shriveled lips.

Terri's formerly soft, silky peaches-and-cream skin was stretched thin and to the breaking point across her skeletal features from a lack of water. Her cheekbones and jawbones bulged; her eye sockets became two dark pits. She looked like she'd been beaten up in a back alley brawl.

Her flesh was red, peeling, and splotchy as if sunburned. And, probably due to her dry sinuses, Terri breathed with her mouth open. She had a completely dry mouth—the roof and gums lacked any natural glistening that would indicate moisture. Her tongue looked like a swollen leather lump with no signs of saliva whatsoever.

I still have difficulty processing the horrifically sad image of a lady who, just a few days earlier, was completely healthy, sitting unaided in a reclining chair, fully awake, alert, and happy.

As I stood there in that surreal moment—with the police hovering over us, the protestors chanting outside, sharpshooters taking up positions on the roof, and a mother grieving over her suffering daughter—I really didn't expect any communication from Terri. Not that she couldn't have interacted as she had done many times before. But with the abuse her system had undergone from the lack of food and water, and with the morphine coursing through her body, I assumed Terri would be incoherent.

I was in for a bittersweet surprise.

Now, as you may recall, Terri's favorite person in the world was her mother. She was always excited to see her mom. In a slow, deliberate motion, I watched as Terri rolled her head toward her mother, who was standing by her side. Terri's eyes got real big and—I'm not sure how she could have summoned it, but I saw a tear roll down Terri's pitted face. She started to sob and kiss her mom with her open, parched mouth. For several long minutes I watched this mother and her disabled daughter sob cheek to cheek as they said their final good-byes. This is the same mother who had told the court, "All I want to do is take care of my daughter."

I stood there completely heartbroken for Mary and, indeed, for our country. *How, in God's name, could we let this happen?* It's an image I'll never get out of my mind. It's a tragedy that never should have happened. Mary and Terri remained in a tearful embrace for eight or ten minutes. Finally, Mary turned and, still choking back her tears, walked out of the room while I stayed behind for just a moment.

According to the regulations set up by Michael—who, incidentally, was provided a comfortable, private room at the hospice for his convenience during Terri's final two weeks[4]—we couldn't linger in the room or hallway for very long. We didn't want to be removed from the visitors list. In light of this, for just a brief minute I looked at Terri and offered a prayer committing her into the care of Jesus. For her part, she looked back at me with those dark, sunken eyes. A desperate plea seemed to settle on her face, as if she were saying, "Isn't there *anything* you can do to help me?" I assured her I was sorry and that we were still doing everything we could to fight for her life.

With a sadness in my heart that defies definition, I joined Mary out in the hallway. She hugged me and put her head on my shoulder for just a moment. "David," she said, "I can't go back. It's just too hard. I can't bear to see her like this. I'm no lawyer, and I'm no doctor, but I just don't understand why they have to kill my little girl." I said, "Mary,

I *am* a lawyer, although I'm not a doctor. I don't understand either. It doesn't make any sense."

I think that's the troubling moral dilemma. Why, with a family wanting to give love and provide help, did Terri have to die this horrific death?

To her credit, Terri was a remarkably strong and healthy woman. She fought to live, to hold on, and to beat the odds. Her inner strength and stamina enabled this brave woman to exceed the expectations of those who predicted a quick death. Indeed, Terri fought until the end—a death that would finally come only a few days later.

THE WORLD WAS WATCHING

The media in the United States treated Terri's last few days much like a deathwatch. They wanted to know all the details about Terri's condition, the family's emotions, the feud between Mr. Schiavo and the Schindlers, and, of course, the money. Rarely was I engaged to debate on a more substantive, big-picture policy level.

By contrast, the international media didn't care about all those details. Keep in mind that I had the opportunity to conduct interviews with members of the media representing Europe, Africa, Central and South America, Australia, Canada, and Asia. Many of these interviews were translated into numerous foreign languages around the world.

Most of these foreign journalists admitted that they didn't understand our court system or our laws regarding the matter. Nor did they really want all of the details. About all they knew was that an otherwise healthy disabled girl was being intentionally dehydrated and starved to death by order of one of the lowest level courts in America. And when the president and the Congress tried to stop this miscarriage of justice, they couldn't do it. That was the essence of what they understood.

Their interest lay outside the family tragedy.

Almost universally, the foreign press was puzzled about the inconsistency between how America, as one of the most compassionate nations in the world, acted on behalf of others around the globe and yet treated one of our own so barbarically. Here's a somewhat typical set of questions they'd ask, along with my responses:

"Mr. Gibbs, is America in Iraq because it's the right thing to do?"

"Yes, our president and leadership thought it was the right thing to do; for human rights, justice, to fight terror, to end the torture and suffering of the Iraqi people under Saddam, and to further the cause of freedom. That's why we're there."

"Did America go to Afghanistan for similar reasons?"

"Yes, indeed."

"Did America, in World War II, come to Europe and stop the Nazis and the advancement of these regimes because it was the right thing to do?"

"Yes," I said, "that's the heart and soul of America. In a sense, we're the voice of morality for the world."

Then they'd ask the question that their international audiences couldn't grasp.

"Mr. Gibbs, by what moral authority, then, does America let this woman die?"

You know what? That is a very telling question. For two hundred years our shores were a safe haven for the oppressed, the maligned, and the disenfranchised. We were a country that stood for life, liberty, and the pursuit of happiness. But almost without warning, America appears to be wandering away from the foundations that made us strong. No, I don't believe there is any moral authority for what happened to Terri Schiavo.

As this case moves into the history books and the years begin to tick by, I hope and pray that Terri's legacy will be that her death birthed a revival, that her struggle gave breath and resolve for a renewed commitment to protect *all* life. I hope that senior citizens and the disabled community will one day look back and say, "Terri, thank you. We have rights too. We may be a people without a voice, but because of your sacrifice, our lives are now protected once again under American law." If that happens, Terri's death will not have been in vain. And I know there's nothing that would bring more joy to her mother's heart.

CHAPTER SIXTEEN

UNTIL WE MEET AGAIN

Today, millions of Americans are saddened by the death of Terri Schiavo. . . . I urge all those who honor Terri Schiavo to continue to work to build a culture of life.
—PRESIDENT GEORGE W. BUSH[1]

On March 30, 2005, as Terri's life was hanging by a mere thread, Bob and Mary Schindler, Bobby, Suzanne, and I were gathered at the hospice. Just before midnight, a phone call delivered heartbreaking news: Our final appeal to the U.S. Supreme Court had been denied. Though we had always known that most of the cases appealed to the Supreme Court are not heard, we had been praying for a breakthrough, a miracle.

We had argued in the federal courts that the removal of Terri's nutrition and hydration was unconstitutional because it deprived her of her constitutionally protected right to life. We had asked the high court to issue a temporary restraining order requiring her feeding tube to be reinserted so that we could have time to file a further appeal and have the federal court take another look at the facts of the case.

But with this unwelcome turn of events coming from our court of last appeal, we knew the Schindlers' fight to save Terri was over—at least as far as the courts were concerned. We were always open to a miracle. That evening we lingered at the hospice until almost one AM, when yet another curveball was hurled at us. At that time, Bobby and Suzanne were abruptly asked to leave Terri's room so that Michael could visit.

Keep in mind, this was a son-in-law who had once lived with Terri in the Schindlers' home—rent free for several years when the young couple's money had been tight. Now, as their daughter entered the final stages of death, Michael refused to endure the family's company under the same roof for a few hours, not even as Terri's death was fast approaching.

Rather than making a scene, I had earlier encouraged Bob and Mary to head home and get some rest. Bobby decided to stay across the street at the thrift store all night because we knew the end was near; he was hoping to get back into Terri's room at the first opportunity. Suzanne, emotionally drained, left to be with her family and planned to return at daybreak.

Just after seven on the morning of March 31, I received a frantic call from Bobby and Suzanne. Hospice officials had just barred them from seeing Terri—at Michael's request. My call to the hospice paved the way for them to return to their sister's side at seven-thirty. At eight-forty-five, my phone rang again. Bobby and Suzanne had been thrown out of Terri's room by Michael once again. When I asked why, Bobby, who was almost frantic, said, "Michael just wants to see her and doesn't want us in the room at the same time. Please, Mr. Gibbs, please. . . . I'll be in the room with him and I'll do whatever. . . . I just don't want to be away from her when Terri dies."

My heart ached for them.

I said, "Bobby, they should let you in there. There's no earthly reason why you shouldn't be by your sister when she dies. The legal battle is over. Let me call the hospice attorney and see if we can't get you in."

I quickly called the hospice attorney and described their predicament. She sounded sympathetic and promised to check on the situation and call me right back. She felt confident something could be worked out so that Bobby and Suzanne could be in the room together with

Michael. Meanwhile, I jumped into my car and headed to Woodside. About ten minutes past nine, the attorney called me back and said, "Mr. Gibbs, I need to tell you that Ms. Schiavo passed away at 9:05."

Terri had been dead for five minutes.

I arrived at the hospice five minutes later. I joined Bobby and Suzanne at the makeshift office across the street. They rallied around me as hope filled their eyes. Bobby said, "Can you get us in to be with Terri? We don't want her to be alone when she dies. I don't care if I have to stand next to Michael. . . . I've just got to get to Terri." I said, "Bobby, I can get you back in, but I need to let you know that I got a phone call on the way over here. . . . Terri's already passed. I am so sorry."

Although not a complete surprise, Suzanne began to cry. For his part, I could see the hope drain from Bobby's eyes. His eyebrows knotted in desperation. "How can we get in, Mr. Gibbs? The police won't let us through." I said, "She's dead now, they *have* to let us in. I'll personally see that you get in there to be with her."

We hurried across the street to the hospice, and thankfully, Bobby and Suzanne were admitted to go see Terri's now lifeless body. After we walked inside, they asked me to wait at the front of the hospice for the arrival of Bob and Mary. Suzanne had called her mom at home and told them to come to the hospice as fast as they could.

Several minutes later, Bob dropped Mary off out front while he parked the car. The fact that I was standing there and that Bobby and Suzanne had asked them to come spoke volumes; Mary already understood that Terri had died. I gave her a brief hug and said, "I'm so sorry, Mary." She covered her mouth with her hand and burst into tears. Being with Mary at that moment was one of the most difficult things I have ever had to do.

Composing herself, she clutched my arm and said, "David, I'll be okay. I just want . . . to be with her. Can I see her?"

I said, "Yes, Bobby and Suzanne are there right now."

Sobbing, she asked, "Will you let Bob know?"

I told her I would and that we'd catch up with them in a moment.

She dabbed her tears with a tissue, turned, and silently made her way inside to grieve with her remaining two children.

Several minutes later Bob shuffled toward me. I could tell that this father, who had crusaded so valiantly for so long, was drained yet remained determined to fight to the finish. Although he was physically weary and emotionally depleted, the fire in his eyes was unmistakable. I wasn't sure, looking at him, if he really comprehended that Terri was gone.

I said, "Bob, we've lost her. . . . Terri is with God now."

Bob seemed startled. "When? Was Bobby with her? Was she alone?"

I was struck by the fact that it mattered very much to him, as a dad, that Terri not die without her family surrounding her. Michael had won what he wanted in terms of a positive press release for him upon Terri's death; but to deny her family the opportunity to be in the room while she was taking her last breath was beyond the pale.

FAREWELL, TERRI

When Terri passed away on March 31, 2005, the security protocol seemed more relaxed—to a degree. But when I reached the door to Terri's room, the police were under instructions, apparently from Michael, not to permit anybody but the immediate family inside. That was odd. I had been on the visitors list for months. Why the abrupt change? The officer, however, informed me that now that Terri had died, I was no longer permitted inside.

Complicating matters was Mary's crying out and Bob's insistence, bordering on screaming at the guards, to allow me to come in to comfort the family. All they wanted was a supportive hug and a few words of encouragement in their hour of great loss. Instead, we were shocked at the news that I had been banned from the room.

Standing just outside the door, I could see Terri's still form. Before her feeding tube was removed, it would have been impossible for me to see her from the doorway. She had been situated out of sight so as to avoid any human contact with the outside world. Once the dehydration/starvation process had begun, however, her bed was repositioned so that the armed guard posted at the door could keep an eye on her at all times—for security reasons.

As I looked over his shoulder at Terri's now lifeless body, my mind drifted back to the first time I'd met her. No longer was she the animated woman whom I had come to know. I couldn't help but notice that this time when Bob went to kiss his daughter, she no longer made her "lemon face." I had so hoped and prayed that we could have prevented this miscarriage of justice even though I knew the case, realistically, had been lost before we were ever asked to get involved.

My heart yearned to reach out to the Schindlers. Watching Bob and Mary wail over their daughter's senseless death was almost too much to bear. As I watched from the doorway as the family continued to weep over their lost loved one, I felt something deep in my soul—I felt a profound loss for our country. As Congressman Mike Pence (R-IN) would say later that day, "With her death, America lost not only a precious citizen, America lost its innocence."

He added, "Although Terri Schiavo's life may be over, the debate over the rights of incapacitated Americans is not over. Congress must right this wrong by ensuring that incapacitated Americans may not be deprived of their inalienable right to life without the assurance of the due process of law that our federal courts were established to protect. This will be Terri Schiavo's legacy."[2]

I couldn't agree more.

Still standing at the door, Mary's sobbing filled the air as she embraced Terri for the last time. Bob Schindler continued to plead that I be permitted to come in to comfort the family. The police stationed around her bed refused to grant his request. In fact, orders had been given by Michael through his lawyer that I was to leave immediately. I said, "But they're obviously very upset. Can't I go in for a few minutes?" The police stood their ground and said, "No."

I couldn't believe what I was hearing.

Terri was dead, right?

I asked if I could at least pray for them. Thankfully, we reached a compromise: I could pray as long as I didn't set one foot inside the room. As I prayed from the doorway, my arms literally outstretched over the officer blocking the door, I was not able to offer the comfort that the Schindlers needed in that very sad moment. It was . . . heartbreaking.

The instant we finished praying the police officers said, "We have our orders. Mr. Gibbs, you need to leave—*now.*" I was escorted out of sight to a side room down the hall. There, I waited for the Schindlers while they, too, were rushed by the security officers to say their final good-byes.

About ten minutes later, the Schindlers walked into the room where I had been waiting for them. We hugged and prayed, and I tried to offer some degree of encouragement. We arranged for a minivan and a motorcycle police escort. The vehicles met us at the rear entrance of the hospice to shuttle Bob and Mary home. After all, the news helicopters were circling overhead trying to capture the first picture of the weeping mother. I'm sure the media frenzy out front would have been devastating.

Right now, this couple needed to be left alone.

They had suffered enough. Media coverage could no longer help Terri.

The family asked if I'd go outside and make the announcement that Terri had died while they headed home. I was honored to help. After ensuring that the transportation was in place, I exited the hospice by the front door to speak with the press. I said, "This is indeed a sad day for the nation; this is a sad day for the family. Their faith in God remains consistent and strong. They are absolutely convinced that God loves Terri more than they do. They believe that Terri is now ultimately at peace with God himself. They intend to comfort themselves with their faith and with their family at this time."

Later that afternoon, we worked together on a more complete family statement. My father always told me in any conflict, you should always do three things:

1. take the right stand
2. the right way
3. with the right spirit

I appreciated the fact that the Schindlers were in full agreement with the spirit of that approach. Here, then, is a portion of the Schindler family statement as read by Bobby and Suzanne at four o'clock the day Terri died:

As you are aware, Terri is now with God and she has been released from all earthly burdens. After these recent years of neglect at the hands of those who were supposed to protect and care for her, she is finally at peace with God for eternity. We are speaking on behalf of our entire family this evening as we share some thoughts and messages to the world regarding our sister and the courageous battle that was waged to save her life from starvation and dehydration.

We have a message for the volunteers that helped our family:
Thank you for all that you've done for our family. Thank you to the hundreds of doctors who volunteered to help Terri. Thank you to the fifty doctors who provided statements under oath to help Terri. Thank you to the lawyers who stood for Terri's life in the courtrooms of our nation. From running our family's Web site, to driving us around, to making meals, to serving in so many ways—thank you to all of the volunteers who have been so kind to our family through all of this.

We have a message for the supporters and people praying worldwide:
Please continue to pray that God gives grace to our family as we go through this very difficult time. We know that many of you never had the privilege to personally know our wonderful sister, Terri, but we assure you that you can be proud of this remarkable woman who has captured the attention of the world. Following the example of the Lord Jesus, our family abhors any violence or any threats of violence. Threatening words dishonor

our faith, our family, and our sister, Terri. We would ask that those who support our family be completely kind in their words and deeds toward others.

We have a message to the media:

We appreciate your taking Terri's case to the nation. Please afford our family privacy to grieve at this time. The patience and graciousness of the on-site media here at hospice has been deeply appreciated by our family.

We have a message to the many government officials who tried to help Terri:

Thank you for all that you've done. Our family will be forever grateful to all of the outstanding public servants who have tried to save Terri.

We have a message of forgiveness:

Throughout this ordeal, we are reminded of the words of Jesus on the cross: "Father, forgive them, for they know not what they do." Our family seeks forgiveness for anything that we have done in standing for Terri's life that has not demonstrated the love and compassion required of us by our faith.

We have a message to parents worldwide:

Our family would encourage parents to spend time with their children and to cherish each and every moment of each and every day with them as a precious gift from God.

We have a message to Terri from her family:

As a member of our family unable to speak for yourself, you spoke loudly. As a member of our family unable to stand under your own power, you stood with a grace and a dignity that made your family proud. Terri, we love you dearly, but we know that God loves you more than we do. We must accept your untimely death as God's will.

Terri, your life and legacy will continue to live on, as the nation is now awakened to the plight of thousands of voiceless people with disabilities that were previously unnoticed. Your family intends to stand up for the other "Terris" around the nation, and we will do all that we can to change the law so that others won't face the same fate that has befallen you.

————

The street in front of Woodside Hospice is no longer barricaded. The crowds have dispersed and the media tents, trucks, and talking heads are gone. The news helicopters are chasing stories elsewhere, and the police are otherwise engaged. While this Florida neighborhood appears to be "back to normal," a part of me wonders about the long-term impact these events have had on the elementary school students who sat in classes just down the street from the hospice while this drama unfolded.

These youngsters continue to study about a block away from this former epicenter of world events. After all, they'd had a bird's-eye view of this tragedy every time their big yellow school bus rolled past history in the making. What did they learn about America's treatment of the disabled? What life lessons will they carry with them? How were their values shaped by the life-and-death struggle that played itself out adjacent to their playground?

Will they understand that every life is important?

Will they know that life is precious in God's eyes?

Or will they believe that killing within a health care environment is acceptable? Will they see Terri as a brain-injured human being who deserved somebody to step up and stand with her parents and her family in the fight for her life? Or will they view such people with contempt? Is it possible some of these children may themselves live in fear of what might happen to them if, one day, they were to become disabled?

Only time will tell.

I pray that somehow these students—indeed, students all across America—would know in their hearts that disabled people matter. Terri mattered. And every life counts. As President Bush said, we all must work to build a "culture of life." That's especially relevant for the next generation. Why? If our young people fail to embrace the worth of every person, then Rush Limbaugh was prophetic. Hours after Terri's death, Rush announced on his syndicated radio program: Americans should mark March 31, 2005, as "the day our country hit rock bottom."[3]

I'm afraid he's right.

While we cannot turn back the clock to undo what has been done to Terri, we do have an opportunity before us to teach the young people of America to cherish life over death. All life.

Especially the lives of the "Terris" of tomorrow.

TIME LINE OF EVENTS: 2004–2005

March 20, 2004: Papal Pronouncement—Pope John Paul II, in a worldwide address, issues a declaration that he specifically intends for Terri Schiavo, stating: "I should like particularly to underline how the administration of water and food, even when provided by artificial means, always represents a *natural means* of preserving life, not a *medical act.*"

April 16, 2004: Death of a Bill—A powerful Florida state senator blocks passage of an updated and permanent version of Terri's Law (bill 692) by preventing it from reaching the Senate floor. Had this legislation been enacted, the Florida Supreme Court might have viewed the constitutionality of Terri's Law in a more favorable light.

May 6, 2004: Governor's Battle—Pinellas-Pasco County Circuit Court voids Governor Bush's executive order protecting Terri and bars the governor from exercising any further authority regarding Terri. The governor immediately appeals, which continues the stay in state court and keeps Terri fed and hydrated.

September 23, 2004: Terri's Law Unconstitutional—The Florida Supreme Court rules that Terri's Law is unconstitutional.

September 27, 2004: *Larry King Live*—Bob and Mary Schindler appear live with attorney David Gibbs III on Larry King's CNN program for the entire hour, taking Terri's case to the nation and the world.

December 3, 2004: Governor's Appeal—Governor Bush appeals the Florida Supreme Court decision in the Terri's Law case to the United States Supreme Court.

December 24, 2004: Christmas Eve Visit—After applying for and being granted permission to be added to Terri's visitors list, the Schindlers' attorneys, David Gibbs III and Barbara Weller, visit Terri at Woodside Hospice for the first time.

Terri's Death Is Again Mandated by the Court: January 24, 2005—The U.S. Supreme Court rejects Governor Jeb Bush's appeal of the Florida Supreme Court's decision in *Bush v. Schiavo*. Judge Greer then orders not only the removal of Terri's feeding tube but also the withholding of all hydration and nutrition by mouth, to begin on March 18, 2005.

March 16, 2005: Death Order Stands—The Florida Second District Court of Appeals rejects the Schindlers' appeal to stay the removal of the feeding tube, allowing the March 18 date to stand. The Schindlers immediately appeal this decision to the U.S. Supreme Court through Justice Kennedy. The Court declines to get involved.

March 18, morning: Summoned to Washington—The U.S. House of Representatives Committee on Government Reform issues subpoenas for Terri Schiavo, her husband, her doctors, and others from the hospice facility to appear at a March 30 hearing in Washington, D.C. This order should result in the reinsertion of Terri's feeding tube to preserve her life, but Judge Greer denies Congress's motion to intervene and ignores congressional subpoenas.

March 18, 1:45 PM: Feeding Tube Removed, Third and Final Time—Terri's feeding tube is removed in the afternoon while hundreds of news media and protestors begin to gather outside her hospice facility.

March 18, afternoon: To the Highest Levels—Attempts to save Terri's life move into high gear after her feeding tube is removed. During this time attempts to save her life are ongoing in the governor's office, in the Florida legislature, in the United States Congress, and with President George W. Bush.

March 20: U.S. Congress Bill—On Palm Sunday, the U.S. Congress delays its Easter recess and works through the weekend to pass a bill, (S686: *An Act for the relief of the parents of Theresa Marie Schiavo*, March 20, 2005: 109th Congress, 1st session). President Bush flies back from Texas to sign the bill into law.

March 21: President Signs Bill—At one AM, President Bush is awakened to sign the federal equivalent of a Terri's Law, intended to give Terri access to a rehearing in federal court, just as a criminal death penalty convict would receive.

March 22: Death Order Stands—Judge Whittemore rules that there is no state action involved in Terri's death order and that Terri has no federal claims that the congressional legislation entitles her to pursue. He refuses to alter the status quo of Terri's death sentence while appeals are pending.

March 23: Eleventh U.S. Circuit Court Appeal—Judge Whittemore's March 22 ruling is immediately appealed to a three-judge panel of the Eleventh Circuit. In a 2-1 decision, the court denies the Schindlers' request to reinsert Terri's feeding tube based on the Palm Sunday Act of Congress. The court also denies the Schindlers' petition in a full court hearing, with only two judges of the full panel siding with the Schindlers.

March 24: U.S. Supreme Court Refuses Involvement—Although clerks at the U.S. Supreme Court, who, with Justice Kennedy, oversee the Eleventh Circuit for the Court, are very gracious and remain open with a clerk on hand to receive petitions for appeals, the U.S. Supreme Court ultimately refuses to become involved. Both decisions of the Eleventh Circuit are appealed to the high Court, but without relief.

March 25: Eleventh Circuit Refuses to Hear Appeal—The Schindlers appeal Judge Whittemore's second ruling to the Eleventh Circuit. This time, the court issues a stern warning that it does not wish to consider this matter again.

March 25: Terri's Attempt to Speak—The Schindlers file a final pleading with Judge Greer on Good Friday. This final hearing is conducted by telephone, as Judge Greer has apparently left the Clearwater area. The affidavits state that on the morning before Terri's feeding tube was removed on March 18, in their presence and in the presence of other visitors in the room, Terri attempted to say, "I want to live," in response to a plea from Mrs. Weller for her to attempt to speak for herself. Judge Greer denies this final motion and accepts the arguments of Michael's lawyer, George Felos, that since Terri is in a persistent vegetative state, she has no ability to communicate.

March 28: Litigating at Light Speed—In total, the Schindlers file ten petitions in ten days in every possible jurisdiction between March 18 and March 28. It has been noted by legal experts that this flurry of activity set a record in U.S. legal history. Terri's plea for life appears to be the only case in American legal history that went through the federal court system to the Supreme Court and back twice in ten days.

March 18–30: Desperate Measures—Nearly a dozen people are arrested attempting to bring water to Terri, including three children. Protesters include the disability community, many of whom conduct their vigil in wheelchairs.

March 30: Second Refusal From High Court—The U.S. Supreme Court refuses to hear a petition for appeal from the Schindlers for the last time, a few hours before Terri dies.

March 31: Terri Passes Away—After thirteen days of valiantly fighting for her life, Terri dies—the first victim of a civil death order by a judge in the history of America.

PART THREE

FIGHTING FOR OUR FUTURE

CHAPTER SEVENTEEN

SUPREME DENIAL

This is a court of law, young man, not a court of justice.
—OLIVER WENDELL HOLMES JR., FORMER U.S.
SUPREME COURT JUSTICE

I 'm often asked why the U.S. Supreme Court refused to protect
Terri's due process rights. Likewise, many people I meet want to
know why a series of lower courts failed to give Terri the same protection afforded to convicted killers on death row, especially after both the
Congress and the president stepped in. After all, Terri's death seemed
to me, as well as to many others, to be a clear miscarriage of justice,
despite the fact that Florida law permitted this outcome. How could the
courts allow this to happen?

The answer is not comforting.

In a word, we do not have *justice* in this country; we have a *system* of
justice.

Tragically, in Terri's case, the system prevailed—justice did not.
What I think many people don't understand is that the judicial system
is just that—a system. And while the goal behind the American system
of justice is to have a "just" or "right" verdict, even the most experienced judge will acknowledge the fact that the system is flawed. A host
of contributing factors can lead to the miscarriage of justice in our

courts. Let's consider the top three: the money, the magistrate, and the morality.

THE FINEST JUSTICE MONEY CAN BUY

You're probably aware of a number of high profile cases in which people have done horrible things and have apparently gotten away with them. How? They had enough money to finance a "dream team." The finest lawyers from the leading law firms and a parade of expert witnesses are flown in from around the country to dazzle the jury. As American poet Robert Frost quipped, "A jury consists of twelve persons charged to decide who has the better lawyer."

Speaking of assembling a dream team, take for example O. J. Simpson or Michael Jackson. Both were celebrities with deep pockets charged with heinous crimes. I don't know whether or not these men actually committed the offenses that they were accused of; the point is that they were in a financial position to afford an aggressive defense to vindicate them at every possible turn.

By contrast, if a single-parent mom, barely making a living and perhaps on food stamps, were to be accused of similar crimes—murder or molestation—she wouldn't have the resources necessary to hire a first-class lawyer. At best she'd be assigned to an overworked public defender who'd be handling literally hundreds and hundreds of cases simultaneously. Most likely, she'd be convicted and jailed simply because she didn't have strong legal counsel.

Clearly, our system of justice provides an unfair advantage to people of wealth.

HERE COMES THE JUDGE

The second factor affecting the kind of justice you or I might receive in court is the magistrate assigned to the case. You see, there is a terrific difference between judges and how they'll rule. There's a mistaken notion in America that somehow the judges are just upholding "the law." In reality, there is no fixed definition of what "the law" is. "The law" is subjective—it's whatever the judge says: "I have interpreted the facts in light of these statutes; here is *the law*." Depending on the personality of the judge, the background of the judge, the politics of the judge, the law and the justice meted out can vary markedly from courtroom to courtroom.

In a personal injury case, one of the first questions some attorneys ask is this: *Which judge did you get?* There are judges who tend to be pro-plaintiff (the people who are suing). There are judges who tend to be pro-defendant. Accordingly, some lawyers believe the anticipated outcome of the financial damages awarded can go up or down depending on the judge that they have. So if you're the defendant being sued for, say, $5 million in damages and you were to draw a pro-plaintiff judge, you might be more tempted to settle out of court. And fast. Conversely, if the judge is pro-defendant, you might be more inclined to take your chances at trial.

How is that equal justice?

The facts should speak for themselves.

The outcome shouldn't depend on the personal views of a judge. That's the tension within the American system of justice. From judge to judge, even from location to location (the big city jurists might handle a case completely different than those in rural regions), *justice is relative.* I realize that may be a difficult idea to embrace, especially since we're so accustomed to expect consistency in daily life.

Think about it. If you stay at a Marriott or a Hampton Inn, or if you eat at McDonald's or an Outback Steakhouse, these hotel and food service chains work hard so that you'll experience the same level of customer service, the same quality of product, and the same degree of excellence across the board. Whether the Golden Arches is franchised or corporately owned, or located in London, England, or London, Indiana, when you sink your teeth into a McDonald's hamburger, you'll instantly recognize the famous taste. If the quality of their food were relative or inconsistent, they'd lose customers.

Let's not overlook the human dimension: Judges are still people.

They have good and bad days. They fight with their spouse. They get flat tires. It would be a mistake to dismiss mood swings, egos, notoriety, and peer review pressure in the judgments that they may make. This explains why there can be enormous inconsistencies in how rulings are handed down. (In all fairness, a great number of judges are aware of this and strive to be both consistent and impartial.)

We've looked at how money and the choice of a judge impacts justice. The third underlying factor is morality. There is no longer an absolute standard of morality in American law. Without a moral foundation, justice is in the eyes of the beholder; what the judge thinks will ultimately control the outcome.

This wasn't always the case.

COMMON LAW VERSUS CIVIL LAW

Back in Duke Law School, one of my earliest civil procedure classes was a real eye-opener. Our professor, who had clerked for two different Supreme Court justices, was a highly respected and successful lawyer. I remember listening to his opening-day speech. Now, as a young law student taking notes, I was much like the others in my class—wet behind the ears. We were just happy to have found the right classroom. We were honored to be there under the teaching of this great man.

In our first class, our professor started off by saying, "I'm going to tell you something that is very important." I thought, *If he thinks it's important, then it's probably going to be on the test.* With pen in hand, I got ready to write down his great insight on my yellow legal pad. With a wave of his hand, he announced, "The common law is dead in America." I thought, *Wow, this is significant. The common law is dead in America.* I wrote that down. He continued: "We now live in an era of statutory law." So I wrote that down, too, although I didn't initially understand the difference.

He explained that American law was originally based upon English law and that English law had been established upon an absolute standard, written down by William Blackstone in a universally used legal textbook called "Blackstone's Commentary." Evidently, Mr. Blackstone quoted from the Bible 80–90 percent of the time in this legal textbook, the first one used in America. So in a pre-computer, pre-law book era, judges established a consistency in the English and early American courts by saying, "If you know the Bible, then you have an understanding of the law."

Even the phrase "One Nation Under God" stamped on our money was designed to demonstrate that this was a nation that recognized God as the ultimate authority. Our president is sworn into office by placing a hand on the Bible. Witnesses about to give testimony in court are sworn to tell the truth by placing their hand on the Bible. These and similar actions reveal our nation's religious roots.

Fifteen years before Terri died, my professor said that the common law in America was dead, that the commitment to absolute truth and the notion of absolute right or wrong are gone. I imagine someone in the class might have wondered, What's the big deal? Times change. The needs of a nation change. What could be so bad about living in a time in which courts base their decisions on statutory law?

What is statutory law anyway?

Statutory law is whatever legislators elected by the people decide is legal at any given moment—and that can change from year to year. It's whatever 51 percent of the leaders, politicians, or courts approve, even if it's inconsistent with what's been done in the past. Which is why prostitution is illegal in forty-nine states, with Nevada permitting it in certain counties. The problem with this approach is that there is no longer any controlling moral authority for American law.

Back in law school the far-reaching implications of a shift from common law to statutory law never really sank in with me. I didn't fully understand it until I began to work within the American justice system. There, I quickly saw that an attorney couldn't walk into a courtroom and say to the judge, "Your Honor, killing a disabled person is not right." Judges today will say, "I'm not going to let your personal opinions or my personal beliefs get in the way here. I will listen to the merits of the case, read the statute, and make my ruling."

But when there is no morality in the law, no absolute standard anchoring it, and with "the law" being decided literally year to year and case by case, it's inevitable that personal opinions are going to be the controlling component because there is no other absolute dominant moral force to say "this is the right" or "this is the wrong."

In short, the court takes the place of God.

When America was anchored to the common law, we could have confidence that the Bible offered the restraining moral influence in our society and in our policies. Today, there is no restraining influence. What does all of this have to do with Terri Schiavo?

Plenty.

The Schindlers lost their fight for Terri's life because they lacked money to wage a proper defense; they found themselves before a judge who saw no value in saving the life of their daughter; and the court was no longer constrained by the biblical notion of the absolute value of human life.

Make no mistake about it: When mortal man denies there is no supreme authority greater than his own mind, he exists in a state of supreme denial. There is a God. He has spoken. He has given us the tools and the basis for law. America once recognized this reality, but over the last fifty years or so, she has been duped into accepting a lower standard of right and wrong. As a result, we are now witnessing the cheapening of human life.

Indeed, as a young law school student, I never dreamed there would come a day when the academic discussion I barely understood then between common law and statutory law would have such profound implications in the fight for life in America. I never fathomed that a day would come when I'd walk into a hospice room and witness the grotesque starvation of a fellow American. In that regard, I was completely unprepared for the most difficult experience of my life: watching a woman dehydrate and starve to death with my own eyes, helpless to save her.

WHAT CAN BE DONE TO SAVE OTHERS?

Six Policy Suggestions

1. At the very least, no court should be permitted to order an innocent person to die by starvation and dehydration without first having a legally sufficient statement such as a written living will or health care surrogate in writing, with signatures and witnesses appropriate to those required for any other legal document.

2. The category of persistent vegetative state (PVS) is reportedly misdiagnosed approximately 43 percent of the time, condemning to death even those people who may have a hope of recovery. At a minimum, states should require an appropriate cognitive assessment review to be done immediately before a feeding tube is removed.

3. A spouse who has entered into another committed relationship and, therefore, has a conflict of interest with the ward, should not be permitted to continue to serve as a guardian for the disabled spouse. In this case, Terri's husband, Michael, had set up a new home with another woman with whom he had two children over a ten-year period. Michael and Terri had been married for only five years before her collapse. When Michael moved on with his life, the better public policy would have been for his decision-making power over Terri to have legally ended.

4. Food and water should never be seen as extraordinary medical treatment but should be treated as ordinary care—something to which every American is entitled, no matter what their physical or mental condition.

5. Whether a person will ever "get better" should not be a valid reason to end their life under the law. It is dangerous to permit a judge to determine the quality of life a disabled person must attain in order to be permitted to live. Many with disabilities will never see their physical condition improve according to standards of the able-bodied. Nevertheless, for millions of disabled Americans, their "quality of life" in the eyes of others should not be a reason to deny them their basic right to life or any other liberty under our Constitution.

6. If ever a court sentences to death an innocent, disabled person who cannot speak for him or herself, the law should provide at least the same judicial review a convicted death row prisoner would be entitled to receive. Such laws do not exist currently in

America. Terri was never provided with an independent legal counsel, nor a trial by jury. Yet by order of a court her life was ended.

There is no rational basis for this fundamental unfairness to continue. Terri's struggle has exposed the problem. Now, our duty as a nation is to work toward the solution.

CHAPTER EIGHTEEN

EXAMINING THE
MEDICAL EXAMINER'S
REPORT

Um, I think I took her engagement ring and her—what do they call it?—diamond wedding band and made a ring for myself.

—MICHAEL SCHIAVO[1]

On June 15, 2005, Pinellas-Pasaco County's chief independent medical examiner (IME), Dr. Jon Thogmartin, filed his findings from Terri Schiavo's autopsy. Both sides in the hotly contested fight over the fate of Terri's life sought answers to a host of questions: Why did she collapse back in 1990? Had she been abused, drugged, or strangled? Did she have a heart attack? Why did Terri have so many bone fractures? Was she terminal? Could she have improved? How extensive was her brain damage?

Was she in a persistent vegetative state?

Dr. Thogmartin took his seat before a vast array of cameras and microphones. The world would be hanging on his every word. Working from a set of prepared comments, he patiently spoke for about an hour, spelling out his thirty-nine pages of findings in both scientific and laymen's terms. Unfortunately, as we soon discovered, many of the nuances in his remarks were lost on impatient analysts, pundits, and those of the public who prefer to view things in black and white. I know some were led to conclude the IME report cleared everything up.

Guess what?

I read the entire medical examiner's report. In fact, I was briefed on it a number of hours before it was released. To be candid, I'm dismayed at how the media portrayed the findings. Keep in mind that Dr. Thogmartin never saw Terri alive. He didn't have the benefit of witnessing what the Schindler family and I saw in her room. He was working on a severely emaciated corpse—in fact, he told me Terri represented the most severe case of dehydration he'd ever seen. One neurologist who read the report told me the autopsy showed unbelievably high levels of dehydration.

While I believe Dr. Thogmartin is a skilled professional, there are some issues raised by the autopsy that an IME cannot resolve. For instance, Dr. Thogmartin noted in his report that Terri's "brain weight was approximately half of the expected weight." When I pressed him about what role the dehydration might have played in the shrinkage of her brain tissue, he conceded he didn't know exactly. I've been told by one neurologist that the brain is highly susceptible to serious medical complications from dehydration. Since 77 to 78 percent of the brain is normally composed of water, shrinkage from such severe dehydration should be expected.

Dr. Thogmartin noted that Terri had "damage and neuronal loss in her occipital lobes, which indicates cortical blindness." In other words, at the time of her death Terri was blind. But *when* did the blindness set in? Bob and Mary had known Terri needed glasses due to her poor eyesight even before her injury. We knew she was visually impaired. Yet Terri could follow the pathway of a balloon as evidenced in videotapes recorded in 2002. A neurologist explained to me that some patients who are cortically blind can retain the ability to track objects—a phenomenon known as "blind sight."

◄ A mother and her disabled son attend a support rally on March 18, 2005.

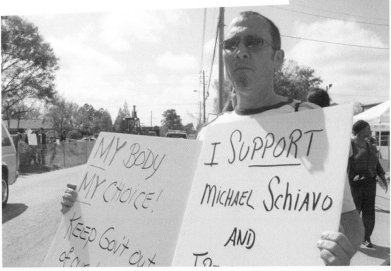

▲ Supporters for Michael Schiavo as well as for the Schindler family attend the rally outside Woodside Hospice on March 18, 2005.

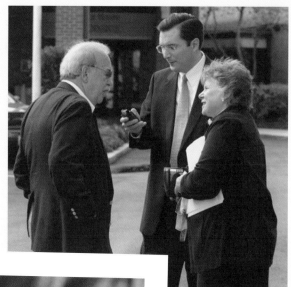

Bob Schindler talks to attorneys David Gibbs and Barbara Weller outside Woodside Hospice on March 18, 2005.

AP Images

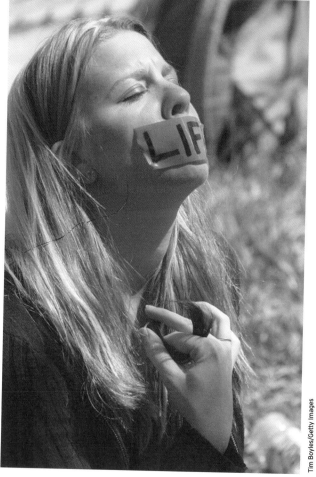

Tim Boyles/Getty Images

Supporters on March 19, 2005, wear red tape bearing the word "life" over their mouths to illustrate how Terri's voice has been silenced.

AP Images

AP Images

Senators Rick Santorum (R-PA), Mel Martinez (R-FL), and Tom Harkin (D-IA) discuss the bill introduced by Senator Martinez that would allow the Schindlers to take their case to a federal judge for a fresh review. Senate Bill S.686 passed unanimously on March 20, 2005.

Representative Dave Weldon (R-FL), Bobby Schindler, and Representative Chris Smith (R-NJ) walk to the House of Representatives on Sunday, March 20, 2005. At 12:34 Monday morning the House overwhelmingly passed S.686: Terri Schiavo Incapacitated Protection Bill.

President Bush returns to Washington from his Texas ranch on March 20, 2005, to be available to sign the emergency legislation to protect Terri's life once both houses of Congress passed it.

Early on Monday, March 21, 2005, House Speaker Dennis Hastert (R-IL), center, gavels to a close the emergency session for debate on the Terri Schiavo case.

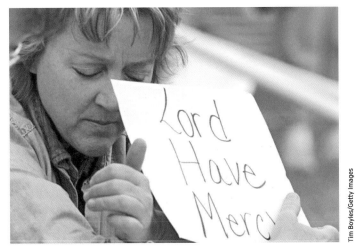

On March 21, 2005, three days after Terri's feeding tube was removed, supporters await a ruling from Federal Court Judge James D. Whittemore on whether Terri's case should undergo a full review.

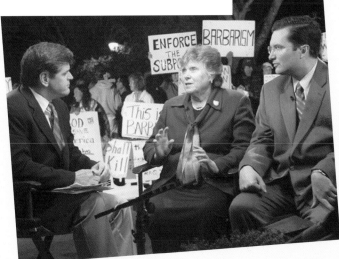

Broadcaster Sean Hannity, left, interviews Barbara Weller, center, and David Gibbs, right, on March 22, 2005.

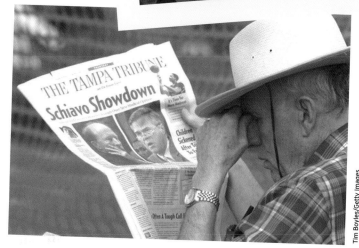

On March 24, 2005, a supporter reads the news that the U.S. Supreme Court has refused to hear Terri's case.

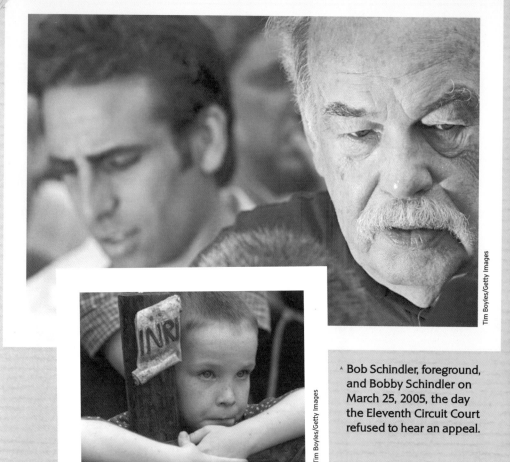

Tim Boyles/Getty Images

Tim Boyles/Getty Images

▲ Bob Schindler, foreground, and Bobby Schindler on March 25, 2005, the day the Eleventh Circuit Court refused to hear an appeal.

▲ A young supporter embraces a cross on March 27, 2005.

▸ Suzanne, Terri's sister, along with Mary and Bob Schindler during a news conference outside Woodside Hospice on March 30, 2005, the day the U.S. Supreme Court refused once again to hear a petition for appeal from the Schindlers.

Tim Boyles/Getty Images

▾ Media surround David Gibbs as he announces that Terri Schiavo has died on Thursday morning, March 31, 2005.

▸ Bulletins from the public memorial service held for Terri on April 5, 2005.

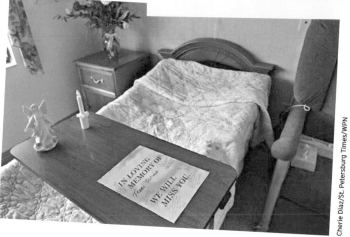

◂ Terri's room at Woodside Hospice, April 1, 2005.

AP Images

‹ Dr. Jon Thogmartin, right, medical examiner, giving his report on Terri's autopsy at a news conference on June 15, 2005, in Clearwater, Florida, with Dr. Stephen Nelson, who assisted with the report.

SCHIAVO

SCHIAVO
THERESA MARIE
BELOVED WIFE

AP Images

› Terri's final resting place, where her remains were buried on June 20, 2005. The gravemarker Michael designed bears the date February 25, 1990, as the day Terri "departed this earth" and March 31, 2005, as the day Terri was "at peace."

This could explain why none of the five doctors who diagnosed Terri for the court in 2002 ever observed that Terri was blind. None of her rehab doctors during the first two years—back before the malpractice trial when Michael actually permitted rehab doctors to attend to her—reported that she was blind. In fact, in the early 1990s, prior to Michael's winning the malpractice award, he is pictured pointing out ducks to Terri at a pond.

So when did the blindness develop?

The medical examiner said, "David, she may have had very finely tuned hearing and sense of smell. She might even have had some poor vision and it's possible that the dehydration did finish it off. I don't know. I'm looking at a corpse. I can only tell you what I'm looking at. I wasn't in the room with you, and I wish I was, because then I'd have a whole different perspective on what I'm looking at."

All that the autopsy can state for certain is that Terri was cortically blind *at the moment of her death.*

Regarding the damage to Terri's brain, Dr. Thogmartin said she was brain-injured, not brain-dead. Many fail to understand that absolutely critical distinction. He described the damage as "irreversible" and concluded "no amount of therapy or treatment would have regenerated the massive loss of neurons." That is not, however, the same thing as saying Terri didn't have any ability to think, hear, or communicate. Or that her capacity to function could not have been maximized by therapy, particularly if she was in a minimally conscious rather than a vegetative state. According to one neurologist I consulted, patients with strokes who also have irreversible brain damage and irreplaceable loss of neurons may still make great strides in functional improvement. Functional assessment is not possible on the basis of pathological specimens, as Dr. Thogmartin himself pointed out in the autopsy report.

Consider this.

The autopsy revealed most of the damage occurred in the area toward the back of Terri's brain where the body's motor skills are controlled. The front of the brain is where higher-level thinking is processed. One neurologist told me this disconnection of higher processing centers from motor expression might make it possible that Terri could not express her thoughts and feelings consistently. At the very least that dynamic should give us pause before racing to conclusions about Terri's mental capacity.

Several other key aspects in the autopsy report were largely overlooked by the press: Dr. Thogmartin could not confirm the notion that Terri had an eating disorder (the basis of Michael's multimillion dollar malpractice lawsuit against Terri's doctors). He ruled out as well the suggestion that a heart attack was the cause for her initial injury in 1990.

In short, he had no medical evidence pointing to what deprived Terri's brain of oxygen for several minutes. In that sense, the IME's report created as many questions as it may have answered. The Schindlers still do not have an answer to what led to the collapse of their otherwise healthy twenty-six-year-old daughter.

Elsewhere, the report stated that Terri was unable to swallow sufficient amounts of food and water without aspiration. Remember, Terri had been denied therapy by Michael for twelve years; muscles will atrophy when they're not used. We'll never know whether or not she could have improved her ability to swallow with therapy. Many therapists would have liked the opportunity to try. The autopsy further confirmed that Terri wasn't terminal and wasn't dying. Terri had a very strong heart. Indeed, Dr. Thogmartin estimated that she could have lived for at least another ten years.

Now, was Terri severely brain-injured?

Absolutely.

While the IME focused on Terri's disability and physical condition, let me remind you that we never argued Terri wasn't disabled. Bob and Mary were under no delusions about Terri's potential. They didn't expect that she would one day jump around or sing in the Sunday choir. Throughout the ordeal, the family's position was that *the degree of a disability is NOT grounds to end life*—especially in the absence of a written advance directive.

Whether you agree or disagree with the issues I've raised about the

IME report, there's a basic moral question before us:

> *Will Americans now accept as routine the practice of starvation and dehydration for the disabled, the blind, and any others whom a court might decide shouldn't be allowed to live?*

Let's be careful here.

While the nation's editorial pages may have led us to the tempting conclusion that Judge Greer actually did Terri a favor when he ordered her to die, there's much more to the story. When the courts consign innocent lives to death by dehydration and starvation against the wishes of loved ones without objective and current medical investigations documenting the absence of consciousness, there will be far-reaching negative consequences for the weak, helpless, voiceless members of society.

TRIAL BY MEDIA

Terri's court case had been decided in two arenas: inside the courthouse, and before the court of public opinion. Clearly, the public's opinion was frequently shaped by a media that either got the story wrong or didn't push hard enough to get the story right. In other words, the press allowed misinformation to be presented as fact. This pattern was especially evident in the wake of the autopsy findings.

Almost universally, the media's reaction had been to vindicate Michael and vilify the Schindlers. For instance, on June 16, 2005, the *New York Post* headline proclaimed, "Terri had no hope—Autopsy supports her husband." On the same day and in a scathing editorial, the editors of the *New York Times* blasted those who fought for Terri's life and opined that the autopsy results "should embarrass all the opportunistic politicians and agenda-driven agitators who meddled in Terri Schiavo's right-to-die case."[2]

Bob and Mary Schindler were "agenda-driven agitators"?

The *New York Times* editors reported that "the medical investigation disproved paranoid theories that Michael Schiavo had injured his wife." They claimed that the report "found no evidence of neglect, abuse, strangulation or other trauma."

No surprise there.

An autopsy is incapable of demonstrating whether Terri experienced "neglect" during her lifetime. But it is a matter of record, as I've said elsewhere, that Terri was isolated and warehoused at a hospice, cut off from human companionship. Unlike the open-door policy that other hospice patients enjoy, she wasn't permitted out of her room. All therapy had been denied since the early 1990s. She couldn't attend her own birthday party.

I'd say that qualifies as neglect.

As for some of the media's haste to absolve Michael from any possible responsibility for Terri's collapse—specifically the so-called "paranoid" theory of strangulation—again, the editors of this prominent newspaper overlooked what the medical examiner actually said in his report:

> Autopsy examination of her neck structures 15 years after her initial collapse did not detect any signs of remote trauma, but, *with such a delay, the exam was unlikely to show any residual neck findings.* (emphasis added)

Put another way, Dr. Thogmartin could not conclusively resolve the issue of strangulation. Too much time had passed. If anything, the autopsy opened the door to more questions about what happened that night now that we know Terri didn't have a heart attack nor did she suffer from bulimia, as was repeatedly asserted.

The inability of the autopsy to answer other key questions points to its limitations. Autopsies can only reveal structural features at the time of death. An autopsy could certainly not make a fine distinction between a minimally conscious and a persistent vegetative state—and Dr. Thogmartin did not claim to have done so. That determination could only have been made on a living human being.

TALKING HEADS

Television coverage of the IME report was equally marred by bias. Case in point: With a touch of his signature smugness, Keith Olbermann proclaimed that Michael Schiavo was "vindicated today by the medical examiner in Pinellas County, Florida, and a neuropathologist brought in to consult on that autopsy. And if you do not believe those doctors, you have to be willing to believe that they would be willing to lose their licenses and jobs if they were proved to be incorrect."

Tossing a jab at the Schindlers, he quipped, "Terri Schiavo's parents apparently believe something like that."[3]

Olbermann then introduced Jay Wolfson, Terri's former court-appointed guardian *ad litem* in 2003. While I'm sure Mr. Wolfson meant well, his comments were often far from objective—or even factually accurate. His mixture of personal editorial and misstatements went unchallenged by Olbermann.

For example, Mr. Wolfson asserted, "What this report does is it helps us, I think, say we've learned as much as we can learn. We've learned as much about this tragic case, clinically, medically, scientifically, and legally, and it closes the door."

It closes the door? Really?

Let me direct you to the concluding statement by the medical examiner on page nine of the autopsy report. Dr. Thogmartin wrote:

> It is the policy of this office that no case is ever closed and that all determinations are to be reconsidered upon receipt of credible new information. In addition to fading memories, the 15-year survival of Mrs. Schiavo after her collapse resulted in the creation of a voluminous number of documents many of which were lost or discarded over the years. Receipt of additional information that clarifies outstanding issues may or shall cause an amendment of her cause and manner of death.

Clearly, the door has been left wide open. Wolfson went on to misstate:

This autopsy did not have to be performed. Michael agreed to have it performed. . . . By allowing it to be done, I think Michael has helped all of us to put some closure on this.

Perhaps Mr. Wolfson was parroting Michael's attorney, George Felos. In a hastily organized press briefing the day before Terri died, Mr. Felos claimed that Michael had requested an autopsy because "he believes it's important to have the public know the full and massive extent of the damage to Mrs. Schiavo's brain."[4]

But Bill Pellan, the director of investigations for the medical examiner's office, dismissed this as grandstanding. Pellan said, "We have determined to be involved because of the statutes . . . not because Michael Schiavo wants us involved."[5] He was referring to Florida Statute 406.11, which requires an autopsy in the case of cremation or if someone dies in an "unusual circumstance." Terri's death most certainly fit that classification.

Let me ask you something.

If Michael wanted the public to know "the full and massive" damage of his wife's brain, why wait until she was dead? He could have more accurately determined this information while she was alive through modern functional brain studies. The Schindlers had repeatedly requested that Terri be reexamined in 2005 before the court's order was carried out. Terri had not been examined since 2002. Functional MRIs, SPECT imaging scans, and other evaluations, neurologists tell me, could have provided more objective information to confirm Terri's awareness of external stimuli. Furthermore, it's confusing how, on one hand, Michael denied Terri visitors, trips to the mall, or appearances in court supposedly because he was trying to protect her privacy. But suddenly he wanted "the public" to know how damaged she was after her death.

And the press went along for the ride.

In my view, what the IME reported doesn't erase the moral shame of what happened. The quality of a person's life and the hearsay testimony of a spouse—who has moved on to another committed relationship—regarding end-of-life medical treatment wishes should never again become the basis for which life can be ended. Ever.

CHAPTER NINETEEN

THE $64,000 QUESTION

Why did Florida put Terri Schiavo to death? Because that
was the demand of a husband who refused to divorce her and
denied her medical care, while he lived with another woman.
Michael Schiavo is the ACLU poster boy for family values.
    —PATRICK J. BUCHANAN[1]

At the outset I mentioned the Schindlers' case hinged upon two simple legal questions:

What was Terri's medical condition?

What were Terri's wishes about ending her life in the case of a medical tragedy?

As to the first question, the court ruled Terri was in a persistent vegetative state (PVS); regarding the second question, Florida law allowed the court to rely upon hearsay evidence to conclude Terri would want to suffer a horrific death rather than live as a disabled person who was loved and cared for by her family. As we saw earlier, Terri left no written instructions expressing her own wishes.

Understandably, when the independent medical examiner, Dr. Thogmartin, filed his autopsy findings, the $64,000 question on everybody's mind was this: Had Terri been in a persistent vegetative state as the court had ruled? Could she feel pain? Could she think? Did Terri really recognize her mother and cry when Mary left the room? Or was Judge Greer right when he insisted that "all of the credible medical evidence this court has received over the last five years"[2] pointed to her being cognitively unresponsive?

Dr. Thogmartin began by making it clear that "PVS is a clinical diagnosis arrived at through physical examination of *living patients*" (emphasis added). Terri was dead. How, then, could Dr. Thogmartin make a definitive postmortem determination as to whether or not Terri was in PVS? He couldn't . . . and didn't.

You might want to read that again.

The IME did *not* declare Terri to be PVS.

About as close as he got was to rely upon the findings of consulting neuropathologist, Dr. Stephen J. Nelson. Let's not forget that Dr. Nelson never saw Terri when she was alive either. Like Dr. Thogmartin, he didn't have the benefit of looking at a "living patient." He only had a severely dehydrated body and brain to work with.

In Dr. Nelson's view, "There's nothing in her autopsy report . . . that is inconsistent with persistent vegetative state."[3] Which is, frankly, like saying, "Maybe she was, but it's impossible to determine that by an autopsy." He also didn't rule out the possibility that Terri might have been in a minimally conscious state (MCS) instead of in PVS. You see, there are no reliable studies on what the PVS brain of a corpse looks like when compared with that of a deceased MCS brain.

I was told by one neurologist that the neuropathological features of MCS are not even known as yet. It is, therefore, impossible to differentiate between a brain that supports minimal consciousness from one that does not through an autopsy. In fact, I am told, the same neurological indications might support different levels of consiousness. Dr. Nelson never claimed to compare Terri's brain with the brain of a deceased MCS patient. The news media, however, eager to justify Terri's death, did not consult knowledgeable neurologists about these subtleties.

Here's my point.

Although it was widely reported that the pathological findings were consistent with PVS, the news media did not report the equally plausible conclusion that the findings could have been equally consistent with MCS—a condition from which patients have improved.

Nevertheless, George Felos was quick to put the best spin on the IME's findings. With the IME report in hand, Mr. Felos trumpeted the news that "in the words of the medical examiners, the results are very consistent with a persistent vegetative state."[4] Mr. Felos got as much mileage as possible out of this nonconclusion in order to lead the public down the road toward a belief that Terri was indeed PVS. I'm not surprised that Mr. Felos placed his spin on the IME's findings. According to his view, Terri had as much life as a "houseplant"—a term he had previously used to characterize Terri.

Here's what's troubling.

The medical examiner was not in any position to confirm or deny whether Terri was in PVS because he never examined her as a *living patient*. PVS is a clinical diagnosis that must be made on a living patient, not a diagnosis that can be based on autopsy findings.

Nevertheless, the media dutifully reported the PVS verdict with little regard for these facts.

CHAPTER TWENTY

A LIFE WORTH LIVING

By 2040, it may be that only a rump of hard-core, know-nothing religious fundamentalists will defend the view that every human life, from conception to death, is sacrosanct.

—PETER SINGER, PRINCETON UNIVERSITY PROFESSOR[1]

Meet Clinton McCurdy.

At age thirteen, Clinton doesn't speak. He can't play ball or ride bicycles with his friends. He can't walk. He can't go to school. He can't dress or feed himself. For the last eleven years, Clinton has been confined to his bed or his wheelchair. You see, when Clinton was twenty-three months old, he fell into a swimming pool and drowned. He was underwater for approximately seven to ten minutes before being pulled out. CPR was performed on him immediately and his heart began to beat again. Being deprived of oxygen for several minutes caused Clinton to suffer severe brain damage, much like Terri Schiavo.

His parents, Tim and Betty McCurdy, brought Clinton with them to hear me speak in Hammond, Indiana. After I had finished my comments, they pushed him in his wheelchair to the lobby of the auditorium to meet me. As we visited, I learned about his injury and the details of his care. I was struck by the similarities to Terri: He was not hooked up to machines nor was he in a coma. All he needed was help with food and water, something that, even in Florida before the new end-of-life legislation was passed in the late 1990s, had always been considered ordinary care, not life support. His parents showed me how Clinton was fed through a small feeding tube inserted under his shirt.

There was one primary difference, however.

I could tell that young Clinton was far less responsive than Terri. For her part, Terri smiled, kissed her parents, cried, and could purposefully interact and respond to external stimuli. But as Tim and Betty shared their story, Clinton didn't respond verbally, nor did he pay any attention at all to our conversation—at least not outwardly. Not wanting to be rude, I bent down to speak with him. As I started to engage him, Betty gently placed a hand on my arm and said, "David, don't worry. He doesn't even know who *we* are."

After allowing her comment to sink in, I told them that they were remarkable parents for loving their boy and for not giving up on him. I asked them, "Has it been tough?" Betty said, "Sure. He has to wear a diaper and we have to bathe and dress him. But Clinton still gives us joy. He may not communicate, but we're still his parents and he's still a part of our family."

His father, Tim, added, "Yes, it's been very difficult, but we made a decision to love and care for Clinton and we will stick by that decision." At that point Tim said something that shocked me. He said, "David, we made the same decision that Michael Schiavo made." For a moment, I thought Tim was confused. I thought he meant to say that they had made the same decision as Bob and Mary Schindler. After all, it was the Schindlers who wanted to save Terri's life while Michael was working to end it.

"No," Tim assured me, "we made the same decision Michael Schiavo did—at first." When I asked what he meant by that, he said, "The night our son was rushed to the hospital as a twenty-three-month-old, we were told that Clinton had suffered a traumatic brain injury. The doctor informed us, 'I think he's going to be severely injured; I'm sorry, he's too far gone. Do you want us to try to save him?'"

I had a hunch where Tim was going with this.

Tim said, "Standing in that emergency room, my wife and I made the same decision that Michael Schiavo made the morning Terri was taken to the hospital. We told the doctors, 'We realize Clinton might not be as healthy as he was. But please do everything you can to save our little boy'—just as Michael asked the doctors to do everything they could to save Terri in February of 1990. That's a decision you have to live with. Once you make a decision to save a life, you're committed."

As the McCurdys shared their story, I remembered reading how Michael stayed by his wife's side for days on end after her brain injury occurred. Without question, he worked hard alongside Mary Schindler to care for Terri. This teamwork went on for the first couple of years. By all accounts Michael was a diligent husband and a faithful caretaker who made sure that Terri was given proper treatment. He even sought rehabilitation therapy in the early days.

Unfortunately, Michael's model behavior ended. I don't pretend to know Michael's heart. What is clear is that he wasn't happy with how his choice turned out; his actions demonstrated that he didn't want to live with the consequences of his initial decision to save Terri's life.

BUYER'S REMORSE

Initially, after learning of her prognosis, Michael could have said, "You know what? Terri's too far gone. Let her go." But he didn't. Michael did the right thing by giving a mandate to the doctors to try to save her. Frankly, I'd be the first in line to congratulate him. He saved Terri's life. She would have died that day in 1990 if Michael, as her husband and guardian, hadn't made the initial decision to do whatever was necessary to keep her alive.

However, I also believe that when you make the choice to save somebody's life, you have a continuing duty to that person. That's where Michael's story deviates from the McCurdys' journey. Michael changed his mind and reversed his decision when he decided he wasn't happy with Terri's "quality of life." To this day, Michael is fond of saying, "I kept my promise" to Terri. In fact, he had that phrase etched on her cemetery headstone.

As for the notion that he kept his promise, I beg to differ. He promised the Schindlers and a jury in a court of law that he intended to care for Terri for the rest of his life. He also said that he had promised Terri on their wedding day before God and man to remain faithful to her "in sickness and in health."

Imagine if the McCurdys had, after five years of unproductive therapy, said, "Clinton is really much more handicapped than we expected. This is a lot harder than we ever anticipated. It's costing us time and money that we can't afford. Let's just starve him to death." Unthinkable, right?

What kind of society would permit such a thing?

After hearing me speak, however, the McCurdys began to wonder whether they were now living in an America that might someday decide to take Clinton away from them and deny them the privilege of caring for him. They were worried that a judge, a social worker, a doctor, or an insurance provider somewhere might decide that Clinton didn't have a quality of life worth the time and resources to maintain. That's a legitimate concern.

Not to be an alarmist, but America is already turning down the road where human life is disposable. It happened openly for the first time in March 2005, when Terri died horrifically before the eyes of all the world, but it is estimated that several thousand Floridians died secretly in the same manner before Terri's public court-ordered death.

This is a roadway that has been traveled before.

Remember what happened under the Third Reich?

LIFE ON A SLIPPERY SLOPE

A troubling doctrine is being advanced in the medical community today. It argues that because Terri, Clinton, and people like them are unable to work and unable to be productive, they're a "burden to society," rather like Hitler's "useless eaters"—a label he used to justify the deaths of the disabled as well as the Jews. The Associated Press cited a new report that found that more than two hundred thousand "physically-deficient" people were eliminated in Nazi Germany simply because of their disabilities.[2]

You might be thinking, *Whoa! Time-out, David. We're nowhere near Hitler's day. We're a reasonable, freedom-loving people who care for everyone.* Really? You might want to press your ear a little closer to the pavement. Many people are now making the decision for others to die, as Michael did. And there's a growing trend in the halls of medicine to disconnect those whose lives appear to have no meaningful place in society.

Today, "progressive thinkers" are informing us that disabled persons "tax the medical system" by draining health insurance dollars for their constant care. We're told these people have no "quality of life" worth preserving, that any medical care would be futile for them. As the seeds of these pro-death ideas take root, the elderly as well as those suffering from dementia, epilepsy, Down syndrome, Alzheimer's, or Parkinson's disease are summarily lumped into the "useless eaters" pot.

Using the logic this school of thought produces, the most expedient solution is to "let nature take its course" (passive euthanasia) by withholding futile medical care and, as in Terri's case, even food and water. The other option frequently advocated is to actively advance a person's death (labeled benignly "terminal sedation" or "assisted suicide").

Is that difficult to believe?

Let's learn from what happened to Terri.

The only "medical treatment" Terri required to stay alive was assistance at mealtime. Even newborn infants cannot feed themselves. Which begs the question: If food and water are now considered "medical treatment," what prevents a doctor from "terminating" a disabled or unwanted baby *after* birth by withholding nutrition? If doctors can purposely starve a woman in Tampa who can't feed herself, why not a baby boy in Boston who is also dependent on someone else to bring him a bottle?

You might not know this, but a number of leading "ethics" professors at America's leading universities are already teaching students that infanticide—the killing of an already born infant—*is* morally acceptable, especially when the infant is debilitated. Take, for example, professor, ethicist, and self-proclaimed atheist Peter Singer at Princeton University's Center for Human Values.

Considered the grandfather of the animal rights protection movement, Singer gives his students some rather inhumane lectures about humanity. Why? Because Dr. Singer believes that there is nothing ethically wrong with "terminating" one-year-old physically or mentally disabled children. You might want to read that again. Mr. Singer is on record saying:

> If you have a being that is not sentient, that is not even aware, then the killing of that being is not something that is wrong in and of itself. I think that a chimpanzee certainly has greater self-awareness than a newborn.[3]

Why stop with infanticide? Marvin Olasky of *World* magazine asked Singer about those who might elect to raise children just to harvest their organs. The exchange revealed something most disturbing about the direction of attitudes toward the preciousness of life. Here's the key part of that interview:

OLASKY: What about parents conceiving and giving birth to a child specifically to kill him, take his organs, and transplant them into their ill older children?

SINGER: It's difficult to warm to parents who can take such a detached view, [but] they're not doing something really wrong in itself.

OLASKY: Is there anything wrong with a society in which children are bred for spare parts on a massive scale?

SINGER: No.[4]

Peter Singer hasn't just stepped onto the slippery slope of moral relativism—he's grabbed his sled and pushed off with gusto. Human life, according to this Princeton professor, isn't necessarily sacred. That's a quaint notion held by "know-nothing religious fundamentalists." In his view, it's possible for animal life to be superior to human life. Writing in the July 1983 edition of *Pediatrics*, Singer said:

> If we compare a severely defective human infant with a non-human animal, a dog, a pig, for example, we will often find the nonhuman to have superior capacities, both actual and potential, for rationality, self-consciousness, communication, and anything else that can plausibly be considered morally significant. Only the fact that the defective infant is a member of the species homo sapiens, leads it to be treated differently from the dog or pig.[5]

But wait, there's more.

In Singer's book *Practical Ethics* he states, "The fact that a being is a human being, in the sense of a member of the species homo sapiens, *is not relevant to the wrongness of killing it*"[6] (emphasis added). How can he arrive at such a statement?

By doing what the courts did in the case of Terri Schiavo: They removed God and any moral considerations from their judgment. Singer makes his hostility toward the Judeo-Christian view of life perfectly clear. He writes: "We can no longer base our ethics on the idea that human beings are a special form of creation, made in the image of God, singled out from all other animals, and alone possessing an immortal soul."[7]

Rather than being fired from Princeton, a school originally founded to promote the gospel of Jesus Christ, for advocating such an outrageous, irresponsible, and pro-infanticide dogma, Professor Singer is considered a visionary in the field of bioethics and throughout academia. Not everyone on the left side of the political spectrum is happy about Singer's message, however. Some have awakened and realized the frightening reality that having a disability may be deadly.

Take Eleanor Smith.

This self-described "liberal agnostic" has been confined to a wheelchair due to childhood polio. In the wake of Terri Schiavo's court-ordered death—a death sentence supported by the American Civil Liberties Union—Smith says, "At this point I would rather have a right-wing Christian decide my fate than an ACLU member."[8] Why? Because she knows that most people of faith view *all* of life as worth living—not just the lives of those ones who are pretty, healthy, or productive. Maybe she also knows that the line between the "right to die" and the "duty to die" is razor thin.

A HIGHER PURPOSE

I could tell that the McCurdys' commitment to their son Clinton didn't come easy for them. As we were about to part company, Betty searched my eyes. She said, "You know, David, it's really hard to have a child that is *this* disabled. As a mother, you want your child to recognize you, to appreciate you, and to communicate with you."

As a father of four children, I understood where she was coming from. What amazed me was where she was going with her insight.

"Whenever I start to feel bad for myself," she said, "I realize everything I'm upset about has to do with things *I* want for *me*. And in those moments, I have to turn my thinking around and say, 'God, you've given me this child. When you gave him to me, he was a healthy boy. You've allowed this disability into his life. I've got to accept the fact that I'm not going to get what I want. He won't recognize me or appreciate me—that's what I want, but not what you've given to me. Help me to embrace what you've given me.'"

The contrast between her unconditional love and the utilitarian worldview espoused by Peter Singer couldn't be more striking.

Tim and Betty McCurdy's silent sacrifice of love is an acknowledgment that life isn't always about getting what we want. It's about accepting what God brings our way. In that respect, Michael Schiavo didn't get what he wanted; he got what God allowed into his life. Rather than accept Terri's disability as a sovereign act of God, he chose to believe that Terri wanted what he wanted for her—namely, to die.

Sadly, Clinton passed away on February 4, 2006. He is survived by his loving parents, Tim and Betty, and his three brothers. His funeral was preached at the First Baptist Church of Hammond, Indiana, just three months after I met him there.

Clinton, you touched my life, and I thank you for that. And thank you, Betty and Tim, for putting Clinton's needs above your own and showing us a wonderful example of unconditional love.

––––––––

The question remains: How might you and I handle a life-and-death decision should God place a severely disabled spouse, daughter, son, or parent into our lives? Would we, like the McCurdys or the Schindlers, and at no benefit to ourselves, help care for, appreciate, and love someone who has little or nothing to give back? If so, to paraphrase Scripture, when you've done this for the least of these, you've done it for God himself.

Let me ask you a question. What if the key that unlocks the door to personal fulfillment in your life just happened to be in giving unconditional love to what the Bible calls "the least of these"?

We have to be very careful when we say disabled people can't contribute to society. Think about this: Terri touched the world because her parents were willing to fight for her life. If they hadn't, if they had said, "Oh well, these bad things happen, we'll just let her go," we never would have heard of Terri. Because of their commitment, Terri Schiavo had a far greater impact than many people who *can* speak or walk.

She touched the nation and the world with her life.

I'd say that's a life worth living.

CHAPTER TWENTY-ONE

EVERY DAY'S A GIFT

The fatalistic attitude toward treating brain disease is very prevalent—and untrue. All too often, people give up. We've all been humbled by the brain's ability to recover.
—Dr. Owen B. Samuels, Chief of Neurointensive Care, Emory University[1]

When Judge George Greer ordered the suspension of Terri's nutrition and hydration on November 22, 2002, he was preoccupied with the quality of Terri's life. He wrote, "The real issue in this case, however, deals with treatment options for Terry [*sic*] Schiavo and whether or not they will have any positive affect [*sic*] so as to 'significantly improve her quality of life.'" He concluded that Terri's chance of improving was slim to none, and therefore, without even offering a window of opportunity to try therapy, she should die.

I wish Judge Greer had invited any one of the following seven living miracles to the witness stand before taking such a dim view of Terri's chances for improvement. Each has emerged from a comatose or persistent vegetative state, often continuing to live amazing lives. Come to think of it, arranging an appearance would have been easy to accomplish. After all, one of these formerly comatose patients attended several days of Terri's trial in Judge Greer's own courtroom.

Meet Brooke Becker of Clearwater, Florida, who lived near to where Terri's tragedy unfolded.

At age twenty, Brooke and her boyfriend were driving home from her summer job when a truck slammed into her car door. Rescue teams struggled for forty-five minutes to cut her free from the mangled vehicle. Precious minutes were lost at a time when life and death were measured in seconds. A helicopter rushed Brooke to the Bayfront Medical Center, where trauma specialists assessed her condition.

In short, Brooke suffered from a ruptured spleen, a fractured liver, a pelvis that had been crushed, a broken collarbone, and a jaw broken in two places. Two collapsed lungs complicated her condition—and that wasn't even the worse part of her injuries. She experienced such traumatic brain damage, she fell into a deep coma. Even though Brooke was given no chance of survival—let alone a quality of life on par with Terri's disabled condition—her doctors performed a seven-hour emergency surgery that required more than thirty pints of blood supplements.

Her parents waited and prayed.

Four months after remaining in a comatose state, fed through a feeding tube, the miraculous occurred: Brooke began to improve. Six months after the near-death accident, in spite of the fact that the doctors had no hope for her survival, Brooke was sent home partially paralyzed yet alert. She remained on a feeding tube for two years while receiving physical therapy.

Today she lives with her parents. Although requiring the aid of a wheelchair, Brooke attends and participates at Calvary Baptist Church with her family. And though her eyesight was damaged by the accident and she cannot speak without the help of a computerized voice synthesizer, Brooke has learned to express herself through art. In fact, her paintings are so stunning, they're frequently sold by commission.

From comatose to competent artist—that's remarkable.

I first met Brooke during a hearing before Judge Greer. I found her smile infectious. Here was a formerly healthy, young college woman whose life had been forever impaired in an instant, yet who felt compelled to support Terri by coming to court. Why? She knew from personal experience what beating the odds was all about. She was living proof. Thankful that her family and her doctors had not given up on her, Brooke hoped her story would encourage the Schindlers in their battle to give Terri the same chance at a new beginning.

I know her presence inspired me.

COMATOSE IN CALIFORNIA

In 1996 twenty-one-year-old Theresa de Vera was a junior at Loyola Marymount University, where she was actively involved in campus life. Volleyball, outdoor water sports, socializing with friends—all of that would change in a split second. Theresa was riding with her mother, Rudy, on the freeway when she passed out from a severe asthmatic attack. By the time Rudy reached Glendale Adventist Hospital, Theresa was blue, unresponsive, and not breathing.

She was slumped over in the backseat, dead.

The nursing staff rushed Theresa inside, where they confirmed she wasn't breathing, she had no pulse, and she had no blood pressure. According to the emergency personnel who first assessed her condition, Theresa was clinically dead, having suffered cardiopulmonary arrest. After aggressive measures to resuscitate her, Theresa jerked back to life and then, thirty minutes later, went into a seizure. She settled into a deep coma and continued on a respirator for two weeks with no change in her condition.

At that point her doctors worked to persuade the family to give up hope and harvest Theresa's organs while they were still viable. A shouting match erupted in the hospital; the family argued for her life while the doctors maintained she was in a persistent vegetative state. They assured the family there was nothing more to be done.

Theresa was gone.

For four months Theresa remained in a deep coma.

She didn't smile. She didn't laugh.

She didn't move. She didn't cry.

She exhibited none of these signs of life that Terri routinely displayed.

As a spokeswoman from the hospital later reported, "Her condition was so severe and her chance of recovery so small—virtually zero—that any recovery would be like Karen Ann Quinlan, really never waking up again. They did recommend that the family terminate treatment."

That would have been a big mistake. Why? With her family and her church praying, Theresa defied the prognosis.

She awakened.

Not only that, she regained her upper body mobility, her speech, and the ability to feed herself. As Theresa is now fond of saying to others with disabilities, "Never allow your disability to become your inability." Those are not empty words. With persistence and hard work, Theresa returned to Loyola Marymount University and graduated with the class of 2004.

Theresa's comeback was so dramatic, she and her family appeared on *Oprah*. One of Theresa's attending physicians sat in the front row of the audience. After confirming the details of her trauma, the clearly stunned doctor said, "I have to tell you, [her condition is] usually associated with really, really severe brain damage. I've never seen anybody come back from something like that. What has happened here defies medical logic. . . . It's a miracle."

His assessment echoed that of the hospital spokeswoman, who said, "This is such an unusual outcome that we call it a miracle because we can't explain it medically. There is no reason this child should have woken up."[2] Of course, while God doesn't always heal in such dramatic ways, He is fully able to do the impossible—medically or otherwise. That's the message of Jeremiah 32:27, "Behold, I am the Lord, the God of all flesh: is there any thing too hard for Me?"

On March 19, 2005, when news reached Theresa that Terri's feeding tube had been removed, she knew what she needed to do. She and her mother packed her wheelchair and took the red-eye flight from California to join Terri's vigil outside the hospice, where she had an opportunity to meet and share her journey of healing and restoration with Bob and Mary Schindler.

TRIAL BY FIRE

The year was 1995. Bill Clinton was in the White House. The Atlanta Braves won their first World Series in almost thirty years. And a jury took less than four hours to acquit O. J. Simpson for a double murder charge. While not national news at the time, that was also the year when firefighter Donald Herbert sustained severe brain damage.

Four days after Christmas, an early morning blaze ravaged a two-story apartment building in the snow-covered town of Buffalo, New York. Donald, a thirty-four-year-old rescue squad veteran, cited numerous times for bravery, strapped on his breathing mask and attacked the flames in hopes of finding any survivors. This time, however, the building fought back, dropping its roof on the rescue effort. Trapped in the attic by fiery debris, knocked unconscious by falling timbers, and deprived of oxygen for six minutes, Donald slipped into a coma for several months. He was later diagnosed as being in a persistent vegetative state.[3]

Unable to feed himself, walk, or talk, Donald was restricted to his bed or a wheelchair. Buffalo firefighters banded together to support his family with chores and financial support. And, they took turns visiting their unresponsive colleague for years on end. While those efforts appeared to be fruitless, his wife, family, and friends continued to lavish love on him.

For the better part of ten years, Donald remained speechless and noncommunicative and resided in a nursing care facility. His wife, Linda, however, was the one who became speechless after the nursing staff called one day to inform her that Donald suddenly "woke up." His first words were, "I want to talk to my wife."[4] Linda and his four sons rushed to the nursing home and, for a marathon fourteen hours of hugs and conversation, got reacquainted. After all, Donald's youngest son Nicholas, thirteen, was a toddler at the time of the accident.

Donald Herbert spent nearly a year reconnecting with his family. And though the initial fourteen hours with his family were his most lucid, he was able to communicate with them and get reacquainted. Sadly, he passed away in February 2006 after a battle with pneumonia. Was his life worth saving? Just ask his wife and children, who had the precious gift of spending nearly a full year with their husband and dad.

When asked to comment about Donald Herbert's amazing recovery by WebMD, neurologist Nancy Childs, who works at the Texas Neuro-Rehab Center in Austin, Texas, admitted that scientists know "practically nothing" about the inner processes of the human brain in an injury case like this. She said, "Some of the basic science and basic questions about what happens with the neurophysiology of the brain as patients move through levels of consciousness are just beginning to be explored."[5] In other words, even highly specialized scientists and neurologists are still learning about the way the brain operates.

Just ask Donald Herbert's family, after his long-dormant tongue was loosened after ten years of nonuse.

Or ask Tracy Gaskill.

On September 3, 2002, Tracy's pickup truck rolled over on a Kansas highway causing extreme trauma to her head and neck. Taken by helicopter to the emergency room at a Wichita hospital, she was placed on a ventilator. The injuries to her brain were so severe, doctors informed the family that she'd be lucky to survive the night. They were wrong. Tracy pulled through, and though semicomatose and unable to speak or feed herself in the years following, she began to heal.

About two and a half years after suffering brain damage, the non-communicative Tracy stunned her doctors and family by suddenly speaking. Her doctor, David Schmeidler, said, "I have never seen this happen in my career. I've read about it happening, the severely brain damaged recovering suddenly, but never seen it until now."[6]

Dr. Schmeidler didn't miss the parallel to Terri Schiavo's case. He said Tracy "is actually able to speak and to speak coherently. In light of all this stuff on Terri Schiavo, it makes you pause and think. For three years or so, [Tracy] was fed through a tube, then she swallowed a little bit and now she speaks."[7] In fact, she's rediscovered the pleasure of strawberry shakes from Sonic.

Tracy's doctor believes four things contributed to her unexplainable return from death's door: constant medical care, prayer, speech therapy, and the daily visits from her grandparents. Tracy's mother had died prior to her accident, and her father lived in a different city. But grandparents Don and Stella Gaskill made Tracy their top priority. I can only imagine what would have happened if Terri had been permitted the same level of medical care and speech therapy afforded to Tracy.

THE PHONE'S FOR YOU

Just after midnight on September 21, 1984, Sarah Scantlin, then eighteen, was crossing the street with friends when she was mowed down by a hit-and-run drunk driver. Her father, Jim Scantlin, reflected upon his first visit to see Sarah that fateful night: "I take one look in there and it's just gruesome. She is horribly mangled, especially in the head because she was hit by a teenager, slung over in the path of another car—and that's the one that really got her, right in the head. I couldn't handle it."[8]

Unlike Terri Schiavo or Donald Herbert, Sarah's oxygen supply wasn't cut off. She could breathe on her own, but that was about the extent of the good news. She was little more than a breathing corpse. Her brain damage was severe and extensive, caused by the impact of two cars and the pavement onto which she fell. Sarah's mother, Betsy, recalled the doctor's ominous verdict in the emergency ward:

"Sarah's not going to wake up tonight."[9]

For reasons nobody could explain, her doctor was wrong. She survived. Six weeks later, this brain-injured college freshman remained motionless and in a coma, fed by a feeding tube. Gradually she progressed, but only to a semicomatose, minimally conscious state where she remained locked out from the rest of the world. Her family, friends, and the nursing staff where she lived never saw Sarah attempt to speak.

For twenty years . . . not one peep.

On February 4, 2005, Jim Scantlin was at his office when his wife arrived and quickly directed him to a conference call from the nursing home. "Someone wants to talk to you," Betsy said, anxiously pointing to the speakerphone. Jim was in for the shock of his life when five precious words spoken by his daughter filled the room:

"Hi, Dad. I love you."

Sarah's next goal? She wants to relearn how to walk.

Sarah's inexplicable emergence from a cocoonlike trance contained another surprise for neurologists: She knew much more about cultural and world events during her "absence" than they ever could have imagined. Sarah knew lyrics from popular songs and was able to describe the significance of 9/11 among other events.

Her father asked, "Sarah, what's 9/11?"

Sarah answered, "Bad ... Fire ... Airplanes ... Building. Hurt people."[10]

You can imagine the geyser of hope that erupted in the hearts of Bob and Mary Schindler as they watched Sarah's recovery unfold. After all, Sarah started speaking six weeks before Terri was to die.

RECOVERY IN ROME

Stories of unexplainable recoveries are not limited to America. While I was writing this book, thirty-eight-year-old Salvatore Crisafulli of Catania, Sicily, awoke after two years in what Italian doctors called a deep coma. The father of four had been hit by a van in 2003. According to one Italian paper, after the accident his doctors considered Salvatore nothing more than a piece of meat formed in the shape of a person on a bed. They asserted that he was unconscious and wrote him off as being virtually dead.

But on July 15, 2005, Salvatore began to regain consciousness. His first word was "momma." In a rather short period of time and with some effort, Salvatore spoke in complete sentences. He proceeded to tell the press he heard and saw everything: "The doctors said that I wasn't conscious, but I understood everything and I cried in desperation"[11] to be heard.

Pietro Crisafulli, who had defended and helped administer the ongoing care of his brother Salvatore, said, "And to think that some doctors said that it was all useless and that he would be dead in three, four months."[12]

Salvatore's recovery came at a time when Italy's National Bioethics Committee (NBC) was wrestling with the question of whether or not to remove artificial feeding and hydration. Unlike what the Florida legislature permitted American courts to decide in the Schiavo case—namely, to starve a disabled woman to death—the NBC overwhelmingly voted to maintain food and water for unconscious patients, including those in a PVS or coma.

What's more, the NBC authorized the feeding and hydration of patients even when such nutrition wasn't desired or requested. Dr. Claudia Navarini, an Italian bioethics professor, explains why the committee arrived at such a conclusion. Her insights are profound:

> Whenever hope for recovery is really vain, the fundamental and inescapable truth remains that a man's life—no matter how sick or disabled, or how precarious his state is—always has immense value, before which man's dominating will must halt.
>
> In the U.S. the whole debate was reduced to the question whether Terri wanted or did not want to die. But here, the NBC stresses, it is a decision for life or for death. Not even if the patient requests it are we authorized to suspend feeding and hydration, because the intrinsic value of human life also exceeds the value attributed to it by the individual. In other words, we are not the owners of our life.[13]

I couldn't agree more.

Besides, we never know when God will decide to baffle us with yet another example of His healing power, nor do we comprehend the mind-boggling ability of our body to recuperate from an extreme injury. Dr. Mark Ragucci's story is a perfect case in point.

WONDERS NEVER CEASE

At thirty-one, Dr. Mark Ragucci had just begun his medical practice when, on December 3, 2001, he experienced an aneurysm in his aorta. With strokes occurring in both sides of his brain, Dr. Ragucci's heart stopped beating. Twenty-four minutes passed without the oxygen-enriched, life-giving blood flowing to his brain.

Dr. Stephan Mayer at Columbia University's medical center worked aggressively with a team of doctors to spare Dr. Ragucci's life based upon his advance written directives. In spite of their valiant efforts, Dr. Ragucci was given no chance of recovering from the cardiac and circulatory arrest, seizures, and paralysis. Dr. Mayer had to break the news to the family that Dr. Ragucci was not going to recover.

"I had no expectation at all that we could help," Dr. Mayer said. Why? Based upon past experience working with other coma patients similar to Dr. Ragucci, "maybe 5% of such patients could follow commands after one year."[14] And though Dr. Ragucci survived the initial round of urgent care, five weeks later he remained unaware and in a coma with no hope of improvement. His wife and family decided to move him to New York University's Rusk Institute of Rehabilitation Medicine.

As far as Dr. Mayer was concerned, the case was closed.

Medically speaking, he was out of options.

He would never see that patient again.

One year later, Dr. Mayer was working in his office at Columbia's medical center when a visitor knocked on the door. Nothing could prepare him for the arrival of his guest: Dr. Mark Ragucci shook his hand and formally introduced himself. Dr. Mayer vividly recalled the moment. "When he walked in, I almost fell over. It was at that point I realized that we knew absolutely nothing about the recuperative power of the brain."[15]

Upon further reflection, Dr. Mayer said, "Mark's great recovery reflects the brain's innate resilience and ability to recover, which I believe has been vastly underestimated to date. It has been underestimated because we never saw any long-term outcomes, because we have always let them die assuming the outcome would be terrible."[16]

Speaking of "outcomes," here's one for the books. Dr. Ragucci returned to his job as a rehabilitation physician at Bellevue Hospital Center and NYU—the very rehab center that had served him as a patient. Like the six fellow survivors mentioned above, Dr. Ragucci has a firsthand appreciation for the wonder, discovery, healing, joy, and purpose that each day holds.

Did you notice the common threads that weave these stories together?

- patients who suffered from a severe brain injury with the dire prognosis of no recovery
- a family who refused to give up caring for and loving one of their own
- a comatose or PVS patient learning to swallow, eat, and speak once again
- gratefulness for a second chance at life

It is true that these and other similar accounts are not as numerous as we would like. Perhaps this is because, as Dr. Mayer stated, we have let the brain-injured die rather than give them the opportunity to live—or as was the case with Terri, they are refused the rehabilitation therapy that could lead to marked improvement.

Could Terri have joined the ranks of these miraculous comebacks? Her parents believed she could have if given the chance. Now, they'll never know.

If there's a lesson to be learned from these seven stories, it's the reminder that modern medicine hasn't begun to comprehend the complexities and capabilities of the human body. As King David said in Psalm 139:14, we are "fearfully and wonderfully made." What's more, we were created "in the image of God." That is why life is sacred and every life is precious to God.

Indeed, as the placard affixed to the wall just outside the entrance to Woodside Hospice where Terri lived and died proclaims: Every Day's a Gift.

CHAPTER TWENTY-TWO

THE LEAST OF THESE

When a person's wishes are not documented, we should err on the side of life; we should assume that living is preferable over dying . . . the quality of one's life should never be a criteria to put them to death.

—JONI EARECKSON TADA[1]

An interesting by-product of Terri's story has been a national debate between the "quality of life" and the "sanctity of life" viewpoints. Far too often these discussions have generated more heat than light. Having walked through the Schindlers' struggle to save their daughter, and having a personal family example to draw upon myself, I'd like to weigh in personally on that debate for a moment.

My grandmother was a high-energy, piano-playing, vibrant woman until she contracted polio in the early 1950s. Prior to the development and usage of a vaccine in 1954, polio was the AIDS of the day—only it was more contagious. Polio could be passed through the air, in food, or in water. Given the high risk of infection, her eight-year-old son (my dad) and his younger sister were sent away to live with relatives.

Even though my grandfather was jeopardizing his own health by entering his wife's bedroom where she was confined, he was committed to caring for her. Polio took its course, but it didn't take my grandma's life, at least not at first. As the disease spread, she became paralyzed from the waist down and was restricted to a wheelchair, never to walk again.

You can imagine the devastation a disease like polio wreaked on a family's life. Grandma couldn't cook, shop, clean the house, or care for the kids. This once spirited woman who had served her family steadfastly for years now needed help with crutches and wheelchairs in order to function. She needed assistance bathing, getting dressed, eating, using the bathroom, and many other activities most of us take for granted.

Sadly, the church where they had attended discouraged her from coming to services anymore. Keep in mind that she had been the devoted piano player at this small country church. As faithful members, my grandparents had never missed a Sunday in years. But understandably, the church folks thought they might catch the disease. And while vaccinations were starting to become available, the church community felt it was best not to risk becoming contaminated themselves. Why take the chance of infecting others? Overnight, my grandparents became virtual outcasts in the fullest sense of the word.

Fast-forward a number of years.

My grandfather stayed married and stayed faithful to my grandmother despite her disability and the daily risk it posed to his own health. He sacrificially cared for her every day for forty-five years, and they remained best of friends for the rest of her life. After my grandmother died in 1997, my grandfather continued to proudly wear his wedding ring and talked about his girlfriend waiting for him in heaven. In late February 2006, my grandfather joined my grandma in heaven; what a sweet reunion that must have been!

What was it about their fifty-three-year marriage that enabled them to stick together? Many turned their backs on them—their friends, their church, and their little slice of society. What's more, my grandpa was a young man when polio crippled his bride. He had a good job in the meat and cattle business. He could have institutionalized her and then moved on to remarry. But he didn't. Why? Evidently, he understood that his wedding vows meant something to God.

And as someone who embraced the sanctity of life, he didn't say, "What's in this relationship for me?" He resisted the temptation to fret about getting the short end of the stick. Never once did he look for a way to get out of the deal. When he stood at the altar, he made a commitment: "Till death do us part." There was no fine print or exception clause that told him, "As long as you remain young, healthy, attractive, or even pleasant to be around, I'll stay with you."

Because he viewed life as a sacred gift from God, my grandfather's marriage became a picture of unconditional love to the generations that followed in our family. I've often reflected on my grandparents' relationship in light of the debate between the quality and the sanctity of life. Let's look at the differences these perspectives present.

QUALITY OF LIFE

If honest, the quality of life position begins and ends with a consideration of "self." If my grandfather was only concerned about himself above the needs of his disabled wife, she would have died a lonely, neglected woman. Instead, something amazing happened: Their relationship deepened in spite of her illness.

You see, the "quality of life" person makes the mistake of trying to hold on to a "normal" lifestyle. These folks want to experience life pretty much the way they want it to go. If they're able to maintain the status quo, then they'll sign on to care for a disabled spouse or a child. But if the price gets too high, or if dealing with the disabled person becomes too difficult, they're not willing to pay the price. In turn, they miss the blessing that awaits those who are willing to make the sacrifice.

At its core, then, the quality of life perspective is self-oriented: concerned primarily about the price required to maintain a life—a price defined by them as money, time, energy, or inconvenience. In short, a quality of life person wants to know:

What will caring for this person cost me financially?

How much of my time will be involved?

How will this added responsibility affect my level of stress?

Will the government provide aid for me?

Is this whole thing going to fall on my shoulders?

Can I still do the things I enjoy doing?

There's one giant problem here. This line of questioning is not consistent with unconditional love. To be unconditional means to serve another regardless of the price. As my grandfather discovered, there's a reward of unparalleled blessing for those who give of themselves to those who can't give anything back.

Let's go a step further.

If you're a quality of life person and you become disabled, you will also be primarily concerned with yourself. That might sound obvious. Indeed, everyone has a degree of self-interest. What I'm driving at here is that the quality of life position essentially says, I want to live life on my terms. If life isn't going my way or if I can't function the way I used to operate, I'd rather not live. That's the ultimate quality of life statement.

Hold on a moment. If life isn't going your way, who gives you the option to choose to end it? Do you have the right to alter what God may want for you? Is it really your choice to short-circuit the impact you might have on your family, friends, and beyond? What gives you or me the right to shrug and say, "I'm unhappy. I want this to be over."

Furthermore, once the quality of life door is opened, what's to stop a host of rationalizations from being used to end a life? Take the teenage girl who is unhappy about being "dumped" by a boyfriend. What if, in the heat of the moment, she wrongly concludes that their breakup is the end of the world? To her, life is no longer worth living. What then? How about the aspiring high school track star who falls and requires knee replacement surgery? What if he can no longer compete and his dreams of going to the Olympics are dashed?

Or what about the sexually abused?

The children of a divorce?

The businessman who loses a fortune?

The woman who is battered by an abusive husband?

The college student suffering from depression?

The victims of a hurricane who have lost everything?

In case you never thought about it, there are trials and misfortunes in life as devastating, or even far worse, than becoming physically or mentally disabled. What then? Should we become a culture that encourages those who have been dealt a difficult hand to give up on life? No. Nor should we be throwing people away merely because of a difficult physical condition.

Consider Terri.

The quality of life advocate scratches his head and wonders, "How can a bedridden, brain-injured woman who can't feed herself for fifteen years have a purpose?" I'll tell you how: God. God doesn't do anything without a grand design in mind. While we may not understand or immediately see His plan, it's there. I do not believe it's our job to question His purposes. Instead, it's our job to find His purposes in these situations. In Terri's case, God had an incredible mission for her life even aside from the simple joy she brought and shared with her family. As I've commented before, Terri's life and death caused America and the world to wrestle with fundamental life issues.

Consider Joni Eareckson Tada.

At seventeen, a severe diving accident robbed this beautiful young woman of the ability to use her hands or to walk. A quality of life advocate would argue that she no longer had a life worth living. Yet the fact that she was a quadriplegic confined to a wheelchair didn't stop Joni from getting married and traveling to forty-one countries as an advocate for those with disabilities. And not only did she learn to paint with a brush clenched between her teeth, her works of art are now collector's items.

Here's a woman who understood that God gave her life. Her accident cost her and her family incredible heartache. She continues to need intensive therapy. Yet early on Joni decided that it wasn't the quality of life but the sanctity of life that would compel her to find God's purpose in her situation. Because of her commitment to go on despite her disability, Joni has ministered to millions of people through a daily radio program and through family retreats for the disabled.

THE VALUE OF LIFE

Those who hold a "sanctity of life" conviction believe that no price is too high when it comes to caring for the disabled or preserving a life. The sanctity of life person says, in effect, there is no discussion of cost. Much like dining at a five-star restaurant where the menu doesn't list the price, the cost is simply not mentioned. Nor does a sanctity of life person calculate the impact of someone else's hardship on their own life. They understand that caring for a disabled person will require a lot; it will radically readjust all of life. That's a given. But the cost is not the determining factor when dealing with these decisions.

For people of faith, there's a spiritual dimension. They demonstrate the power and compassion and love of God by ignoring the cost (as the Schindlers did), by paying the price (as the Schindlers did), and by not being concerned about what it's going to do to them. While some members of the press and several pundits blasted the Schindlers' motives as being selfish, the exact opposite was true. They paid a huge price in their fight to care for Terri:

It cost them financially: They fought an uphill legal struggle without deep pockets.

It cost them an enormous amount of time: They spent countless hours visiting their daughter and doing whatever was necessary to save her life.

It cost them emotionally: They constantly worried whether or not Terri was being properly cared for by those who were legally in charge of her well-being.

Furthermore, as I observed working alongside Bob and Mary, there is never a discussion of "me" in the sanctity of life equation. Why? Because those who hold this perspective view their life as a living sacrifice; admittedly, that's a countercultural position. The only consideration the sanctity of life person makes is to follow what God says in the Bible. Here, then, are three guiding principles from Scripture:

- God is the giver of all life.
- God is the allower of any disability.
- God and God alone should decide when life ends.

Whenever I share those insights with an audience, a number of folks will say, "Mr. Gibbs, you're 100 percent correct. That's what the Bible teaches and that's probably what I should believe if faced with such a situation. But I'm not that good of a person." Guess what? While I admire them for their honesty, the truth is this: I don't believe anybody is that good of a person.

However, when we by simple faith step forward and say, "I am going to live what I say I believe," at that point God will divinely empower and help us to do what must be done, even when it appears that what is required of us isn't humanly possible. Demonstrating our willingness to line up with His principles and truthfully confessing that we can't do it in our own strength miraculously unlocks His divine provision.

As the saying goes, "Where God guides, God provides." Whenever there is a calling from God, He divinely equips and provides exactly what we need to get the job done.

LEAN ON ME

Before leaving this discussion, there's a subtext to the quality versus sanctity of life debate that's easily missed. Have you noticed how American society seems to place a premium on the "beautiful people"? We aggrandize those who are exceptionally gifted, talented, athletic, wealthy, or attractive. Their picture-perfect faces and Aquafresh smiles dominate the newsstands. We follow their every move with an almost religious devotion.

In sports, for instance, enthusiasts memorize the latest team statistics and player trades and collect enough memorabilia to fill a room. In the music and entertainment industries, fans binge on the latest juicy morsel of gossip. Entire television shows focus solely on the houses in which these rich and famous live. Magazines have built massive circulations reporting the "inside scoop" on today's popular icons as the paparazzi go to bizarre lengths to catch these celebrities on film.

But there's a downside to this all-consuming stargazing.

The fact that we cherish such an external standard of worth means we're bound to diminish the value of those who are weak, handicapped, impoverished, orphaned, or even those who are—dare I say—just plain old average. Is it any wonder, then, that we're tempted to think primarily in terms of the quality of life? We're predisposed to value those who measure up to this false standard of "worthiness."

By contrast, the Bible is replete with commands to care for the widows, the orphans, the underprivileged, the downtrodden—those whom God calls "the least of these." No question, Terri Schiavo would fall into that category. So whenever people approach me and ask why I'd fight for Terri Schiavo—a woman who is most likely not going to be able to get a job or be productive, and who will always be, in a certain respect, a burden—I point them to the gospel of Matthew, chapter 25.

Briefly, it's Judgment Day and God is talking to the righteous. God says: "For I was an hungered, and ye gave me meat: I was thirsty, and ye gave me drink: I was a stranger and ye took me in: Naked, and ye clothed me: I was sick, and ye visited me: I was in prison, and ye came unto me" (35–36). The righteous are standing before God completely baffled at His statement.

They respond by asking, "Lord, when saw we thee an hungered, and fed thee? or thirsty and gave thee drink? When saw we thee a stranger, and took thee in? or naked, and clothed thee? Or when saw we thee sick, or in prison, and came unto thee?" (37–39). In other words, the righteous are saying, "We don't remember doing any of this for you." Notice God's response in verse 40: "And the king shall answer and say unto them, Verily I say unto you, inasmuch as ye have done it unto one of the least of these my brethren, you've done it unto me."

Who are the least of these?

Anybody who can't give something back to you.

That could be a Terri Schiavo. A senior citizen. A drug addict. A homeless family living in a rescue mission. A single parent. A child living in poverty at home or abroad. The unemployed. Certainly the disabled among us. To care for them requires an acknowledgment that this life is not about us. Instead, like my grandfather, we make a decision to accept whatever God brings into our path, especially the least of these. On Judgment Day, God will say that whatever we have done for these "unwanted" and "undesirable" people, we will have done it for the King of Kings himself.

Talk about an unmatched privilege!

CHAPTER TWENTY-THREE

IF THERE'S A WILL
THERE'S A WAY

The thirty years of literature on living wills has shown very disappointing results. The shortcomings of living wills are real. Dying is just too complicated.

—CHARLES SABATINO, ASSISTANT DIRECTOR, AMERICAN BAR ASSOCIATION'S COMMISSION ON LAW AND AGING[1]

In the wake of Terri's death, it's safe to say that millions of us scrambled to make sense out of our end-of-life wishes as well as our instructions in the case of a medical emergency. Ironically, Michael Schiavo has joined the chorus of those preaching the virtues of having a living will. I say ironically because Terri never had her wishes spelled out in writing, which was a fundamental flaw in this case. That said, you might be surprised to know that I'm not a fan of the living will.

Here's why.

When I graduated from law school, one of my first jobs as a young lawyer was to create wills for our clients. I was handed an official-looking template for a last will and testament and a sample living will. At first I wasn't sure there was a difference. They sounded similar in name.

As I began to read exactly what these legal documents contained, I discovered that they're radically different. The last will and testament makes a tremendous amount of sense. All adults would do well to obtain one, regardless of age or marital status. More on that in a moment. But there was something about the living will even back then that caused me to have serious reservations. The language seemed to favor death over life. As it turns out, my instincts were right on target.

You see, the first living will was created by the Euthanasia Society of America in 1967. While this pro-death organization changed its name to "Choice in Dying" and then morphed into something called the "Partnership for Caring," the group's goals of physician-assisted suicide and their push to see the public widely using these living wills should raise more than a few red flags.

Originally sold as a device to articulate a person's wishes when she could no longer speak for herself, in some cases the living will has turned into a permission slip for doctors to legally withhold medical care and even hasten death in situations that most patients never anticipated. That should come as no surprise since Choice in Dying has been actively lobbying for direct euthanasia.[2] Looking beyond their agenda, there are a number of practical reasons why living wills have fallen into disfavor.

First, advances in medicine and technology are constantly changing. There was a time when a heart transplant was unthinkable. If back then your living will had said, "Never put me on a ventilator in the case of heart failure," you would have missed the opportunity to be provided a new heart in the wake of emerging surgical procedures that are now considered almost routine. These living wills are locked in time, making them out-of-date with every new treatment and cure that comes along.

Second, it's not possible to anticipate all of the health care scenarios you might face if you were to be incapacitated. By stipulating a set of directives and preferences in advance, you might inadvertently tie the hands of a professional who could otherwise provide a new appropriate treatment. The withholding of medical care occurs far too frequently due to a vague and poorly worded living will.

Third, the law governing medical care is constantly changing. In Terri's case, the provision of food and water was not considered medical treatment or artificial life support at the time of her injury. Over time, euthanasia advocates worked to revise state law so that "artificially provided sustenance and hydration" would be redefined as a "life-prolonging procedure" rather than ordinary care, as it was previously medically categorized for at least half a century. Almost overnight in Florida, offering food and water through a feeding tube was legislatively reclassified as "medical treatment" in the context of a medical setting. That change gave the courts new authority to end lives in situations such as Terri's.

I'm not the only person who recognizes these and other disadvantages of the living will. Far too often we wrongly think that drafting a living will is no different from ordering a Whopper at Burger King—you know, have it your way. The problem is that we cannot anticipate all the complexities of a future medical emergency. Charles Sabatino, the associate director of the American Bar Association's Commission on Law and Aging, put it this way:

> These documents were written as if you'd know what you want, kind of like ordering a salami and cheese: you want provolone, mayo, no mustard, lettuce but no tomato. You have the ability to be that specific in your document, but in reality [the living will] has very little connection with what you'll be facing.[3]

Here's an added concern. From my vantage point as a Christian, the living will completely removes God from the process. I don't believe in signing anything that would accelerate my death. I don't fear death, mind you. I know that to be absent from the body is to be present with the Lord (2 Corinthians 5:8). To be pro-life does not mean that I refuse to acknowledge death. Our bodies will fail; nobody gets out of here alive. But unlike the atheist who has no hope, my conviction as a believer is that death is not the end—it's the beginning.

I readily acknowledge that there is "a time to be born and a time to die." I also agree with the saying: Not everything that can be done should be done to prolong a life. But since my life as a Christian is not my own (1 Corinthians 6:19–20), at no point should I embrace a back-door suicide by taking steps to hasten death. The living will is almost like putting such an intention in writing. Considering the goals of those who invented it, I'd say that shouldn't come as a surprise. As you'll see, there is a better alternative.

In case you are tempted to say, "If I'm ever incapacitated like this, please let me go," I'd like for you to consider the story of Pat Rummerfield. Here's a remarkable young man who, when faced with a near-death experience, clung to the "will to live" rather than a living will. You just never know what God might want to do with your life.

NEVER GIVE UP

In 1974 Pat Rummerfield hopped in the passenger seat of his sleek Corvette and handed the keys to his best friend. The two buddies had been drinking, and under the influence of alcohol, they rocketed down the highway at 135 mph. Losing control, the car crashed and rolled, causing a near-fatal accident. Pat broke his neck in four places, fractured all his ribs, shattered his collarbone, and almost lost an eyeball, which had popped out of its socket and had to be reinserted.

With massive head injuries, four crushed cervical vertebrae, and unable to move from the neck down, Pat's doctors gave him seventy-two hours to live. Although he was mentally alert, his physicians wanted to put the brakes on any additional treatment. Instead, they recommended that this twenty-one-year-old receive convalescent care to live out whatever remaining time he had in peace. Unlike Terri Schiavo, however, Pat could speak for himself. Lying flat on his back, unable to move or feed himself, he refused to accept such a dire prognosis. Instead, he insisted on giving rehabilitation his best shot—just in case.

At that point I imagine his family, friends, and doctors felt he wasn't being realistic. Privately, they may have fretted about the "quality of life" he'd have if he survived. He was, after all, a total quadriplegic—

unlike Terri, who could sit in a reclining chair, clutch stuffed animals, and turn her body to face her mother or a guest.

In a day and age where insurance companies and hospitals desire to cut costs when such care appears "futile," Pat's life would be at the top of the list of a life "not worth living." And if our courts continue to make judgments from the bench as to which lives are of value, and if medical ethics committees determine what is futile care in any given situation, I wouldn't be surprised if one day soon a judge didn't step in and deprive a person like Pat of having the chance to improve—even though he could speak for himself.

As Pat tells the story, he was lying in his bed just dreaming of playing basketball once again. He even pictured himself becoming a NASCAR driver. He told God that he'd use his life to help those less fortunate if he was given a second chance. The last thing he wanted was to surrender to the hopelessness that others projected on his situation. In the stillness of night while entertaining these thoughts, something amazing happened.

He moved his big toe.

Three years later, through sheer determination and daily physical therapy, Pat relearned how to walk. He also regained the strength and use of his hands. His doctors were astonished and were completely without a medical explanation for his recovery. But Pat didn't stop there. After seventeen years of maintaining a grueling workout regimen, Pat regained almost complete functionality of his body and decided to enter a number of triathlons.

In 1992 Pat entered the world famous Ironman triathlon in Hawaii. Only the fittest of the fit will attempt this annual Herculean event. To compete, contestants must first swim 2.4 miles, then complete a 112-mile bike race, followed by running a 26.2-mile marathon. In what was a phenomenal feat bordering on the miraculous, Pat finished the race—not bad for a guy who was told he'd never walk again.

Five years later Pat went on to complete the 1997 Antarctica Marathon—a course so difficult, only eighty-two participants have ever managed to run its 26.2 miles of glaciers and frozen streams. You have to wonder what Pat was thinking as he battled the 45-mph winds and sub-zero temperatures to go the distance. After all, there was a time when just wiggling his big toe was big news.

As if overcoming these challenges wasn't enough, Pat set the world land speed record at the Bonneville Salt Flats for electric cars and has raced in two NASCAR competitions. His accomplishments have been recorded by Ripley's Believe It or Not, ESPN, the History Channel, Discovery, and a host of publications including *GQ, Runner's World,* and *Popular Science.* He now travels widely sharing his inspirational testimony.

Admittedly, Pat's story is an unusual display of healing. Nevertheless, I'd like for you to ponder something. Imagine if he had been denied the rehabilitation and physical therapy that he desired. Imagine if he had bought into the notion that there was no chance his quality of life would ever improve. Imagine if he couldn't speak and couldn't articulate his will to live. And imagine the mistake he would have made had he signed a living will that limited or prevented his care and rehab. Clearly, the world would have been deprived of an unbelievable story of faith, hope, and healing.

LAST WILL

At the outset I touched on the importance of executing a last will and testament. So before offering an alternative to the living will, let me explain why I'd encourage you to put a last will in place and how you might use this document to advance your personal convictions.

Simply put, the last will and testament is a legally binding device that properly disperses your assets to your heirs upon your death. In it you spell out who gets the house, the car, the stocks and bonds, the dog—in short, all of your "stuff."

Of particular importance are the provisions for your minor children, including naming who their guardians will be. I also view the last will as a wonderful tool to share your heart one final time after you are gone from this earth. When crafting their wills, I encourage Christians to think of ministry opportunities in addition to spelling out the distribution of their assets. There's no reason this has to be just a legal document.

For example, you might want to include a statement of what you believe—a statement of faith or a personal creed. Sharing a favorite passage of Scripture or insight into the Christian life are great opportunities for you to witness to your loved ones. These declarations don't change the legal weight or meaning of the document. Mentioning several personal aspirations for your kids if you have youngsters in your care is also a good idea.

You might consider saying: "I'd like for my kids to attend church," "I'd like for my children to receive a Christian education," or "I'd like for them to be raised to follow the Lord." Of course, the expression of these desires is not legally binding. No judge is going to order the children to go to church. No guardian can force them to attend a Christian school or college.

Nevertheless, there's something special when children have a piece of paper from their dad or mom that clearly lays out where their parents stood and what their hopes were for them. There's something comforting when a young person knows "This is what my dad believed," or "These are the people my mom wanted to look after us."

A very common last will for the married father of young children might read: "I leave everything to my wife. My kids will be under the control of their mother. If we both die, then [name grandparents or aunts or uncles or friends who would be willing to look after the kids]." Whatever meager assets there might be in a young couple's life can be placed in a trust. If you are older and have amassed a great deal of wealth, this document can help you minimize inheritance taxes while maximizing your resources for the use of your heirs or for the charities you desire to support.

Without a last will and testament, the state will step in and make these decisions for you; I'm sure you can imagine the nightmare scenario that can present for those left behind. Without question, a properly executed will is a must for everyone. Now, you might be thinking,

"David, if a last will is a good thing because it protects our assets, and the living will is a bad thing because it more often than not fails to protect our well-being in health-related situations, what am I to do? How do I avoid what happened to Terri Schiavo?" Read on.

WISDOM IN MANY COUNSELORS

Soaring health insurance coverage, the trend to manage care by managing costs, and limited hospital space places incredible pressure to terminate a life that doesn't meet some arbitrarily determined standard of value. Likewise, there are those for whom a conflict of interest—such as an heir to your estate—impairs an objective assessment of your condition.

The very best way to protect yourself from these forces is the **Designation of a Health Care Surrogate**. This individual or team of individuals will speak on your behalf when you are unable to speak for yourself, especially if that decision knowingly ends your life. I fully realize that any surgery could result in your death. That's not what I'm talking about here. I'm talking about a crisis situation where there's a question about the removal of life support (taking you off of a ventilator) or the decision whether to initiate a life-saving surgery (a heart or lung transplant) or, as in Terri's case, an attempt to remove food and water.

While you could choose one trusted individual such as your spouse to serve as your proxy, we saw in the Schiavo case that people change. A husband who swore under oath that he wanted to provide medical care for his wife did a complete U-turn. That's why I prefer a team approach; three people seems like a good number because it places the decisions about your life "in the multitude of counselors," where, as Scripture says, "there is safety."

Could there be five? Sure. Could there be just two? Yes. Again, it's your decision. Whether there are two, three, or more surrogates, your safety valve is to require them to unanimously agree on the medical course of action in cases where that decision was intended to result in your death. If one of your surrogates, for instance, thinks your feeding tube should be removed but two disagree, the tube stays in. Even if two agree the tube should be removed and one disagrees, the tube still stays in if your document requires unanimity. The spirit of this document is the presumption of life or at least the presumption that one of your surrogates will not want to kill you if other options exist.

Thankfully, the vast majority of Americans will never need to worry about being so incapacitated that they require someone to step into their shoes and make medical decisions for them. But if, God forbid, a situation were to arise where you were unable to make your own decisions, at that moment this team of loved ones—your spouse, your parents, a family member, a close friend and/or pastor—can speak with the doctors, gather information, seek the Lord, and then jointly decide.

Several benefits over the living will immediately emerge. This approach takes the burden of the decision-making process off your spouse. He or she will be surrounded by loving, caring friends and family who will share the load. It clarifies from a legal standpoint who the decision makers are. Likewise, you don't have to be fearful. You don't have to be concerned about whether or not someone might try to hurry you along to heaven to get you out of the way. And if, at some point, one of the individuals you selected were to betray your trust by acting irresponsibly, the others provide a corrective measure of accountability.

For a Designation of Health Care Surrogate sample form, please see Appendix B.

Terri's passing has prompted the nation to wrestle with these and a host of other critical issues. I believe that's a good thing. Yet her death has exposed something lethal lurking in the dark corners of our souls: America has become far too calloused toward the sacredness of life. In our arrogance, we play God. In our foolishness, even as believers we often ignore His claim upon our lives and, in so doing, provoke His judgment. Now is the time when we must call upon the Great Physician to lance this festering wound and heal our land—and our souls.

CHAPTER TWENTY-FOUR

LIFE SUPPORT
IN VIEW OF ETERNITY

Every Day's a Gift
— PLACARD AFFIXED TO WALL OUTSIDE WOODSIDE
HOSPICE

W hen faced with the decision whether or not to remove the life support of a loved one, there's one perspective few take into view: Eternity. Let me ask you this question: If you knew a person who had not yet made their peace with God, meaning they would go to hell if you removed them from their life support, would you still pull the plug? Does that question at least cause you to pause and weigh the eternal finality of such a decision?

I believe it should.

Eternity is forever. And while talking about "rights" and "choice" and "living wills" has value, it's easy to overlook the immense gravity of stepping from this life into the next without settling the question of the eternal destination.

A dear friend of mine for many years, Helen Barber, was faced with that very dilemma. Helen's father, Sterling Johnson, was a strong man who milked a dozen cows by hand every day. Helen described him as a "moral" person and yet one who remained without Christ throughout his life. For forty years Helen prayed for her dad's salvation.

As Sterling got older, he developed significant health issues and, at one point, made it clear verbally that he did not want to be placed on life-support machines to prolong his life. He did not put those wishes in writing. As Sterling's health began to deteriorate more dramatically, his doctor pulled Helen aside and said, "Your father is dying. He will not live fifteen minutes unless we put him on a respirator to breathe for him. And when he's removed from the respirator, he will die. What do you want us to do?"

Helen's mind rushed into an immediate whirlwind of conflict and stress. Helen knew what her father had said—basically his was a request to let him die sooner as opposed to later. But Helen also knew that if her dad died tonight, he would die without ever having trusted Jesus Christ as his Savior. His eternity was at stake as the doctor asked the question. For forty years her dad had rejected the gospel message, but with one more night of life, Helen and her husband would have a final opportunity to tell him about Jesus.

Helen's decision was immediate and resolute: "Put him on the respirator! Put him on anything that will keep him alive."

Helen's husband, Raymond, raced to the hospital and entered the room where Sterling was now hooked up to a life-support machine. Raymond was a pastor who had won many people to Christ in hospitals over the years, and as Sterling's son-in-law, he would do all he could. Helen remained in the hallway, praying and begging God for her dad to trust Jesus Christ in his final moments on earth. Was it too late to do any good? I'll let Helen tell what happened next:

> When Raymond came out, he said, "Your dad trusted Christ as his Savior!" I said, "No, I don't think he really did trust Christ. I think he just told you that because he knows it will break my heart if he dies without Christ." But I was so wrong. My dad was taken off of the life support several days later and fully expected to die. Interestingly, he continued to live and was

dismissed from the hospital to come live in his own home.

Amazingly, my dad lived a normal life in New Mexico for another eighteen months and attended church every Sunday. He read his Bible, and for the first time in my life, I heard my dad pray. He was a changed man. His greatest regret was that he had wasted his life not knowing the full joy of a close relationship with Christ. I am so thankful that God put it on my heart to place my dad on life support in order to give him one more chance at a new life in Christ. When my daddy passed away eighteen months later, I had no doubt in my mind that he knew Jesus Christ as his Savior.

Here, then, is a simple blueprint for the Christian to consider when confronted with a situation similar to that of Helen Barber's dad or Terri Schiavo. We begin with the question, "Are they terminal?" Notice I didn't ask, "Are they sick?" or "Will they improve or recover?" For me "terminal" means this: There is a reasonable amount of medical certainty they will die fairly soon. Examples of a terminal condition would include advanced stages of cancer, AIDS, or Alzheimer's.

If a person is terminal, I believe we have a duty to do what would reasonably sustain life (such as providing food and water), but the dominant goal is to keep them comfortable and properly cared for with dignity. If the person is unsaved, sharing the gospel with them as quickly as possible should be the highest priority. Remember the thief on the cross next to Jesus? He confessed his faith in Christ literally moments before he died as a convicted criminal. Jesus turned to him and said, "Verily I say unto thee, Today shalt thou be with me in paradise" (Luke 23:43).

Now, if a person is not terminal, every opportunity to introduce them to Jesus Christ before their death should still remain the ultimate priority. With respect to the medical decision-making process, I believe that we should aim to preserve, enhance, and prolong the life of non-terminal patients. Granted, there are no guarantees that a sick or disabled person will ever fully improve or recover.

A good rule of thumb is to always err in favor of life. When in doubt as to what to do, make the decision that favors preserving a life. If a new technology now emerges that could have dramatically improved Terri Schiavo's mental and physical condition, it's too late. The decision to let her die has already been acted upon.

Helping people remain alive is a worthy goal that drives firefighters, police officers, and military personnel to often risk their own lives to save others. In like fashion, nonterminal patients deserve our best efforts to keep them alive.

CHAPTER TWENTY-FIVE

BRAVE NEW WORLD?

The care of human life and happiness, and not their
destruction, is the first and only legitimate object of good
government.

—THOMAS JEFFERSON[1]

I magine it's the year 2040.

A seismic shift in the American cultural landscape has occurred. As a nation, we've slipped into an era where moral relativism has completely replaced the Ten Commandments as the foundation for law. God is out, and arbitrary legislative and judicial rulings are in. American church attendance has dropped to European levels; less than 10 percent participate in weekly services. And on the political front, so-called liberal blue states outnumber conservative red states two to one.

After several decades of relentless legal challenges by the ACLU, the last vestiges of our Judeo-Christian heritage have been stripped from public view. Churches and war memorials may no longer exhibit crosses visible from the road. Our historical monuments in Washington, D.C., have been sandblasted to remove their centuries-old references to God and Scripture. Likewise, the money in circulation no longer says, "In God We Trust." And Christmas has been replaced by the Winter Holiday.

In the public schools, the Christian faith of our Founding Fathers, initially noted at Plymouth Rock and in the later historic documents drafted by our founders' able hands, has been replaced by a generic nod toward a universal spirit. Even the textbooks used by private Jewish and Christian schools have been neutered from their faith-based orientation in order to meet a strict, court-mandated educational standard. Religion classes must include the exploration of all faiths—especially Islam.

For its part, the federal government has caved under intense pressure to provide socialized medicine for every citizen—as well as for millions of illegal aliens. As a result, the national budget is strapped. Record deficit spending is necessary to pay for universal health care, which, in turn, threatens to stall the economy.

The solution?

A congressional subcommittee has been called to explore measures to curb spending on health-related issues. A parade of expert testimony is assembled. Ultimately, these doctors, social workers, caregivers, and economists recommend three cost-cutting, albeit controversial, measures. First, they propose emptying all nursing homes; the elderly will be asked to fulfill their duty to the next generation by expediting their deaths. Their adult stem cells will be harvested for research.

Second, the subcommittee recommends suspending hospital treatment when the "quality of life" of a patient fails to meet a minimum standard set by a medical ethics committee. These hard luck cases will receive morphine while being deprived of food and water until nature takes its course.

Finally, the subcommittee proposes that newborns be terminated if they are diagnosed with chronic illness, show evidence of birth defects, or if their parents are without sufficient financial means to provide for their care.

Not everybody is pleased with this proposal.

A lawsuit challenging these new laws based on the constitutional right to life is filed by the pastor of your church with the help of a dedicated Christian legal team. In spite of the anti-Christian bias that has dominated the courts for decades, a judge eventually agrees to hear the case. Your pastor intends to make the argument that America's founders believed that life is a gift from God; and as such, it is sacred and must be treated with the utmost respect. He believes that only God should determine when life begins and ends and that a higher moral authority than the courts or a doctor's "educated guess" must govern end-of-life decisions.

The opposition will argue that humans are nothing more than an evolved extension of the animal kingdom. People are not a special creation of God deserving of extraordinary care. In the final analysis, humans have no more intrinsic value than a dog or cat and, in some cases, are less beneficial to society than animal life. This is not entirely unexpected since decades before, professors like Princeton's Peter Singer had laid the foundation for this view in ethics classes.

To help your pastor establish his case that God created life and that human life is sacred, he asks you as a member of his church to be a witness. You agree. You study what the Bible teaches about the origins of life, the uniqueness of the human soul, and what the Bible says about God's divine plan for each person.

The big day comes. Your name is called and you take a seat in the witness stand. You're sworn in with a pledge to tell the whole truth. It's kind of a scary moment. The lawyer representing the other side approaches and starts by quizzing you with a series of background questions. For the record, he asks you to state your name, your address, your date of birth, and then he covers a handful of innocuous issues. You begin to relax when he asks if you belong to a particular church. Let's pick up the hypothetical exchange at that point.

"How did you become a member of your church?"

"Well, I attended several new members' classes and was told I had to be saved, baptized, and agree with the doctrine of the church before I could join."

"I see," he says, making a mental note. "So what does it mean to be 'saved'?"

You think about that for a moment and then give the short version.

"I believe that you have to confess that you are a sinner and you must put your faith and trust in Jesus Christ." That's odd, you think. You're in open court explaining the plan of salvation when you thought you were here to explain why you believe all life is sacred. But instead of moving on to that topic, the lawyer continues to probe.

"So what happens if you don't get saved?"

You shift in your seat, unsure how much to say. "In simple terms, when we die there's a hell to avoid and a heaven to be gained based upon the choice we all make on this side of eternity."

"Are there several choices to get to heaven, as you put it?"

"No. Just one."

"Really. What's that?"

"Well, you have to believe in Jesus and what He did on the cross. When He died, He took the punishment my sins deserve."

The lawyer turns toward the defense table where your pastor is sitting and then asks you, "Did your preacher just cook all of this up? Was this some sort of a marketing campaign or perhaps a guilt trip the church leadership designed to get people to show up on Sundays?"

"No. What our pastor preaches—and what I believe—is all based on the Bible, God's Word."

The lawyer is enamored with the fact that you actually believe God wrote a book. He says, "Now, let me get this straight. You really believe that God wrote a book?"

You look at the judge for a moment. "Do you actually want me to go into all of that? I thought—"

The judge cuts you off. "Please, answer the question."

"Well, not to get too technical," you say, "but I believe God breathed His Spirit on the holy men of old—you might say He inspired them with His thoughts. They took it all down, and others have carefully preserved what they wrote over thousands of years." Suddenly, you're glad you stayed awake during the foundations of the Christian faith sermon series.

The lawyer says, "Is God going to write another book anytime soon?"

"No, the Bible even addresses that. It says that no one should add or take away from what's there. And it says that 'not one jot or tittle'— not one of the smallest marks in the original Hebrew text—is going to pass away. This book is going to stand for eternity. It's the Word of God." At this point, you feel your testimony is going great.

The lawyer takes a step closer and, placing a hand on his hip, says, "Have you ever read the entire Bible through even one time in your life?"

A hush falls over the courtroom. All eyes are fixed on you. "Well, I do read the Bible, if that's what you mean." You offer a weak smile.

"That's not what I asked," the lawyer says. "I asked if you ever read the entire thing through, just one time?"

You shift in your seat, wishing your pastor didn't have to hear your answer. "Well, most Christians who go to church have never read the entire Bible through."

"I'm not interested in what most people do," he says, clearly intent on securing a direct response. "Have you read it one time cover to cover?"

"Um, I don't know if I've read the whole thing, it's a pretty big book."

"I assume you own a copy. Is that correct?"

"I do."

"Several copies?"

"Yes. Three or four."

"How long have you owned these copies?"

You blink. "About ten years."

"So we could say you've owned at least one copy for the last three thousand, six hundred fifty days?"

"Sounds right." Now your heart is racing. You have no idea where this line of questioning is going or what the relevance of it is to the sanctity of life testimony you thought you were going to provide.

"How many pages are in your Bible?"

"Um, I don't know . . . maybe twelve hundred?"

"Alright. You've said that you haven't read God's Word through one time. You've said it's a large book. And you've owned a copy for ten years. Is that a fair summary so far?

"Yes."

"Let's say you were to read just one-third of one page per day," he says, consulting his yellow legal tablet. "Mathematically speaking, at that rate you could finish reading the whole Bible in ten years, correct?"

"Yes . . . that sounds right."

"How long does it take you to read a page?"

At this point you have an idea of where he's going and decide to get creative. You say, "Look, I went to a very bad school. They were messing around with that whole phonics fad and I never did get to be a strong reader."

The attorney pauses for emphasis. "I think it's safe to estimate that the average person might take one minute a day to read a third of a page. Agreed?"

You nod and then whisper, "Yes."

The judge, looking down at you over the top of his glasses, says, "Please repeat that louder for the benefit of the jury."

"Yes. I could read a third of a page per day. Sure."

"According to these calculations," the lawyer says, driving home his point by ticking them off with his fingers, "you could have read the only book that God ever wrote, the source of your faith, the source of what your church believes, had you spent just sixty seconds a day over a ten-year period. Is that true or false?"

"Well, according to your math, yes. It's true."

"And I believe you already testified that you didn't."

"No sir, I didn't."

"Why didn't you?"

"Well, I . . . I was busy. I had a lot of things going on. I feel bad about it now. I should have had more time."

"Do you own a television?"

"Yes."

"You own more than one?"

"I do. Three to be exact."

"Do you pay money to run a cable or a satellite dish or antenna to it?"

"Doesn't everybody? We have cable."

"Do you get a lot of channels?"

"Sure, but we're not big TV viewers."

"Do you ever watch television sixty seconds in a day? What about five minutes? An hour? Two hours?"

———

Before you know it, you'd be grilled about how much time you spend listening to the radio, reading a newspaper, reading a magazine, or surfing the Internet. And in the end, the other side will demonstrate that you and I have all of the time we want to do what matters most to us. The judge and jury will come to see that believers ignore their God and His Word all the time. They'll conclude that we believers are not guided by the strength of our convictions after all.

You know what?

Sloppy Christian living is killing our testimony.

The vast majority of Bible-believing people neglect to faithfully study God's Word, seek His face through prayer, and make choices about life and living that reflect His priorities. This is how Paul describes the spiritual bankruptcy of his day: "They profess that they know God; but in works they deny him" (Titus 1:16a). Sounds like us, doesn't it? Is it any wonder that we're not experiencing the revival that our nation needs?

America is at a crossroads. There are forces working from within, pushing a culture without God, a culture of death over life, folly over wisdom, and secularism over faith. In the history of our nation, it was the church that was in the forefront of defending the helpless and the poor, tending the sick and feeding the hungry. Churches established the first hospitals and schools, both in America and in many other lands. When the church again defends the disabled, the struggling, the weak, the poor, the hopeless, and the orphan, America will experience a blessing and continued freedom from the hand of God.

How can we awaken the church?

Read on.

CHAPTER TWENTY-SIX

IF MY PEOPLE

There was nothing I could personally do to change what was happening to Terri. I just totally put myself in God's hands. I put 100 percent of my confidence in God, and whatever He decided, that was the way it was going to be.

—BOB SCHINDLER

The interest in Terri's fight for life reveals that we are a deeply divided nation. This is obvious everywhere I travel. There are some typical responses when I speak about her struggle. The first group of people think we should have left well enough alone. A man in Tallahassee, Florida, said, "Mr. Gibbs, I realize you and the Schindlers are making a big deal over Terri's life. But, frankly, it's creating a problem." When I asked him what he meant by that, he said, "Well, you know, seven to eight thousand people a year are starved to death in the state of Florida. Many are senior citizens whose lives are ended at the request of their family."

He added, "Terri Schiavo would have been one of those eight thousand if you guys had just kept your mouths shut. If you had just said, 'There's nothing we can do,' then none of us would have had to view this as an issue. And Terri would have slipped quietly away without all the fuss in the media too." Here's a guy more concerned about the nuisance that Terri's story created than with the fact that so many thousands of the disabled and elderly are being starved to death in his own backyard.

Other folks are overwhelmed at the scope of the problem; with a shrug, they give up in frustration. To them, the entire court and political system is broken beyond repair. Like Dorothy in *The Wizard of Oz*, they wish they could just click their heels together three times and be transported to safety. Knowing that is not an option, they decide to tune out the whole debate.

Thankfully, there's a better option. This response has to do with making changes from the inside out; it begins with the hearts and minds of each of us. Here's the good news: God supplies the means to heal our land—if we are willing to do it His way. His blueprint is found in 2 Chronicles 7:14:

If my people, which are called by my name, shall humble themselves, and pray, and seek my face, and turn from their wicked ways; then will I hear from heaven, and will forgive their sin, and will heal their land.

Did you catch it? God doesn't say, "If the judges . . . if the politicians . . . if the police . . ." No. I don't think we're going to change the courts until we change the hearts and minds of the American people. I don't think we're going to change the leadership in Washington, D.C., or in your state capital until we first change the convictions and values of Americans.

Put another way, the best way to influence the laws of the land is to pursue a change of heart among the people of the land. This powerful verse begins by sounding a clarion call to the church. The cure for our nation's ills begins not with the courts or with the government but with the people of God. Indeed, God says, "If my people" do four things, He promises to heal our land. Let's briefly unpack those four steps.

1. HUMBLE OURSELVES

This is easier said than done. True humility before God occurs when we say, "It's not my way—it's your way. It's not what I think that matters most, it's discovering what you've said and then doing it." Humility, therefore, grows every time we defer to what God has said in His Word and then obey it. That's tough. Watch how easy it is to get this backward.

For example, the Bible says that husbands are to love their wives as Christ loved the church. Let's say a husband reads that but his first thought is, "Yeah, I know what the Bible says. But you don't know my wife—she's distant and she constantly bad-mouths me to her friends. We just aren't happy. We should stop pretending anything will get better."

Time-out. Did you see what just happened? He elevated his personal opinion above God's Word.

Let's say a parent has unruly children. She might say, "I know the Bible says I need to discipline my kids and raise them to know the Lord. But frankly, I just don't have the energy to constantly be disciplining." Watch out. Those feelings are about to take precedence over what God has made clear: "The rod and reproof give wisdom: but a child left to himself bringeth his mother to shame" (Proverbs 29:15).

Consider the disabled. Terri Schiavo was starved to death before our eyes. Guess what? While she was in the last days of suffering a most uncivilized death, a *Time* magazine poll found that 53 percent of "Americans surveyed who call themselves born again Christians or Evangelicals agreed with the decision to remove Terri Schiavo's feeding tube."[1]

That should break our hearts.

How is it possible that so many believers in Jesus Christ appear undisturbed by the euthanasia of a disabled, nonterminal person? Are we more concerned about what we think than about what God says? I imagine the rationalization process might look like this: "Well, she was brain-injured. Who would want to live in that condition? So I think . . ."

261

Here's an interesting dynamic. When we humble ourselves, the "least of these" look a whole lot more important. Humility, then, begins when we put an end to our constant quibbling over what God has allowed into our lives. The well-known story of Job comes to mind. Here was a man who had everything. But in the blink of an eye, God permitted it all to be swept away. Houses. Possessions. Livestock. Wealth. Children. Even his health. You might say Job's wife was the original right-to-die advocate. She said, "Dost thou still retain thine integrity? curse God, and die" (Job 2:9).

Notice Job's reaction: "But he said unto her, Thou speakest as one of the foolish women speaketh. What? shall we receive good at the hand of God, and shall we not receive evil? In all this did not Job sin with his lips" (v. 10). What Job didn't know was that his life was being scrutinized by an audience in heaven. By humbling himself in obeying the words of God rather than by taking his life in his own hands, he brought honor to God and proved Satan wrong.

The best model of humility, of course, is seen in Jesus' life, the One who "humbled himself, and became obedient unto death, even the death of the cross" (Philippians 2:8).

2. PRAY, PRAY, PRAY

What do you think I'd do if the president of the United States were to call and say, "I'd like to see David Gibbs in the Oval Office this afternoon"? I'd be on the next plane, car, or train. You'd probably have the same reaction. We'd do whatever we had to do to take advantage of that opportunity. Talk about a real honor.

Yet you and I have a far greater privilege to come into the presence of the King of Kings through prayer every single day. In fact, this is not a onetime invitation to speak with the One who holds our breath in His hands. The apostle Paul encourages believers to "pray without ceasing" (1 Thessalonians 5:17).

Do you know when most people pray? Aside from perhaps at mealtime, most people pray when they get really scared. You see, when life is rolling along smoothly, we tend to do everything in our own strength. We rely upon our own talents and giftedness to get ahead in the workplace. We take comfort in our relatively good health. We draw a sense of security from a fully funded retirement account. With everything going so well, why pray?

Then, without warning, we feel chest pains—can't breathe, the room seems hot, we're dizzy, tingly, numb—as the dismaying and terrifying realization dawns on us that we're experiencing what only happens to "other people." We're having a heart attack. Or perhaps it's a diagnosis of cancer, or our home is flooded, or we're the victim of identity fraud. Whatever the crisis, our world has just lurched out of the control we thought we had of it. And when that world crashes down around us, we find time to cry out to God, don't we?

I'm sure the Lord is pleased to hear those prayers. But His invitation to go deeper in a day-by-day conversation with you and me is what His heart longs for. God is looking for those who will say, "By faith I'm going to start totally depending on you for my daily bread rather than relying upon myself." The humbling of ourselves and the commitment to prayer go hand in hand because they demonstrate that all of life is about God, not about us.

Here's a practical tip: Use your "wait time" to pray. Stuck at a long red light? Use those moments to pray for your spouse or a friend in need. Trapped behind a long line of shoppers at the cash register? Thank God you have food you are waiting to buy, a home to eat it in, and friends and family to eat it with. In the morning, waiting for your coffee to brew, greet the Lord; ask for His wisdom as you make decisions in the hours that stretch ahead of you.

3. SEEK HIS FACE

The word "seek" in this context connotes a "passionate excitement" or a "burning desire." Unfortunately, in some churches it looks like the people are all in pain.

Grown men who will yell and holler at a ball game or women who become elated over a shopping sales event can't so much as give a holy grunt for God. Believers who can memorize a mountain of statistics about their favorite athlete seem to have difficulty remembering the general location of the various books of the Bible.

You know what?

The world is not going to get any more excited about Jesus than we are. The idea behind seeking His face is that we are to pursue Jesus with the same passion, the same energy, and the same single-mindedness as anything else that thrills our soul in this life. One indicator of our priorities and what captures our hearts is where we spend our time. The Barna Group found that "born again Christians spend *seven times* as much time on entertainment as they do on spiritual activities"[2] (emphasis added).

Let's contrast that with the story of the pearl of great price. Jesus was speaking to His disciples about the passionate pursuit of God's kingdom. He says, "Again, the kingdom of heaven is like unto a merchant man, seeking goodly pearls: who, when he had found one pearl of great price, went and sold all that he had, and bought it" (Matthew 13:45–46). Do you see the difference?

King David set a wonderful example of seeking God with passion and a holy gusto. In Psalm 63:1–2, David compares the seeking heart to the yearnings of a thirsty man: "O God, thou art my God; early will I seek thee: my soul thirsteth for thee, my flesh longeth for thee in a dry and thirsty land, where no water is; To see thy power and thy glory, so as I have seen thee in the sanctuary." Why is David so captivated by God? He writes, "Because thy lovingkindness is better than life" (v. 3a).

4. TURN FROM OUR WICKED WAYS

From the beginning of the Bible to the last page, one thing is perfectly clear, and it can be found in every book of the Bible. Simply stated: God will bless righteousness; God must judge sin. It's His very nature as a holy God that if someone is living holy and right, He will bless that; and if there is sin, He must judge it.

When God looks at our country, what does He see?

Do you think He hears the cry of the 1.5 billion aborted babies? Does He see the Supreme Court sanctioning behavior that He clearly denounces as sin? Does His heart break when He watches His people nod in approval of Terri's death? Does He see the pastors of our churches living private lives that contradict their public preaching?

The tension is that we want to live like the world, but when we die we still want to be admitted into heaven. We don't want to live like Christians here. We'd rather live life on our own terms than obey God. Does that sound like I'm overstating the condition of the church today? A number of years ago, George H. Gallup surveyed the attitudes and behavior choices within our churches. Here's a summary of what he found:

> There's little difference in ethical behavior between the churched and the unchurched. There's as much pilferage and dishonesty among the churched as the unchurched. And I'm afraid that applies pretty much across the board: religion, per se, is not really life changing. People cite it as important, for instance, in overcoming depression—but it doesn't have primacy in determining behavior.[3]

If the church is flirting with sin while asking God to move in her midst, she's asking God to violate His very nature and His Word. I often wonder if we've gotten so sloppy with our spiritual lives that, in a measure, much of the prayer we're engaged in is not having the impact we think it has before the Lord.

We can watch in disbelief, in horror, or in silent apathy while the courts, the ethicists, and the social engineers play God with life-and-death decisions. Or we can fight for dear life. How? By becoming agents of change who start with seeking a changed heart. And by humbling ourselves and committing ourselves to prayer, by seeking God's face and repenting of our negligence. In turn, America will experience the hand of blessing from a loving Savior who promises to heal our land.

God has said: "I call heaven and earth to record this day against you, that I have set before you life and death, blessing and cursing; therefore choose life, that both thou and thy seed may live" (Deuteronomy 30:19).

What kind of country will we leave our children and grandchildren? Will we be a nation that defends the value and purpose of every life? Will we speak for those who have no voice—for the disabled and the unborn? Will we reorient our priorities to cherish and sacrificially love those the world says don't have a life worth living? Will we strive with everything we have—our hearts, our homes, and our resources—to preserve life and, in so doing, point others to the Author of Life?

If we want to continue to experience the Lord's blessing in America, if we desire His healing touch, and if we long to see our courts protecting life, we must humble ourselves, pray, seek His face, and repent. If we do, a revival will sweep across this land like a much-needed rain in a time of drought.

It's happened before in our country and it can happen again. That is my fervent hope and prayer for God's people. Yes, today is the day to adopt the heart of God and to fight for dear life.

For the least of these.

For Terri.

APPENDIX A

FREQUENTLY ASKED QUESTIONS: TERRI AND THE CASE*

Did Terri Schiavo ever execute a living will or put her wishes in writing?
Answer: No, she did not.

What did Judge Greer have to determine since there was no writing?
Answer: Florida law required him to find "clear and convincing" evidence of Terri's wishes.

Why couldn't Terri divorce Michael?
Answer: Florida law would not allow it without Michael's permission, and he would not consent to it.

Why couldn't a new guardian be appointed to care for Terri?
Answer: Although the Schindlers asked Judge Greer several times to remove Michael as Terri's guardian, based on a number of potential conflicts of interest between Michael and Terri, the judge consistently denied their petitions.

Why couldn't the media see Terri?
Answer: Michael Schiavo and Judge Greer would not allow them in.

Why wasn't Terri taken outside?
Answer: Michael Schiavo would not allow her to be seen in public. He also chose to not have her wheelchair repaired or replaced.

Why wasn't Terri getting therapy?
Answer: Michael Schiavo did not think it would help her, and the court

---

*Permission to photocopy granted

267

did not require him to provide it for Terri.

Why couldn't Terri get a new trial with a different judge?

Answer: The appeals courts affirmed Judge Greer's rulings, and Judge Greer refused to recuse himself from the proceedings.

Why did the appeals courts not overturn Judge Greer?

Answer: The appeals courts review the law (not the facts of a case). They determined that Judge Greer had followed Florida law as he interpreted the facts.

Why did Judge Greer never go see Terri for himself?

Answer: He did not think it was necessary or prudent.

Where did the videos that were shown repeatedly on TV come from?

Answer: They were clips that had been shown in a court hearing in 2002, making them a public record.

Was Terri ever in a coma?

Answer: Yes, after her initial trauma in 1990, Terri was comatose for a few months.

Was Terri ever on a ventilator?

Answer: Yes, after her initial trauma in 1990, Terri was on a ventilator for approximately three months before she began breathing on her own.

When Terri was removed from the ventilator and came out of the coma, what was her diagnosis?

Answer: Terri was diagnosed as being in a "persistent vegetative state."

What is the difference between a coma and a persistent vegetative state?

Answer: A coma is a profound or deep state of unconsciousness. The affected individual is alive but is not able to react or respond to life around him/her. Coma may occur as an expected progression or complication of an underlying illness, or as a result of an event such as head trauma.

A persistent vegetative state, which sometimes follows a coma, refers to a condition in which individuals have lost cognitive neurological function and awareness of the environment but retain noncognitive function and a preserved sleep-wake cycle.

It is sometimes described as when a person is technically alive, but his/her brain is dead. That description, however, is not completely accurate. In a persistent vegetative state the individual loses the higher cerebral powers of the brain, but the functions of the brain stem, such as respiration (breathing) and circulation, remain relatively intact. Spontaneous movements may occur and the eyes may open in response to external stimuli, but the patient does not speak or obey commands.[1]

Can a person ever recover from a coma or PVS?

Answer: The outcome for coma and vegetative state depends on the cause and on the location, severity, and extent of neurological damage: Outcomes range from recovery to death. People may emerge from a coma with a combination of physical, intellectual, and psychological difficulties that need special attention.

Recovery usually occurs gradually, with patients acquiring more and more ability to respond. Some patients never progress beyond very basic responses, but many recover full awareness.[2]

Was Terri in PVS?

Answer: This is in dispute. Michael Schiavo believes she was. Terri's family believed she was in a minimally conscious state.

What is a minimally conscious state?

Answer: This state of consciousness was first defined in 1996. In this condition, patients show occasional moments of awareness, such as attempting to communicate through speaking, writing, or using yes/no signals (other than eye blinks). A recent study in the journal *Neuroscience* revealed that people in this state may be quite aware, although trapped in a body that is largely nonfunctioning.[3]

The researchers from New York Presbyterian Hospital used brain imaging technology to show that, when played audiotapes of their loved ones' voices, people in this state have brain activity similar to that of a fully conscious person. When no recording was played to the patients, however, their brain activity was less than half that of healthy people.

How would a doctor decide whether Terri was in PVS or MCS?

Answer: At least one criterion should be present and occur on a reproducible or sustained basis to diagnose MCS:

1. follows simple commands
2. gestural or verbal yes/no responses (regardless of accuracy)
3. intelligible verbalization
4. movements or affective behaviors that occur in contingent relation to relevant environmental stimulus and are not attributable to reflexive activity[4]

Any of the above behavioral examples provide sufficient evidence, although this list is not meant to be exhaustive.

Did anyone beside the Schindlers see Terri respond at an MCS level?

Answer: Yes, there were a number of nonfamily members who watched Terri interact meaningfully with her environment. These people included doctors, nurses, attorneys, and clergy.

Did the autopsy performed on Terri answer the question whether she was in PVS or MCS?

Answer: No, it did not. This type of diagnosis can only be made on living patients who can be observed. The autopsy stated, "PVS is a clinical diagnosis arrived at through physical examination of living patients."

APPENDIX B

SAMPLE FORM:
DESIGNATION OF HEALTH CARE SURROGATE

The laws governing health care surrogates may vary from state to state. This form provides a general starting point that you and/or your lawyer may tailor to fit your state's requirements. It's also a good idea to carry in your purse or wallet the name and phone number of the surrogate who is to be contacted in the event of an emergency.*

---

*Permission to photocopy granted.

Designation of Health Care Surrogate of:

In the event that I have been determined by health care providers to be incapacitated to provide informed consent for medical treatment and surgical and diagnostic procedures, I designate as my surrogate for health care decisions:

Name, Address, and Telephone Number of Surrogate:

Name _____

Address _____

Telephone Number _____

Alt. Number _____

In the event that my Health Care Surrogate proposes a course of action or medical treatment or procedure, or the removal of the same, which is intended to result in my death (such as, for illustrative purpose, the removal of nutrition and hydration), the following named individuals must give unanimous consent to said proposed decision.

1. _____   _____
   Name   Street Address

   _____   _____
   Relationship to Declarant   City, State, Zip Code

   _____
   Telephone number

2. _____   _____
   Name   Street Address

   _____   _____
   Relationship to Declarant   City, State, Zip Code

   _____
   Telephone number

3. _____   _____
   Name   Street Address

   _____   _____
   Relationship to Declarant   City, State, Zip Code

   _____
   Telephone number

If any one of these named individuals refuses to consent, the action that will result in my death may not be taken.

In the event that my Health Care Surrogate is unable or unwilling to act in said capacity or is determined to have a conflict of interest, whether moral, financial, or any other, by a majority of the following named individuals:

1. _____   _____
   Name   Street Address

   _____   _____
   Relationship to Declarant   City, State, Zip Code

   _____
   Telephone number

2.

Name	Street Address
Relationship to Declarant	City, State, Zip Code
Telephone number	

3.

Name	Street Address
Relationship to Declarant	City, State, Zip Code
Telephone number	

I designate as my alternate surrogate for health care decisions:

Name, Address, and Telephone Number of Alternate Surrogate:

Name _____

Address _____

Telephone Number _____

Alt. Number _____

I fully understand that this designation will permit my Health Care Surrogate to make health care decisions for me and to provide, withhold, or withdraw consent to medical procedures on my behalf; to apply for public benefits to defray the cost of health care; to authorize my admission to or transfer from a health care facility; and to have access to medical records pertaining to me and to authorize the release of medical information and medical records to third parties as directed by my Surrogate.

I understand the full import of this declaration, and I am emotionally and mentally competent to make this declaration.

Signed this _____ day of _____, 20_____.

_____
Declarant

STATEMENT OF WITNESSES

We declare, under penalty of perjury, that the Declarant is personally known to us, or has produced a driver's license as identification, that the Declarant signed or acknowledged this Designation of Health Care Surrogate in our presence, that the Declarant appears to be of sound mind and under no duress, fraud, or undue influence, and that we are not the person appointed as Health Care Surrogate by this document or related to the Declarant by blood or marriage.

_____   _____
Witness Signature   Printed Name of Witness

Date: _____   _____

                                     _____

_____   _____
Witness Signature   Printed Name of Witness

Date: _____   _____

                                     _____

STATE OF _____

COUNTY OF _____

The foregoing instrument was acknowledged before me this _____ day of _____, 20____, by _____, who personally appeared before me at the time of notarization, and who is personally known to me or who has produced a driver's license as identification and who did take an oath.

                        _____
                        Notary Signature

                        _____
                        Printed Name

My Commission Number: _____
My Commission Expires: _____

APPENDIX C:
Terri's Law

EXECUTIVE ORDER NUMBER 03-201

WHEREAS, on October 21, 2003, the Florida Legislature passed House Bill 35-E (to be published as Public Law 03-418), signed this date by me, authorizing the Governor to issue a one-time stay in certain cases where, as of October 15, 2003, the action of withholding or withdrawing nutrition or hydration from a patient in a permanent vegetative state has already occurred and there is no written advance directive and a family member has challenged the withholding or withdrawing of nutrition and hydration; and

WHEREAS, under House Bill 35-E a person may not be held civilly liable and is not subject to regulatory or disciplinary sanctions for taking any action to comply with a stay issued by the Governor pursuant to House Bill 35-E; and

WHEREAS, in the case of Theresa Marie Schindler Schiavo, Robert Schindler and Mary Schindler, the parents of Theresa Marie Schindler Schiavo, have requested that the Governor enter a stay prohibiting further withholding or withdrawing of nutrition or hydration; and

WHEREAS, a court has found that Theresa Schiavo is in a persistent vegetative state as of October 15, 2003; and

WHEREAS, Theresa Schiavo had no written advance directive as of October 15, 2003; and

WHEREAS, nutrition and hydration have been withdrawn from Theresa Schiavo, and continues to be withheld as of October 15, 2003; and

WHEREAS, the Schindlers have challenged the withdrawal and withholding of nutrition and hydration as of October 15, 2003; and

WHEREAS, an immediate and urgent need has arisen to address the removal of nutrition or hydration, because death due to lack of nutrition and hydration is imminent;

NOW THEREFORE, I, JEB BUSH, Governor of the State of Florida, by the powers vested in me by the Constitution and laws of the State of Florida, specifically House Bill 35-E, do hereby promulgate the following Executive Order, effective immediately:

Section 1

A. Effective immediately, continued withholding of nutrition and hydration from Theresa Schiavo is hereby stayed.

B. Effective immediately, all medical facilities and personnel providing medical care for Theresa Schiavo, and all those acting in concert or participation with them, are hereby directed to immediately provide nutrition and hydration to Theresa Schiavo by means of a gastronomy tube, or by any other method determined appropriate in the reasonable judgment of a licensed physician.

C. While this order is effective, no person shall interfere with the stay entered pursuant to this order.

D. This order shall be binding on all persons having notice of its provisions.

E. This order shall be effective until such time as the Governor revokes it.

F. The Florida Department of Law Enforcement shall serve a copy of this Executive Order upon the medical facility currently providing care for Theresa Schiavo.

IN TESTIMONY WHEREOF, I have hereunto set my hand and have caused the Great Seal of the State of Florida to be affixed this 21st day of October, 2003.

Appendix D

109TH CONGRESS
1ST SESSION

S. 686

For the relief of the parents of Theresa Marie Schiavo.

IN THE SENATE OF THE UNITED STATES

MARCH 20, 2005

Mr. FRIST (for himself, Mr. MARTINEZ, and Mr. SANTORUM) introduced the following bill; which was read twice, considered, read the third time, and passed

---

AN ACT

For the relief of the parents of Theresa Marie Schiavo.

1 *Be it enacted by the Senate and House of Representa-*

2 *tives of the United States of America in Congress assembled,*

3 **SECTION 1. RELIEF OF THE PARENTS OF THERESA MARIE**

4   **SCHIAVO.**

5   The United States District Court for the Middle Dis-

6 trict of Florida shall have jurisdiction to hear, determine,

7 and render judgment on a suit or claim by or on behalf

8 of Theresa Marie Schiavo for the alleged violation of any

9 right of Theresa Marie Schiavo under the Constitution or

10 laws of the United States relating to the withholding or

1 withdrawal of food, fluids, or medical treatment necessary

2 to sustain her life.

3 **SEC. 2. PROCEDURE.**

4   Any parent of Theresa Marie Schiavo shall have

5 standing to bring a suit under this Act. The suit may be

6 brought against any other person who was a party to State

7 court proceedings relating to the withholding or with-

8 drawal of food, fluids, or medical treatment necessary to

9 sustain the life of Theresa Marie Schiavo, or who may act

10 pursuant to a State court order authorizing or directing

11 the withholding or withdrawal of food, fluids, or medical

12 treatment necessary to sustain her life. In such a suit, the

13 District Court shall determine de novo any claim of a vio-

14 lation of any right of Theresa Marie Schiavo within the

15 scope of this Act, notwithstanding any prior State court

16 determination and regardless of whether such a claim has

17 previously been raised, considered, or decided in State

18 court proceedings. The District Court shall entertain and

19 determine the suit without any delay or abstention in favor

20 of State court proceedings, and regardless of whether rem-

21 edies available in the State courts have been exhausted.

22 **SEC. 3. RELIEF.**

23   After a determination of the merits of a suit brought

24 under this Act, the District Court shall issue such declara-

25 tory and injunctive relief as may be necessary to protect

1 the rights of Theresa Marie Schiavo under the Constitu-

2 tion and laws of the United States relating to the with-

3 holding or withdrawal of food, fluids, or medical treatment

4 necessary to sustain her life.

5 **SEC. 4. TIME FOR FILING.**

6 Notwithstanding any other time limitation, any suit

7 or claim under this Act shall be timely if filed within 30

8 days after the date of enactment of this Act.

9 **SEC. 5. NO CHANGE OF SUBSTANTIVE RIGHTS.**

10 Nothing in this Act shall be construed to create sub-

11 stantive rights not otherwise secured by the Constitution

12 and laws of the United States or of the several States.

13 **SEC. 6. NO EFFECT ON ASSISTING SUICIDE.**

14 Nothing in this act shall be construed to confer addi-

15 tional jurisdiction on any court to consider any claim re-

16 lated—

17   (1) to assisting suicide,

18   (2) a State law regarding assisting suicide.

19 **SEC. 7. NO PRECEDENT FOR FUTURE LEGISLATION.**

20 Nothing in this Act shall constitute a precedent with

21 respect to future legislation, including the provision of pri-

22 vate relief bills.

1   **SEC. 8. NO EFFECT ON THE PATIENT SELF-DETERMINA-**

2   **TION ACT OF 1990.**

3   Nothing in this act shall affect the rights of any per-

4   son under the Patient Self-Determination Act of 1990.

5   **SEC. 9. SENSE OF THE CONGRESS.**

6   It is the Sense of the Congress that the 109th Con-

7   gress should consider policies regarding the status and

8   legal rights of incapacitated individuals who are incapable

9   of making decisions concerning the provision, withholding,

10 or withdrawal of foods, fluid, or medical care.

○

NOTES

CHAPTER ONE

1. Ken Connor, "Government's Chief Role: To Protect Life," *WorldNetDaily,* March 26, 2005, http://worldnetdaily.com/news/article.asp?ARTICLE_ID=43503.

2. Nat Hentoff, "Terri Schiavo: Judicial Murder," *Village Voice,* March 29, 2005.

CHAPTER TWO

1. George Felos, "Should Terri Schiavo's Feeding Tube Be Removed?" *Burden of Proof,* CNN, May 3, 2001.

2. Michael Schiavo, interview by Larry King, *Larry King Live,* CNN, October 27, 2003.

3. Keith Andrews, Lesley Murphy, Ros Munday, and Claire Littlewood, "Misdiagnosis of the Vegetative State: Retrospective Study in a Rehabilitation Unit," *British Medical Journal* 313 (July 6, 1996): 13–16.

4. Jeff Johnson, "Schiavo's 'Dr. Humane Death' Got 1980 Diagnosis Wrong," *Cybercast News Service,* April 12, 2005, http://www.cnsnews.com/View SpecialReports.asp?Page=%5CSpecialReports%5Carchive%5C200504%5CS PE20050412a.html.

5. Ibid.

CHAPTER THREE

1. Joe Kovacs, "Mel Gibson on Schiavo: It's Modern Crucifixion" (quoting a radio interview by Sean Hannity, *Sean Hannity Show,* March 30, 2005), *WorldNetDaily,* March 31, 2005, http://www.worldnetdaily.com/news/article.asp?ARTICLE_ID=43576.

CHAPTER FOUR

1. Dr. Laura Schlessinger, *Dr. Laura Schlessinger Program,* March 24, 2005.

2. Steve Schiavo, radio interview by Glenn Beck, *Glenn Beck Program,* October 16, 2002.

CHAPTER FIVE

1. Sean Hannity, "Foul Play in Terri Schiavo Case?" *Hannity & Colmes,* October 27, 2003.

CHAPTER SIX

1. CNN News, "Time Running Out for Terri Schiavo; Governor Jeb Bush Holds News Conference Addressing Schiavo Case," *Live From . . .* , CNN, March 23, 2005.

CHAPTER SEVEN

1. Diana Lynne, "The Whole Terry Schiavo Story," *WorldNetDaily,* March 24, 2005, http://www.worldnetdaily.com/news/article.asp?ARTICLE_ID =43463.
2. Ibid.
3. Jackie Rhodes, interview by Greta Van Susteren, *On the Record With Greta Van Susteren,* FOX News, March 21, 2005.
4. Larry King, "Interview With Mary, Robert Schindler," *Larry King Live,* CNN, September 27, 2004.

CHAPTER EIGHT

1. Representative Joseph Pitts of Pennsylvania, *For the Relief of the Parents of Theresa Marie Schiavo,* 109th Cong., 1st. sess., *Congressional Record* 151 (March 20, 2005): H 1714.

CHAPTER NINE

1. Patricia Heaton, "Patricia Heaton Pleads for Terri Schiavo," press release, Feminists for Life of America, March 19, 2005.

CHAPTER TEN

1. "Kevorkian: Terri a Potential Patient," *WorldNetDaily,* October 1, 2005, http://www.worldnetdaily.com/news/article.asp?ARTICLE_ID=46613.
2. Michael Schiavo, interview by Chris Bury, "Husband at the Heart of the 'Right to Die' Case Speaks to Chris Bury," *Nightline,* ABC, March 15, 2005.
3. Andrew C. McCarthy, "Beyond a Reasonable Doubt," *National Review Online,* March 25, 2005, http://www.nationalreview.com/mccarthy/mccarthy200503250823.asp.
4. Ibid.
5. Ibid.
6. John Schwartz, "Experts Say Ending Feeding Can Lead to a Gentle Death," *New York Times,* March 20, 2005.

CHAPTER ELEVEN

1. "Man Offers $1 Million to Save Terri Schiavo," *WorldNetDaily,* March 10, 2005, http://www.worldnetdaily.com/news/article.asp?ARTICLE_ID =43235.

2. Ibid.

3. Steven Ertelt, "Terri Schiavo's Parents Discuss Rejection of Million Dollar Offer," *LifeNews.com,* March 11, 2005, http://www.lifenews.com/ bio773.html.

4. Anne Lindberg, "Hospice Pays Schiavo Bill," *St. Petersburg Times,* April 20, 2005.

5. Anne Lindberg, "Council Won't Waive Hospice Bill, For Now," *St. Petersburg Times,* April 17, 2005.

6. Sarah Foster, "No Easter Basket for Terri Schiavo," *WorldNetDaily,* April 12, 2004, http://www.worldnetdaily.com/news/article.asp?ARTICLE_ID =37992.

CHAPTER TWELVE

1. Manuel Roig-Franzia, "Gov. Bush Is Rebuffed in Schiavo Case," *Washington Post,* March 24, 2005.

2. Ted Barrett, Bob Granken, Joe Johns, Bill Mears, and John Zarrella, "Schindlers' Lawyer: Legal Fight Near End," CNN, March 26, 2005, http:// www.cnn.com/2005/LAW/03/26/schiavo/index.html.

3. Michael Schiavo, interview by Chris Bury, "Husband at the Heart of the 'Right to Die' Case Speaks to Chris Bury," *Nightline,* ABC, March 15, 2005.

4. John Schwartz, "Experts Say Ending Feeding Can Lead to a Gentle Death," *New York Times,* March 20, 2005.

5. Ibid.

6. "The Battle Over the Fate of a Comatose Patient," *Burden of Proof With Greta Van Susteren,* CNN, May 7, 2001.

7. Kate Adamson, *Kate's Journey: Triumph Over Adversity* (Redondo Beach, CA: Nosmada Press, 2004).

8. Kate Adamson, interview by Bill O'Reilly, "She Recovered From a Persistent Vegetative State," *O'Reilly Factor,* FOX News, November 5, 2003.

9. George Felos, *Litigation As Spiritual Practice* (Nevada City, CA: Blue Dolphin, 2002).

10. Ibid.

11. Ibid.

12. Eric Pfeiffer, "Odd Felos: Michael Schiavo's Very Strange Lawyer," *National*

Review Online, March 30, 2005, http://www.nationalreview.com/comment/pfeiffer200503301030.asp.

13. George Felos, speaking to the West Palm Beach County Bar Association, West Palm Beach, Florida, September 31, 2005.

14. Carl Limbacher, "Felos: Starving Terri Looks 'Beautiful,'" *NewsMax.com,* March 27, 2005, http://www.newsmax.com/archives/ic/2005/3/27/95930.shtml.

15. "Felos: This Death . . . Was for Terri," *WorldNetDaily,* March 31, 2005, http://www.worldnetdaily.com/news/article.asp?ARTICLE_ID=43594.

16. "George J. Felos Turning Heads and Opening Hearts on National Speakers Circuit," press release, November 29, 2005.

17. Allan Lengel, "Sniper Goes on Hunger Strike," *Washington Post,* August 26, 2005.

18. Karen Kennedy-Hall, "S.J. Officials Consider Starved Youth's Future," *South Jersey Courier-Post,* November 14, 2003.

19. Geoff Mulvihill, "N.J. to Give $12.5M to Boys Found Starving," Associated Press, September 30, 2005.

CHAPTER THIRTEEN

1. Unless otherwise noted, all congressional debate included in this chapter is from *For the Relief of the Parents of Theresa Marie Schiavo,* 109th Cong., 1st. sess., *Congressional Record* 151 (March 20, 2005).

2. "Statement of Senator Tom Harkin (D-IA) on the Case of Terri Schiavo," press release, March 18, 2005.

3. Ken Connor, "Government's Chief Role: To Protect Life," *WorldNetDaily,* March 26, 2005, http://worldnetdaily.com/news/article.asp?ARTICLE_ID=43503.

4. "Pelosi Statement on Congressional Involvement in Terri Schiavo Case," Nancy Pelosi press release/U.S. Newswire, March 20, 2005.

5. "Emergency Vote Puts Schiavo Case in Federal Court," CNN, March 21, 2005.

6. Carl Hulse and David D. Kirkpatrick, "Congress Passes and Bush Signs Legislation on Schiavo Case," *New York Times,* March 21, 2005.

7. "Emergency Vote Puts Schiavo Case in Federal Court," CNN, March 21, 2005.

8. Ibid.

CHAPTER FOURTEEN

1. Representative Joseph Pitts of Pennsylvania, *For the Relief of the Parents of Theresa Marie Schiavo*, 109th Cong., 1st. sess., *Congressional Record* 151 (March 20, 2005): H 1714.

2. "President Calls 'March for Life' Participants," news release, White House Office of the Press Secretary, January 23, 2006.

3. Steven Ertelt, "Zogby Poll: Americans Not in Favor of Starving Terri Schiavo," Zogby International, April 1, 2005, http://www.zogby.com/soundbites/ReadClips.dbm?ID=11131.

4. "Poll: Keep Feeding Tube Out," CBS News, March 23, 2005, http://www.cbsnews.com/stories/2005/03/23/opinion/polls/main682674.shtml.

5. "Poll: Do You Approve or Disapprove of Congress' Involvement in the Terri Schiavo Case?" CNN/USA Today/Gallup Poll, *USA Today*, April 6, 2005.

6. Available at http://www.pollingreport.com/news.htm#Schiavo.

CHAPTER FIFTEEN

1. Michael Schiavo, interview by Larry King, *Larry King Live*, CNN, October 27, 2003.

2. Michael Schiavo, interview by Chris Bury, "Husband at the Heart of the 'Right to Die' Case Speaks to Chris Bury," *Nightline*, ABC, March 15, 2005.

3. "Terri's Brother: Felos in Love With Death," *WorldNetDaily*, March 29, 2005, http://www.worldnetdaily.com/news/article.asp?ARTICLE_ID=43535.

4. Jane Roh, "Terri Schiavo Dies in Florida Hospice," FOX News, March 31, 2005, http://www.foxnews.com/story/0,2933,152032,00.html.

CHAPTER SIXTEEN

1. "President Discusses Schiavo, WMD Commission Report," news release, White House Office of the Press Secretary, March 31, 2005.

2. Mike Pence, "Statement From Congressman Mike Pence on the Death of Terri Schiavo," press release, March 31, 2005.

3. Rush Limbaugh, *The Rush Limbaugh Show*, March 31, 2005.

4. "Felos: This Death . . . Was for Terri," *WorldNetDaily*, March 31, 2005, http://www.worldnetdaily.com/news/article.asp?ARTICLE_ID=43594.

CHAPTER EIGHTEEN

1. Joan Didion, "The Case of Theresa Schiavo," *New York Review of Books* 52, no. 10 (June 9, 2005). Note: Mr. Schiavo was responding to a question regarding the disposition of his wife's personal jewelry in a 1993 deposition.

2. Editorial, "Autopsy on the Schiavo Tragedy," *New York Times,* June 16, 2005.

3. Keith Olbermann, *Countdown With Keith Olbermann,* MSNBC, June 15, 2005.

4. David Karp and Stephen Nohlgren, "Autopsy Issue Part of a Day of Sparring," *St. Petersburg Times,* March 30, 2005.

5. Ibid.

CHAPTER NINETEEN

1. Patrick J. Buchanan, "The Culture of Death Advances," *WorldNetDaily,* March 30, 2005, http://www.worldnetdaily.com/news/article.asp?ARTICLE_ID=43541.

2. James Ridgeway, "Schiavo Judge Has Reason to Fear," *Village Voice,* March 28, 2005.

3. Sandy Bauers and Stacey Burling, "Schiavo Autopsy Finds 'Massive' Brain Damage, No Abuse," *Philadelphia Inquirer,* June 15, 2005.

4. "Felos: Michael Schiavo 'Very Pleased to Hear Results,'" Tampa Bay News 9, June 15, 2005, http://www.baynews9.com/content/36/2005/6/15/93389.html.

CHAPTER TWENTY

1. "Prof: Right to Assisted Suicide 'Irresistible,'" *WorldNetDaily,* December 3, 2005, http://www.worldnetdaily.com/news/article.asp?ARTICLE_ID=47719.

2. Nat Hentoff, "The Disabled Sound the Alarm for the Nonreligious," *Free Inquiry,* August/September 2005.

3. Marc Morano, "Christianity Harmful to Animals," *Cybercast News Service,* July 1, 2002, http://www.cnsnews.com/Culture/Archive/200207/CUL20020701b.html.

4. Marvin Olasky, "Blue-State Philosopher," *World,* November 27, 2004.

5. Peter Singer, "Sanctity of Life or Quality of Life," *Pediatrics* 72, no. 1 (July 1983): 129.

6. Peter Singer, *Practical Ethics* (Cambridge: Cambridge University Press, 1993).

7. Singer, "Sanctity of Life or Quality of Life," 129.

8. James Tarentino, "Who Will Remember Terri?" *Wall Street Journal,* April 1, 2005.

CHAPTER TWENTY-ONE

1. Thomas M. Burton, "In a Stroke Patient, Doctor Sees Power of Brain to Recover," *Wall Street Journal,* November 23, 2005.

2. All quotes in this section were taken from video clips provided by Theresa May de Vera's Web page: http://homepage.mac.com/tisamay/Menu18.html.

3. Miranda Hitti, "Firefighter's Miracle Recovery Rare in Long-Term Coma Cases," FOX News/WebMD, May 6, 2005, http://www.foxnews.com/story/0,2933,155608,00.html.

4. Associated Press, "Brain-Damaged Man 'Wakes Up' After 10 Years," FOX News, May 3, 2005, http://www.foxnews.com/story/0,2933,155344,00.html.

5. Ibid.

6. Associated Press, "Woman Speaks First Words in Two Years," FOX News, May 12, 2005, http://www.foxnews.com/story/0,2933,156344,00.html.

7. "Schiavo-like Woman Speaks After 2 years," *WorldNetDaily,* May 13, 2005, http://worldnetdaily.com/news/article.asp?ARTICLE_ID=44244.

8. "Awake After 20 Years, Sarah Speaks," CBS News, August 4, 2005, http://www.cbsnews.com/stories/2005/08/04/earlyshow/series/main757388.shtml.

9. Ibid.

10. "Coma Patient Sings Way to Health," CBS News, August 5, 2005, http://www.cbsnews.com/stories/2005/08/05/earlyshow/series/main760296.shtml?CMP=ILC-SearchStories.

11. Phil Stewart, "Italian Coma Victim Says Heard Everything," Reuters, October 5, 2005.

12. Ibid.

13. "In Italy, Support for Those in a Vegetative State," *ZENIT News,* October 10, 2005, http://www.zenit.org/english/visualizza.phtml?sid=77987.

14. Burton, "In a Stroke Patient, Doctor Sees Power of Brain to Recover."

15. Ibid.

16. Ibid.

CHAPTER TWENTY-TWO

1. Joni Eareckson Tada, "Terri Schiavo's National Legacy," press release, March 31, 2005, http://www.joniandfriends.org/apcm/APCMviewer.asp?a=128&z=4.

CHAPTER TWENTY-THREE

1. Michael Vitez, "Living Wills Fail To," Knight Ridder, November 27, 2005.
2. Lindsey O'Connor, "Dying Smart: Why Your Living Will May Not Be Good Enough," *Christianity Today*, August 2005.
3. Vitez, "Living Wills Fail To."

CHAPTER TWENTY-FIVE

1. Thomas Jefferson, "To the Republican Citizens of Washington County, Maryland," March 31, 1809.

CHAPTER TWENTY-SIX

1. "Time Poll: A Majority (53%) of Those Who Call Themselves Evangelicals Support Removing the Feeding Tube, 41% Oppose Removal of the Feeding Tube," *Time*, March 27, 2005, http://www.time.com/time/press_releases/article/0,8599,1042435,00.html.
2. Barna, "The Year's Most Intriguing Findings."
3. George H. Gallup, "Vital Signs," *Leadership* (Fall 1987): 17.

APPENDIX A

1. National Institute of Neurological Disorders and Stroke, National Institutes of Health at www.ninds.nih.gov.
2. Ibid.
3. J. T. Giacino and others, "The Minimally Conscious State: Definition and Diagnostic Criteria," *Neurology* 58 (2002): 349–353.
4. Ibid.